To
ANDY, TOM, and AMY
and
DIANNE and MY MOTHER and FATHER

To
ANDY, TOM, and AMY
and
DIANNE and MY MOTHER and FATHER

Brief Contents

Contents

Preface

Organization development is the applied behavioral science dedicated to improving organizations, and the people in them, through the theory and practice of planned change. Today, organizations face multiple challenges and threats—threats to effectiveness, efficiency, and profitability; challenges from turbulent environments, increased competition and changing customer demands; and the constant challenge to maintain congruence among organizational dimensions such as technology, strategy, culture, and processes. Keeping organizations healthy and viable in this world is indeed a daunting task.

Individuals in organizations, too, face multiple challenges—finding satisfaction in and through work, fighting obsolescence of one's knowledge and skills, maintaining dignity and purpose in the pursuit of organizational goals, and developing connectedness and community in the workplace. In the face of constant layoffs and cutbacks, simple survival has become a major challenge today. Although new jobs are being created at record rates, old jobs are being destroyed at an accelerating pace. "Knowledge" work is replacing "muscle" work. In short, organizations and the individuals in them, face an enormously demanding present and future.

Fortunately, a variety of solutions exist to help people and organizations cope, adapt, survive, and even prosper in these vexing times, and organization development (OD) is one of them. Organization development is a process for teaching people how to solve problems, and take advantage of opportunities. OD focuses on issues related to the "human side" of organizations by finding ways to increase the effectiveness of individuals, teams, and the organization's human and social processes.

Organization development is not just about improving organizations, but also about developing individuals. This dual focus is a unique strength of OD. It is possible for the people within an organization to collaboratively manage its culture in such a way that the goals and purposes of the organization are realized at the same time that human values of individuals within it are furthered. OD channels the intelligence, experience, and creativity of organization members in systematic and participative programs where they create solutions to their own most pressing challenges—a powerful formula for change. Behavioral science theory and practice and were applied in a trial-and-error fashion until a coherent improvement strategy, now called organization development, evolved.

Organization development, a relatively recent invention, started in the late 1950s when behavioral scientists steeped in the lore and technology of group dynamics attempted to apply that knowledge to improve team functioning and intergroup relations in organizations. Early results were encouraging, and attention was soon directed toward other human and social processes in organizations such as the design of work tasks, organization structure, conflict resolution, strategy formulation and implementation, and the like. The field of OD grew rapidly in the 1970s and 1980s with thousands of organizations in the private and public sectors using the theory and methods of OD with great success. Today, organization development represents one of the best strategies for coping with the rampant changes occurring in the marketplace and society. We predict that organization development will be a preferred improvement strategy well into the twenty-first century. Given the rapid and dynamic changes in the workforce profile, nature of work and organizational structures, there have been additions to the arsenal of the organizational development interventions too.

This book tells the story of what OD is, how it works, its values, its change techniques (called interventions), and what the future of OD might be. We have attempted to present a concise but complete exposition of the theory, practice, and research related to organization development with the belief that leaders, students, and OD practitioners can use these concepts. With the growing presence of OD in India, they will find the addition of Indian case studies in this book particularly valuable.

ORGANIZATION OF THE BOOK

Chapters 1–7 provide an overview of OD and its changing context. Sequentially, the reader is provided with illustrations of OD efforts; definitions of OD; a history of OD; its underlying values, assumptions, and beliefs; its theoretical and research foundations; managing the OD process; the history and utility of action research; and an overview of OD interventions.

Chapters 8–11 describe interventions in some detail. Chapters 8 and 9 detail OD interventions of importance to teams and to intergroup and interpersonal relationships. Chapter 10 describes interventions that involve the entire organization, including "getting the whole system in the room" and appreciative inquiry (AI). It also includes a discussion of Schein's cultural analysis as well as transorganizational development. Chapter 11 focuses on structural (or "technostructural") interventions, including work redesign, sociotechnical systems (STS), self-managed teams, parallel learning structures, total quality management (TQM), "high-involvement work systems," and large-scale systems change. A discussion of reengineering is included along with the dilemmas this change strategy poses for OD practitioners. Chapter 12 focuses on training interventions of relevance to OD, including the T-group, instrumented training, and coaching and mentoring.

Chapter 13 looks at issues in consultant-client relationships, including the nature of the consultant's expertise, depth of intervention, and ethics. Chapter 14 deals with the sensitive issue of power and politics in OD.

The book ends with discussions about OD research and the future of OD in Chapter 15. This chapter on the future of OD includes a section on "the search for community" and its relationship to OD.

ACKNOWLEDGMENTS

We acknowledge our debt to the work and writings of the pioneer practitioner-scholars about whom we write in Chapter 2 "Definitions and Historical Overview of Organization Development." Correspondence and interviews with several of these leading figures provided us with invaluable information and helped us unravel the threads of the early history of OD. In particular, we want to thank Chris Argyris, Richard Beckhard, Kenneth Benne, Robert Blake, Rensis Likert, Ronald

Lippitt, Jane Mouton, Eva Schindler-Rainman, Herbert Shepard, and Robert Tannenbaum. We are grateful to the following people for their review of the manuscript: William L. Tullar, University of North Carolina at Greensboro; Raymond Hill, Eastern Michigan University; Steven Vitucci, University of Central Texas; Bob Herring, Radford University; Lisa Scherer, University of Nebraska at Omaha; and Robert Schappe, University of Michigan at Dearborn. We also wish to thank other authors and clients and internal and external consultants with whom we have worked over the years. They have taught us much about this field.

Special mention has to be made of the consent of Mr Udai Pareek to allow the inclusion of his Role Efficacy Lab intervention. We would also like to acknowledge the contribution of case studies by Mr A. S. Vasudevan who has been involved with his colleagues in carrying out OD work with Madura Coats (now Madura Garments), L&T Cements, Murugappa Group's Tube Investments etc.

Dr Ranjana Mittal, faculty member (PMI–NTPC) has furthered our cause by providing the case study of NTPC which she has authored with Dr Suneeta Singh, senior faculty member (PMI–NTPC). Various other sources such as the electronic media and earlier published material have also contributed to this effort in different ways. We are also grateful for the secretarial support of Ms Janice Fernandes. The patience and support of our families has made this edition possible.

Wendell French
Cecil Bell
Veena Vohra

CHAPTER I

The Field of Organization Development

Organization development is a systematic process for applying behavioral science principles and practices in organizations to increase individual and organizational effectiveness. This book tells the brand story of organization development—its history, nature and characteristics, theory, methods and values. The focus is organizations and making them function better, that is, total system change. The orientation is action-achieving results as a consequence of planned activities. The target is human and social processes, the human side of organizations. The setting is real organizations in the real world. We want you, the reader, to have a complete understanding of organization development (OD): What it is; how it works; why it works; and how you can use the information in this book to improve the performance of your organization and/or your client organizations.

To begin the story, this chapter introduces the field of OD, shows some of its major features in broad outline, and presents several illustrations of OD programs. Later chapters round out the story.

OVERVIEW OF THE FIELD OF ORGANIZATION DEVELOPMENT

Organization development is an organizational improvement strategy. In the late 1950s and early 1960s, it emerged out of insights from group dynamics and from the theory and practice of planned change. Today the field offers an integrated framework capable of solving most of the important problems confronting the human side of organizations.

Organization development is about how people and organizations function and how to get them to function better. The field is based on knowledge from behavioral science disciplines such as psychology, social psychology, sociology, anthropology, systems theory, organizational behavior, organization theory, and management, OD practitioners are consultants trained in the theory and practice of organization development, with knowledge from the underlying behavioral sciences.

OD programs are long-term planned, sustained efforts. Such efforts begin when a leader identifies an undesirable situation and seeks to change it. The leader contacts an OD professional, and together they explore whether organization development suits the task at hand. If the answer is yes, they enlist others in the organization to help design and implement the change program. The participants develop an overall game plan or strategy that includes a series of activities, each intended to achieve an outcome that moves the organization toward its goals. The two major goals of OD programs are (1) to improve the functioning of individuals, teams and the total organization, and the total organization, and (2) to teach organizations members how to continuously improve their own functioning.

Organization development deals with the gamut of "people problems" and "work systems problems" in organizations; poor morale, low productivity, poor quality, interpersonal conflict, intergroup conflict, unclear or inappropriate goals, inappropriate leadership styles, poor team performance, inappropriate organization structure, poorly designed tasks, inadequate response to environmental demands, poor customer relations, inadequate alignment among the organization's strategy, structure, culture, and processes, and the like. In short, where individuals, teams and organizations are not realizing their potential, OD can improve the situation.

A PREVIEW OF THE MAJOR THEMES OF THE BOOK

Several themes underlie the theory and practice of organization development. One theme is planned change; another is the distinctive nature of OD consulting. A cluster of themes describes OD as a process that focuses on organizational culture, processes, and structure using a total system perspective. A final theme is "action research." We will examine these themes in turn.

Planned Change

Change means the new state of things and is different from the old state of things. Change is everywhere, change will be the one of the few constants during the end of this century and into the next. This book is about planned change for organizations and the people in them. The field of organization development was established to help leaders address and embrace change, to view change as an opportunity rather than a threat. Demands for change come from forces both external and internal to the organization. External forces include regulators, competitors, market forces, customers, technology, and the larger society. Internal forces include obsolescence of products and services, new market opportunities, new strategic directions, an increasingly diverse workforce, and the like. Regardless of the source, the result is rapid and turbulent change.

Change has different facets; for example, it can be deliberate (planned) or accidental (unplanned). Its magnitude can be large or small. It can affect many elements of the organization or only a few. It can be fast (abrupt, revolutionary), or slow (evolutionary). The new state of things can have an entirely different nature from the old state of things (fundamental, quantum, or "second-order" change). each of these facets calls for different actions from leaders and OD practitioners.

Early OD efforts primarily addressed first-order change—making moderate adjustments to the organization, its people, and its processes. Today the demands on organizations were being reinvented, work tasks reengineered, and the rules of the marketplace rewritten. The fundamental nature of work and organizations is changing. Indeed, the new state of things is already vastly different from the old state of things, and the changes are just beginning.

Organization Development as a Distinctive Consulting Method

A fundamental difference between organization development and other organization improvement programs is found in the OD consultant's role and relationship to clients. OD consultants establish a collaborative relationship of relative equality with organization members as they together identify and take action on problems and opportunities. OD consultants co-learners and collaborators: they work with people in the organization to discover what needs to be changed and how to go about it. The role of OD consultants is *to structure activities to help organization members learn to solve their own problems and learn to do it better over time.* OD consultants typically do not give substantive solutions to problems. Rather they create learning situations in which problems are identified and solutions are developed. OD consultants are experts on organizational change and organizational dynamics, and on structuring learning situations for problem solving and decision making.

The aim of leaving the organization members better able to solve their own problems is a distinctive feature of organization development. This process is called " self-renewal" or "learning how to learn" or "organizational learning" in the literature, and it means teaching clients the key skills and knowledge required for continuous self-improvement. OD consulting thus fosters increased competence, growth, learning, and empowerment throughout the client system.

Organization Development as a Process That Focuses on Organizational Culture, Processes, and Structure Using a Total System Perspective

You will find this cluster of themes throughout the book—its focus on organizational culture, processes, and structure captures the essence of OD. Organization development is a process in the sense that a process is an identifiable flow of interrelated events moving over time toward some goal or end.[1] OD is a journey, not a destination. It is an unfolding and evolving series of events. Every OD program is unique because every organization has unique problems and opportunities. Yet all OD programs *are identifiable flows of interrelated events moving over time toward the goals of organizational improvement and individual development.*

Major events in the process include sensing that something is wrong and should be corrected; diagnosing the situation to determine what is happening; planning and taking actions to change the problematic conditions; evaluating the effects of the actions; making adjustments as necessary; and repeating as necessary; and repeating the sequence. OD is thus an iterative process of diagnosing, and taking action. All organizational improvement programs are complex processes of goals → actions → redefined goals → new actions.

A powerful insight into the practice of OD is that some elements of the organization are more important than others as sources of effectiveness and ineffectiveness. Specifically, the organization's culture, processes, and structures are key leverage points for determining how well or how poorly the system functions.

Organization culture is defined as the values, assumptions, and beliefs held in common by organization members that shape how they perceive, think, and act. Every organization has a culture. Culture strongly influences individual and group behavior—how people act depends on how they perceive and think about things, which is often embedded in the organization's culture. The culture must be altered if permanent change is to occur, Warner Burke considers culture change to be the hallmark of OD: "... *organization development is a process of fundamental change in an organization's culture.*"[2] Thus norms, values, and assumptions help determine behavior and effectiveness in organizations. OD interventions that have the power to change culture can thereby change individual and organizational performance. Being able to diagnose, understand, and change organization culture is increasingly important in organization development.

Organizational processes are also crucial leverage points for achieving organizational improvement. Processes are how things get done in organizations, the *methods* for arriving at results. Important processes in organizations include communication, problem solving and decision making, resource allocation, conflict resolution, allocation of rewards, human resource practices, strategic management, exercise of authority, and self-renewal or continuous learning. *How* things are done in organizations (organizational processes) is as important as *what* is done.

Peter Vail believes that the genius of OD is its focus on organizational processes, He views OD as "a process for improving organizational processes."[3] A major thrust in organization development is improving organizational effectiveness by improving organizational processes. The power and importance of processes were discovered during research or group dynamics and laboratory training. Investigators found it useful to distinguish between "task" and "process." Task was *what* the group was working on. To improve the group's functioning it was usually necessary to improve the processes the groups was using. This same relationship holds for improving organizational functioning.

Organization structure refers to the overall design of the organization, that is, the "wiring diagram" for how the parts are connected to producer the whole. Structure also refers to how individual work tasks are designed and how these tasks are integrated in a coherent manner. A number of OD interventions help leaders redesign the organization's structure to make it function better. Traditional ways of structuring work and organizations have found wanting; they are associated with excessive waste, inefficiency, inflexibility, and high costs. In addition, certain structures promote responsibility, innovation and initiative whereas other structures thwart these behaviors. Getting the structure right produces immediate, substantial improvements in performance. Organizational structure is an active area of experimentation in OD today.

Organizations are complex social systems interacting with the environment, and OD efforts usually focus on improving the total organization, or large parts of it. The target of change is the organization as a system, not its individual members, even though individuals are the instruments of change. Systems theory is an important foundation for OD theory and practice. Shafritz and Ott describe the systems perspective as follows: "The systems school views an organization as a complex set of dynamically intertwined and interconnected elements, including its inputs, processes, outputs, feedback loops, and the environment in which it operates. A change in any element of the system inevitably causes changes in its other elements."[4]

A systems perspective directs OD practitioners to be aware of interdependencies, interrelatedness, multiple causes, and multiple effects. For example, systems theory suggests that a change in one element of the system, say, strategy, will require changes in other elements such as structures, processes, and culture if the change in strategy is to be effective. If this explanation makes organization change sound complicated, it is, but the systems paradigm helps leaders to understand complicated organizational dynamics and take actions.

A primary goal of OD programs is to optimize the system by ensuring that system elements are harmonious and congruent. When organization structure, strategy, culture, and processes are not aligned, performance suffers. Different OD interventions focus on aligning the individual and the organization, aligning organizational elements, and aligning the organization with environmental demands.

Organizations are examples of open systems, that is, systems interacting with their environments. Many problems of organizations today stem from rapid changes in environmental demands, threats, and opportunities. As the environment changes, the organization must adapt. But that gets harder to do as the pace of change quickens and as the number of shareholders increases. (Stakeholders are groups and individuals who are affected by the organization's activities and who want a say in what the organization does; these units include, for example, labor unions, government regulators, environmentalists, and investors) OD practitioners therefore have to be knowledgeable about both systems thinking and open systems thinking.

The Action Research Model

Earlier in the chapter we described OD as a process of diagnosing, taking action, rediagnosing, and taking new action. This process assumes a distinct form in OD called *action research*. Action research is essentially a mixture of three ingredients: the highly participative nature of OD, the consultant nature of OD, the consultant role of collaborator and co-learner, and the iterative process of diagnosis and action. The action research model as applied in OD consists of (1) a preliminary diagnosis, (2) data gathering from the client group, (3) data feedback to the client group, (4) exploration of the data by the client group, (5) action planning by the client group, (6) action taking by the client group, and (7) evaluation and assessment of the results of the actions by the client group—with an OD practitioner acting as a facilitator throughout the process. The action research model is powerful; seeking the ideas and energies of a large number of people produces superior results. Participation by client group members ensures better information, better decision making and action taking, and increased commitment to the action programs.

Action research yields both change and new knowledge: Change occurs based the actions taken, and new knowledge comes from examining the results of the actions. The client group learns what works, what does not work, and why.

This introduction to organization development is intended to give you a basic understanding of what the field is about and how it operates. The themes and characteristics in this chapter will become more familiar as we continue through the book.

The following illustrations of actual OD programs provide examples from our experience and from the work of others. Notice how the programs are initiated, how they are planned and executed, and how the central themes of OD are translated into action.

ILLUSTRATION I: PROBLEMS IN A BUSINESS FIRM

Lack of cooperation between subunits, increasing complaints from customers, sagging morale, and rapidly increasing costs induced the president of a medium-sized company to confer with an OD consultant about ways to improve the situation. The two talked at length, and it became apparent to the consultant that the executive, while having some apprehensions, was generally agreeable to examining the dynamics of the situation, including decision-making processes and his own leadership behavior. He and the consultant agreed that certain organization development efforts might be worthwhile. They decided that a three-day workshop away from the usual routine, with the executive and his entire work team, might be an appropriate way to start.

The president then sounded out several of his subordinates about the possibility of the workshops, and reactions ranged from enthusiasm to some uneasiness. The team agreed to have the consultant meet with the executive and all his immediate subordinates to explain the typical format of such a meeting and to discuss the probable content of a workshop. At the end of this meeting, the group decided to give it a try.

A few days before the off-site session, the consultant spent an hour interviewing each member of the team. In essence he asked them, "What things are going well?" and "What things are getting in the way of this group and this organization being as successful as you would like to be?" The purpose of these interviews was to obtain the data around which to build the design of the workshop.

At the beginning of the workshop, the consultant first reported back to the group the general themes in the interviews, which he had grouped under these problem headings: "The Boss," "Meetings," "Administrative Services," "Customer Relations," "Relations Between Departments," and "Long-Range Goals." The group then ranked these problem themes in terms of importance and immediacy and chose the problem areas to work on. With the consultant acting more as a coach than as a moderator, the group examined both the underlying dynamics of each problem area and optional solutions to the problems. In addition to making suggestions for breaking into subgroups to tackle certain agenda items, and in addition to providing several 10-minute lectures on such topics. As decision making and team effectiveness, the consultant, upon request, intervened from time to comment on the way the group was working together and to help make explicit the norms under which the group was together and to help make explicit the norms under which the groups seemed to be operating.

During the three days, the participants had time for recreation activities, such as jogging, basketball, swimming and billards. On two of the three days, the group worked until 6:00 or 6:30 p.m. and then adjourned for a relaxed dinner and socializing. By and large, the three days, although involving intense work, were worked through in the group setting; others were worked out informally during breaks from the work agendas. It seemed to the consultant that the group experienced a sense of enhanced camaraderie and team spirit.

The last morning was spent developing "next action steps" for a dozen or so items discussed under the problem headings. One decision was to spend half a day with the consultant three months in the future to review progress toward problem solutions.

During a subsequent meeting between the company president and the consultant, the executive reported that group morale was up substantially and customer complaints and costs were beginning to go down, but that "we still have a long way to go, including making our staff meetings more effective." The two then agreed to have the consultant sit in on three staff meetings before the three-month review session.

The three-month review session with the consultant showed significant progress had been made on some action steps. However, improvement seemed to be bogged down, particularly in areas requiring the president to delegate certain functions to key subordinates. This matter was extensively worked on by the group, and the president began to see where and how he could "loosen the reins," thus freeing himself for more long-range planning and more contacts with key customers.

During the following years, the top-management team institutionalized an annual three-day "problem-solving workshop" involving the consultant. In addition, all the top managers used the consultant's services in conducting comparable workshops with their own subordinates. Over this period, the consultant and the human resources director, whose hiring was a direct outgrowth of one of the sessions, began to work as a consulting team to the organization, with the human resources director gradually assuming more and more of the role of a "change agent." In addition to having planning and control responsibilities for employment and compensation and other traditional personnel functions, the new human resources director coordinated a management development program decided to supplement the company's problem-solving workshops. For example, managers could request to attend specialized seminars in such areas as budgeting and finance, group dynamics, and long-range planning. The human resources director thus assumed an expanded role in which he served as an internal OD consultant to the operating divisions, as a linking pin with the external (original) consultant, and as a coordinator of the traditional human resources functions.

ILLUSTRATION 2: FROM "MUDDLING THROUGH" TO MAKING MILLIONS

The president and seven senior executives of a parts manufacturing company spent a year and a half working through a strategic planning process facilitated by an OD consultant. At the end of that time they had a clear and uplifting mission; specific goals for customer relations, quality, employee relations, and profits; and a well-conceived strategy for achieving the goals and fulfilling the corporate mission. It was a long, arduous journey; intense three-day work sessions every three to four months were combined with "homework" assignments to prepare for the network session. They made tough decisions, launched new initiatives, and streamlined product lines. As the new strategy was implemented, profits, which had been minimal for years (make a million dollars this year, lose a million dollars next year), started to soar. Profitability increased substantially every year for a number of years.

The story began with a phone call to the consultant from an assistant to the president. The assistant explained that the company's top management team had decided that its single most important problem was lack of a clear, agreed-upon strategic plan, that the executives wanted to conduct a thorough strategic planning process, and that they needed to help of an outsider, previous do-it-yourself strategic planning attempts had ended in frustration and stalemate. The consultant replied that outside help on strategic planning comes in two forms: from an expert on strategic planning content, or from an expert on facilitating a process in which the executives themselves generated the content. "I can facilitate a strategic planning process if that is the kind of help that is wanted," the consultant said.

Several phone calls later, a two-day visit was arranged. The consultant met with the president and each executive individually for lengthy interviews and exploration. At a meeting of the top management team on the second day, the consultant reported in general terms what he had learned, stated that strategic planning was indeed appropriate, and described a process for creating a strategic plan. The process called for five three-day planning sessions stretched over about a year and a half. He explained in detail the activities and desired outcomes for each session.

The team made a "go" decision. The consultant supplied reading materials on strategic management, and the first session was arranged. Information on company performance was prepared for the session.

Three goals of the first session were (1) to understand the industry, the competitors, and critical success factors for the industry; (2) to determine what the executives wanted the company to be and to do; and (3) to generate the first draft of a corporate mission statement embodying their aspirations for the company. The consultant structured activities to achieve the three goals and gave assignments to individuals, sub-groups, and the total group throughout the three days. It quickly became apparent that the executives did not work well as a group: Several strong personalities pushed hard for their positions without compromise, considerable scapegoating and intimidating occurred, people did not listen to or accept the opinions of others, the group jumped from topic to topic without getting closure on subjects, and people held vastly different opinions about what the company should be and do.

One half day focused on the industry and the competition. The group explored the following questions: What are industry trends? What are industry success factors? Who are the main competitors? What are their strategies? What do they do well? What do they do that we want to avoid? Next, the group conducted a specific environmental analysis using a SWOT analysis (company strengths/weaknesses, environmental opportunities/threats).

Discussions and activities centered on the question: What do we want the company to be and to do? Differences of opinion were great, as was the strength of conviction shown by the various executives. The consultant's major tasks were to keep the group focused on the topic at hand, to highlight areas of disagreement, and to ensure that all ideas were given a fair hiring.

The charge for the third day was to complete the first draft of a corporate mission statement that incorporated what the group wanted the company to be and to do. Individuals wrote their own versions of a mission statement: subgroups used these versions to construct a subgroup mission statement; next to total group discussed the subgroup reports. In a second iteration subgroups wrote revised statements, and then the total group hammered out a draft. The executives were generally pleased with their progress and with the mission statement. Arrangements were made for the next three layers of management to critique the mission statements before the next work session.

The goals of the second session three months later were to finalize the mission statement based on three months of reflection and on the inputs from additional managers, and to agree on corporate goals for the next two to five years. Finalizing the mission statement was difficult because this document would constitute the guiding principles for the corporation. The input from additional managers provided a healthy reality check, but old differences of opinion among the executives surfaced and were explored until resolved. (In retrospect, the most valuable feature of the strategic planning process was to surface, confront, and resolve differences among the executives. They could not move forward as a company as they resolved their differences and were all committed to a common course of action. But agreeing on the common course of action had never been achieved in the past.)

After finalizing the mission statement, the group set goals for quality, customer relations, employee relations, and company profitability. The executives agreed it would be impossible to achieve gains in profits without attending to the foundation of profits: employees and customers. The final task was to decide how to report the results of the second work session to the next three levels of management.

The goal of the third session four months later was to develop the strategy or strategies to enact the corporate mission and achieve the corporate goals. The consultant's main tasks were to cause exploration of multiple possibilities, prevent premature closure on disclosure of new ideas, and test for commitment to the mission and goals that had been developed in prior sessions. The executives identified five new strategic initiatives that would enable the company to achieve its goals. To ensure implementation and follow through, a "champion" was assigned responsibility for each initiative.

The goal of the fourth session three months later was to assess progress on the five initiatives. Each champion reported on progress to date. Refinements, needed adjustments, additional clarification, and obstacles were all explored. If necessary, additional resources were allocated to the initiatives. Recommitment to the mission, goals, and strategy was obtained. The executives felt good about what they had done because significant positive results were beginning to occur.

The fifth and final session was held four months later. The goals were to assess progress on implementation, to build support mechanisms for the five initiatives, and to revisit the corporate goals for the present year. Because profitability was greater than expected, and because they had five months until the end of the fiscal year, the executives decided to set new, ambitious performance goals for the current year. They subsequently achieved these goals, made a significant profit for themselves, the company, and the employees (who had a gainsharing program in place) and started a record of achievement that the company had never seen before.

Strategic planning is really about alignment with environmental demands and opportunities, and alignment and agreement among the top executives about what they want to do and how they intend to do it. The OD approach to strategic planning is to facilitate a process whereby the key executives align their efforts toward common goals and a common "game plan."

ILLUSTRATION 3: TAKING ON GLOBAL CHALLENGES WITH THE HELP OF OD

Providing IT services is where India has a proven competitive advantage. With all the requisites like technically qualified people, English-speaking professionals, and the other competencies required in the services sector, India should do well by concentrating in the service sector and once the industry matures, software products and consulting could be taken up more seriously.

A major disadvantage of the Chinese software industry, it is reported, is a lack of fluency in English among its professionals; this in turn may hamper their growth. Otherwise they have a good infrastructure and a proactive government support which aids in the development of the software industry. So if China resolves its language barrier, it will certainly give a tough fight to the Indian software industry in the future.

Given this scenario, software organizations are priming their systems and work processes and gearing themselves to meet future challenges. KPIT is trying to bring about a change by carrying out Organisation Development activities in its work place.

The OD work in KPIT is a proactive approach. It was initiated in 2000 to facilitate KPIT in its quest to become a global IT services player. OD basically helps take proactive steps for introducing planned change that cuts across departmental and hierarchical boundaries and thus increases transparency. It brings change in the company's culture, mindset, skills, and organization.

OD was taken up as a planned change management exercise. The OD interventions began with a diagnostic phase (survey) followed by process consultation. The services of an OD consulting firm was used for the initial interventions. After a diagnostic survey, a top management workshop, followed by workshops cutting across the company was conducted. These workshops put people through the concepts of change and its management, as well as other areas like collaboration, team building and inter-personal expectations and their fulfillment. A restructuring of the compensation and benefits package followed these workshops, and in future, it will be followed by structural changes and a focus on organizational roles played by software experts and consultants.

Basically, the OD function in KPIT is a formal process, which aligns the people towards business imperatives. But before proceeding with the action plan the company had a blue print ready with it.

There are two ways in which change can be viewed—Transactional and Transformational. Companies with vision would go for transformational change that is in-depth and enduring. This applies to KPIT who basically believed in initiating changes in structure, systems, skills and the other S's described in the 7 S framework, rather than think that the right strategy and structure will automatically lead to business success.

The control mechanisms involve periodic review of the performance of the organization. They have a business review every month and a more strategic review held at the top level twice in a year. Besides this, four quarterly reviews are also held when the entire staff of KPIT is invited. This is essentially a participative and an interactive session that updates everyone on the latest developments and initiatives.

OD has definitely changed the organization. However, one should remember that this is a process and a journey and not a destination. Change brings bigger challenges, which requires even greater changes.

OD has brought about structural changes in the organization, a better collaboration and communication, a better orientation to business and quite a bit of positive energy, which is important to the success of the organization. This could become even more important in the challenges lying ahead of the serious players in the IT services industry as KPIT takes up the task of becoming very competitive.

OD in the present context is very essential if an organization wishes to sustain itself in the long run, rather than be focused only on the short term.

CONCLUDING COMMENTS

In this chapter, we examined the nature of organisation development and its central themes to establish a foundation for understanding the field. OD is a strategy for change that intervenes in the human and social processes of organizations. The illustrations demonstrate the themes in action—the use of action research, of teams of various configurations, of a consultant-facilitator, and of interventions into the organization's culture, structure, and processes.

In later chapters we will look more closely at the techniques, at the underlying theory and assumptions of OD, and at some of the pitfalls and challenges involved in attempting to improve organizations through behavioral science methods.

NOTES

1. Wendell L. French, *Human Resources Management*, 4th ed. (Boston: Houghton Mifflin, 1998), p. 6.
2. W. Warner Burke, *Organization Development: A Process of Learning and Changing*, 2d ed. (Reading, MA: Addison-Wesley Publishing Company, 1994), p. 9.
3. Peter B. Vaill, "Seven Process Frontiers for Organization Development," in *The Emerging Practice of Organization Development*, Walter Sikes, Allan B. Drexler, and Jack Gant, eds. (La Jolla, CA: Copublished by NTL Institute and University Associates, 1989), p. 261.
4. Jay M. Shafritz and J. Steven Ott, *Classics of Organization Theory*, 2d ed. (Chicago: The Dorsey Press, 1987), p. 234.

CHAPTER 2

Definitions and Historical Overview of Organization Development

The literature contains numerous definitions of organization development. We examine several here and present one of our own. A good way to gain an Appreciation for what OD is all about is to see how various authors have described the field over the years. No single accepted definition of OD exists, but there is general agreement on the nature of the field and its major characteristics.

Some early definitions of organization development follow.[1]

> Organization development is an effort (1) *planned,* (2) *organization – wide*, and (3) *managed from the top*, to (4) *increase organization effectiveness and health* through (5) *planned interventions* in the organization's "processes," using behavioral – science knowledge. (Beckard, 1969)
> *Organization development* (OD) is a response to change, a complex educational strategy intended to change the beliefs, attitudes, values, and structure of organizations so that they can better adapt to new technologies, markets, and challenges and the dizzying rate of change itself. (Bennis, 1969)
>
> OD can be defined as a planned and sustained effort to apply behavioral science for system improvement, using reflexive, self–analytic methods. (Schmuck and Miles, 1971)
> Organization development is a process of planned change–change of an organization' s culture from one which avoids an examination of social processes (especially decision-making, planning and communication) to one which institutionalizes and legitimizes this examination. (Burke and Hornstein, 1972)

More recent definitions of organization development are these.[2]

> [The aims of OD are] ... (1) enhancing congruence between organizational structure, processes, strategy, people, and culture.: (2) developing new and creative organizational solutions; and (3) developing the organization's self–renewing capacity.
> Organization development is an organizational process for understanding and improving any and all substantive processes an organization may develop for performing any task and pursuing any objectives.... A "process for improving processes"–that is what OD has basically sought to be for approximately 25 years. (Vaill, 1989)
>
> *Organizational development* is a set of behavioral science–based theories, values, strategies, and techniques aimed at the planned change of the organizational work setting for the purpose of

enhancing individual development and improving organizational performance, through the alteration of organizational members' on-the-job behaviors. (Porras and Robertson, 1992)

[OD is] ... *a systematic application of behavioral science knowledge to the planned development and reinforcement of organizational strategies, structures, and processes for improving an organization's effectiveness.* (Cummings And Worley, 1993)

Organization development is a planned process of change in an organization's culture through the utilization of behavioral science technologies, research, and theory. (Burke, 1994, p.12)

As you can see, these definitions overlap a great deal (that's encouraging), and contain several unique insights (that enlightening). All authors agree that OD applies behavioral science to achieve planned change, likewise, they agree that the target of change is the total organization or system and that the goals ate increased organizational effectiveness and individual development.

Schmuck and Miles provide an important insight with the words "reflexive, self-analytic methods." In OD, organization members systematically critique how they are doing to learn how to do better. Burke and Hornstein's idea of "legitimizing" an examination of social processes" speaks to the same issue of becoming more self-analytical.

Several definitions emphasize the importance of organization processes (Beckhard, Burke and Hornstein, and Vaill). Vaill depicts OD as a "process for improving processes"-a keen observation. Likewise, several definitions emphasize the crucial role of organization culture (Burke and Hornstein and Burke). Organization culture and processes are high-priority targets in most OD programs.

Beer and Cummings and Worley emphasize achieving congruence among the components of the organization such as strategy, structure, culture, and processes. Cummings and Worley suggest getting the components right (planned development), and keeping them right (reinforcement). Porass and Robertson suggest that OD is a "package" of theories, values, strategies and techniques. This package gives OD its distinct character compared to other improvement strategies.

Bennis calls OD both a response to change and an educational strategy intended to change beliefs, attitudes, values, and organization structure—all directed toward making his organization better able to respond to changing environmental demands. His definition is as relevant today as when it was first written. Porras and Robertson state that the aim of OD is to alter people's behaviors by changing organizational work settings. Beer's definition is the only one to mention, "developing the organization's self-renewing capacity"—a central goal in all OD programs—but all these authors agree with the desirability of creating self-renewing, "learning organizations."

Collectively, these definitions convey a sense of what organization development is in and does. They describe in broad outline the nature and methods of OD. There is no set definition of OD and no agreement on the boundaries of the field, that is, what practices should be included and excluded. But these are not serious constraints given that the field is still evolving, and that practitioners share a central core of understanding as shown in the preceding definitions.

Now let's turn to our definition of organization development. We do not propose it as the "right" definition, but as one that includes characteristics we think are important for the present and future of the field. *Organization development is a long-term effort, led and supported by top management to improve an organization's visioning, empowerment, learning, and problem-solving processes, through an ongoing, collaborative management of organization culture—with special emphasis on the culture of intact work teams and other team configurations—using the consultant-facilitator role and the theory And technology of applied behavioral science, including action research.* This definition is lengthy, but it includes a number of components we consider essential. We will explain this definition in some detail.

By *long-term effort* we mean that organizational change and development take time— several years in most cases. Ralph Kilmann's book, *Beyond the Quick Fix*, tells the story correctly: There is no "quick fix" when it comes to lasting organizational improvement.[3] In fact, it is more accurate to describe "improvement" as a never- ending journey of continuous change. One program or initiative moves the organization to a higher plateau; then another moves to yet a higher plateau of effectiveness.

The phrase *led and supported by top management* states an imperative: Top management must lead and actively encourage the change effort. Organizational change is hard, serious business; it includes pain and setbacks as well as successes. Top management must initiate the improvement "journey" and be committed to seeing it through. Most OD programs that fail to do so because top management was ambivalent, and, lost its commitment, or became distracted with other duties.

By *visioning processes*, we mean those processes through which organization members develop a viable, coherent, and shared picture of the nature of the products and services the organization offers, the ways those goods will be produced and delivered to customers, and what the organization and its members can expect from each other. Visioning means creating a picture of the desired future that includes salient features of the human side of the organization and then working together to make that picture a reality.

By *empowerment processes* we mean those leadership behaviors and human resource practices that enable organization members to develop and use their talents as fully as possible toward individual growth and organizational success. By empowerment, we mean involving large numbers of people in building the vision of tomorrow, developing the strategy for getting there, and making it happen. For empowerment to become a fact of life, it must be built into the very fabric of the organization—its strategy, structure, processes, and culture.

By *learning processes* we mean those interacting, listening, and self–examining processes that facilitate individual, team, and organizational learning. Peter Senge describes learning organizations as "... organizations where people continually expand their capacity to create the results they truly desire, where new and expansive patterns of thinking are nurtured, where collective aspiration is set free, and where people are continually learning how to learn together.[4] "As Chris Argyris advises, people and organizations must avoid the trap of "defensive routine" those habitual reactions that prevent embarrassment and threat, but that also prevent learning.[5]

Problem–solving processes refer to the ways organization members diagnose situations, solve problems, make decisions, and take actions on problems, opportunities, and challenges in the organization's environment and its internal functioning. Michael challenges in the organization's environment, and its internal functioning. Michael Beer's definition called for "developing new and creative organizational solutions." We believe solutions to problems are enhanced by tapping deeply into the creativity, commitment, vitality, and common purposes of all members of the organization, in contrast to having only a select few involved. We further believe that having a compelling, widely shared vision of a desired future creates the best climate for effective problem solving by all the organization's members. Empowerment means involving people in problems and decisions and letting them be responsible for results.

By *ongoing collaborative management of the organization's culture* we mean, first, that one of the most important things to manage in organizations is the *culture*: the prevailing patterns of values, attitudes, beliefs, assumptions, expectations, activities, interactions, norms, sentiments, and artifacts.[6] And second, managing the culture should be a collaborative business, one of widespread participation in creating and managing the culture that satisfies the wants and needs of individuals at the same time that it fosters the one, not just a small group, has a stake in making the organization work. Just as visioning, empowerment, learning, and problem-solving processes are opportunities for collaboration in organization development, so is managing the culture.

By including culture so prominently in our definition, we affirm our belief that culture is the bedrock of behavior in organizations. The reciprocal influence among culture, strategy, structure and processes make each important, and each influences the others. Still, culture is of primary importance. Edgar Schein clarifies the nature and power of culture in his definition: "Culture can now be defined as (a) a pattern of basic assumptions, (b) invented, discovered, or developed by a given group, (c) as it learns to cope with its problems of external adaptation and internal integration, (d) that has worked well enough to be considered valid and, therefore (e) is to be taught to new members as the (f) correct way to perceive, think and feel in relation to those problems."[7] So culture consists of basic assumptions, values, and norms of behavior that are viewed as the correct way to perceive, think, and feel–that is why culture change is necessary for true organizational improvement.

Our definition also places considerable weight on organizational processes. Processes are *how* things get done, we highlight the importance of visioning, empowerment, learning, and problem-solving processes. Processes are relatively easy to change, so they are the place OD programs often begin–getting people to stop doing things one way and start doing them a different way. But change becomes permanent when the culture changes and people accept the new ways as the "right" ways. We believe that when the culture promotes collaboration, empowerment, and continuous learning the organization is bound to succeed.

By *intact work teams and other configurations* we recognize the teams are central to accomplishing work in organizations. We think teams are the basic building blocks of organizations. When teams function well, individuals and the total organization function well. Further, team culture can be collaboratively managed to ensure effectiveness.

The most prevalent form of teams in organizations is intact work teams consisting of superior and subordinates with a specific job to perform. Team building and role and goal clarification interventions are standard activities in OD programs directed toward intact work teams. But in many organizations today, intact work teams do not have a boss in the traditional sense—the teams manage themselves. These self-directed teams assume complete responsibility for planning and executing work assignments. In addition to team building and role and goal clarification, members are trained in competencies such as planning, maintaining quality control, and using management information. Over time, self-directed teams control performance appraisals, hiring, firing, and training. The results are usually gratifying both for the team members and for the organization.

Today's organizations increasingly use ad hoc teams that perform a specific task and disband when the task is completed. The current method for getting complex tasks done in organizations is to assemble a cross-functional team comprised of members from all the functional specialists required to get the job done, such as design, engineering, manufacturing, and procurement. The old method was to have functional specialists work, on the problem sequentially. When one function finished with its part of the project, the process "threw the results over the wall" to the next functional unit. This method resulted in loss of synergy, wasted time much rework, and considerable antagonism among the separate functional specialists. The skills required to work effectively in teams will be at a premium in such a world.

The phrase *using the consultant–facilitator role* conveys our belief that leaders can benefit from seeking professional assistance in planning and implementing OD initiatives. In the early phases, at least, the services of a third-party consultant-facilitator are desirable. The third-party role is powerful: That person is typically seen as bringing objectivity, neutrality, and expertise to the situation. Also, the third party is not captive to the culture of the unit undertaking the program. This need of objectivity does not mean that the third party cannot be a member of the organization: rather, it means that he or she should not be a member of the particular unit initiating the OD effort.

Part of an effective OD effort is a growing appreciation of the consultant–facilitator role and the growing capability of many organizational members to perform that role, whether on and ad hoc or a more formal basis. Numerous members should be encouraged to increase their consultation skills and use these skills in various ways, such as helping to run more effective meetings or providing counsel to peers. We are thus calling attention to the facilitator role in organizations as well as facilitator *persons*.

By *the theory and technology of applied behavioral science*, we mean insights from the sciences dedicated to understanding people in organizations, how they function, and how they can function better, OD *applies* knowledge and theory. Therefore, in addition to the behavioral sciences such and psychology, sociology, and so on, applied disciplines such as adult education, psychotherapy, social work, economics, and political science make contributions to the practice of OD. Porras and Robertson state:

> Organizational development (OD) is the practical applications of science of organizations. Drawing from several disciplines for its models, strategies, and techniques. OD focuses on the planned change of human systems and contributes to organization science through the knowledge gained from its study of complex change dynamics.[8]

And finally, by *action research* we mean the partIcipative model of collaborative and iterative diagnosis and taking action on which the leader, organization members, and OD practitioner work together to define and resolve problems and opportunities. Because of the extensive applicability of this model in OD, another definition of organization development could be *organization improvement through participant action research*.

The definition we have just analyzed contains the elements we believe are important for OD. To summarize, here are the primary distinguishing characteristics of organization development.

1. OD focuses on culture and processes.
2. Specifically, OD encourages collaboration between organization leaders and members in managing culture and processes.

3. Teams of all kinds are particularly important for accomplishing tasks and are targets for OD activities.
4. OD focuses on the human and social side of the organization and in so doing also intervenes in the technological and structural sides.
5. Participation and involvement in problem solving and decision-making by all levels of the organization are hallmarks of OD.
6. OD focuses on total system change and views organizations as complex social systems.
7. OD practitioners are facilitators, collaborators, and co-learners with the client system.
8. An overarching goal is to make the client system able to solve it problems on its own by teaching the skills and knowledge of continuous learning through self- analytical methods. OD views organization improvement as 0an ongoing process in the context of a constantly changing environment.
9. OD relies on an action research model with extensive participation by client system members.
10. OD takes a developmental view that seeks the betterment of both individuals and the organization. Attempting to create "win-win" solutions is standard practice in OD programs.

These characteristics of organization development depart substantially from traditional consultation modes. Schein identifies the three following basic models of consultation–the first two are not OD, the third model is a good description of OD.[9]

In the "purchase of expertise model" a leader or unit identifies a need for information or expertise the organization cannot supply and hires a consultant to meet that need. Examples includes hiring a consultant to (1) survey consumers or employees about some matter, (2) Find out how organizations organize certain units, or (3) search out information such as the marketing strategy of a competitor. The consultant then makes recommendations.

In the "doctor-patient model" a leader or group detects symptoms of ill health in a unit, or more broadly in the organization, and employs a consultant to diagnose what is causing the problem or problems. The consultant, like a physician, then prescribes a course of action to remedy the ailment.

In the "process consultation model" the consultant works with the leader and group to diagnose strengths and weaknesses and to develop action plans. Furthermore, in this model the consultant assists the client organization to become more effective in diagnosing and solving problems.

The first two models depict traditional management consulting: the third model is more typical of OD consulting. In OD the clients receive help in the ways they go about solving problems. The consultant suggests general processes and procedures for addressing problems. The consultant helps the clients generate valid data and learn from them. In short, the OD consultant is an expert on *process*—how to structure effective problem solving and decision-making.

A HISTORY OF ORGANIZATION DEVELOPMENT

The history of organization development is rich with the contributions of behavioral scientists and practitioners, many of whom are well known, as well as the contributions of many people in client organizations. Even if we were aware of all the significant contributors, which we are not, we could not justice to the richness of this history in a short essay. Therefore, all we can do is write about what we believe to be the central thrusts of that history, based on our research to date, and hope that the many people who are not mentioned will not be offended by our incompleteness. Our focus will be largely the origins of OD plus some discussion of current trends and the current extent of application.

Systematic organization development activities have a recent history and, to use the analogy of a mangrove tree, have at least four important trunk stems. One trunk stem consists of innovations in applying laboratory-training insights to complex organizations. A second major stem is survey research and feedback methodology. Both stems intertwined with a third, the emergence of action research. Paralleling these stems, and to some extent linked, is a fourth stem—the emergence of the Tavistock sociotechnical and socioclinical approaches. The key actors in these stems interact with each other and are influenced by experiences and concepts form many fields, as we will see.

THE LABORATORY TRAINING STEM

The T-Group

Laboratory training, essentially unstructured small-group situations in which participants plants learn from their own actions and the group's evolving dynamics, began to develop about 1946 from various experiments in using discussion groups to achieve change sin behavior in back-home situations. In particular, an Inter-Group Relations workshop held at the State Teachers College in New Britain, Connecticut, in the summer of 1946 influenced the emergence of laboratory training. This workshop was sponsored by the Connecticut Interracial Commission and the Research Center for group Dynamics, then at MIT.

The Research Center for Group Dynamics (RCGD) was founded in 1945 under the direction of Kurt Lewin, a prolific theorist, researcher, and practitioner in inter-personal group, intergroup, and community relationships.[10] Lewin had been recruited to MIT largely through the efforts of Douglas McGregor of the Sloan School of Management, who had convinced MIT President Carl Compton of the wisdom of establishing a center for group dynamics. Lewin's original staff included Marian Radke, Leon Festinger, Ronald Lipitt, and Dorwin Cartwright.[11] Lewin's field theory and his conceptualizing about group dynamics, change processes, and action research profoundly influenced the people associated with the various stems of OD.

Through a series of events at the New Britain workshop of 1946, what was later to be called the "T-group" ("T" for training") began to emerge. The workshop consisted of Kurt Lewin, Kenneth Benne, Leland Bradford, and Ronald Lipitt. The latter three served as leaders of "learning groups" (sometimes called "l-groups"). Each group, in addition to group members and a leader, had an observer who made notes about interactions among members. At the end of each day, the observers met with the staff and reported what they had seen. At the second or third evening session, three members of the workshop asked if they could sit in on the reporting session, and were encouraged to do so. One woman disagreed with the observer about the meaning of her behavior during the day's sessions, and a lively discussion ensued. The three workshop members then asked to return to the next reporting session, and, because of the lively and rich discussion, Lewin and the staff enthusiastically agreed. By the next evening, about half of the 50–60 members of the workshop attended the feedback session. These sessions soon became the most significant learning experiences of the conference.[12]

This experience led to the National Training Laboratory in-group Development, organized by Benne, Bradford, and Lipitt (Lewin died in early 1947). They held a three–week session during the summer of 1947 at the Gould Academy in Bethel, Maine.[13] Participants met with a trainer and an observer in Basic Skill Training Groups (later called T-groups) for a major part of each day. The work of that summer evolved into the National Training Laboratory, later called NTL Institute for Applied Behavioral Science, and into contemporary T-group training. Out of the Bethel experiences and NTL grew a significant number of laboratory training centers sponsored by universities. One of the first was the Western Training Laboratory, headed by Paul Sheats and sponsored by UCLA.

In addition to Lewin and his work, extensive experience with role-playing and Moreno's psychodrama influenced Bradford, Lipitt, and Benne's invention of the T-group and the subsequent emergence of OD.[14] Further, Bradford and Benne were influenced by John Deweys' philosophy of education, including concepts about learning, and change and about the transactional nature of humans and their environment.[15] Benne, in collaboration with R. Bruce Raup and others, built on Dewey's philosophy, focusing on the processes by which people who differ reach policy agreements.[16] In addition, Benne was influenced by the works of Mary Follett, an early management theorist, including her ideas about integrative solutions to problems in organizations.[17]

As a footnote to the emergence of the T-group, the widespread use of flip–chart paper as a convenient way to record, retrieve, and display data in OD activities and in training sessions was invented by Ronald Lipitt and Lee Bradford during the 1946 New Britain sessions.

In a sense, the T-group emerged from an awareness that had been growing for a decade or more, awareness of the importance of helping groups and group leaders focus on group and leadership processes. This growing awareness was particularly evident in adult education and group therapy.[18] As the use of the laboratory method evolved, stated goals of T-group experiences tended to include such statements as "(1) self–in sight ... (2) understanding the conditions which inhibit or facilitate group functioning. (3) understanding interpersonal operations in groups, and (4) developing the skills for diagnosing the individual, group, and organizational behavior.[19]

While these insights and skills were practical and relevant for most participants, one driving force for the rapidly growing popularity of T-groups was probably their spiritual and therapeutic (therapy for normals) aspects.

Over the next decade, as trainers began to work with social systems of more permanency and complexity than T-groups, they began to experience considerable frustration in transferring laboratory behavior skills and insights of individuals into solving problems in organizations. Personal skills learned in the "stranger" T-groups setting were difficult to transfer to complex organizations. However, the training of "teams" from the same organization emerged early at bethel and undoubtedly was a link to the total organization focus of Douglas McGregor, Hebert Shepard, Robert Blake, and Jane Mouton and subsequently the focus of Richard Beckard, Chris Agyris, Jack Gibb, Warren Bennis, Eva Schindler- Rainman, and others.[20] All had been T-group trainers in NTL programs.

Growth of T-groups in India

Rolf Lynton in 1957 conducted initial groups in India. He established "Aloka" in Mysore in order to develop the capacity of youth. He implemented leadership training for 12 weeks, including unstructured group exercise.

In North India, Max Coley, Dean of Teachers, College, Columbia University, USA, and a member of NTL, stayed in Delhi from 1959 to1962 as a consultant to the Ministry of Education. He conducted T-Groups in his house, and Udai Pareek was one of participants. With the help of a recommendation from Coley, Pareek visited USA in 1961 for a half-year and was trained by NTL. He became a member and subsequently a Fellow of NTL. After his return to India, the first full-scale Laboratory Training in India was implemented in 1962 in Ferozpur by Coley and Pareek. In 1960 Lynton shifted to SEIT Institute and Pareek also joined him there.

They started "L-groups" in SEIT Institute from 1964. In 1960s, SEIT Institute became a central organization of Laboratory Training.

At the same time, Indian Institute of Management, Calcutta (IIM-C) invited some NTL members as visiting professors, and they implemented Laboratory Trainings there. After that, Behavioral Sciences Group in IIM–C had offered many labs, and this group became a base of Laboratory Training in eastern India.

Robert Tannenbaum

Some of the earliest sessions of what would now be called "team building" were conducted by Robert Tannenbaum in 1952 and 1953 at the U.S. Naval Ordnance test Station at China Lake, California.[21] According to Tannenbaum, the term *vertically structured groups* was used with groups dealing with "personal topics" (such as departmental sociometrics, interpersonal relationships, communication, and self analysis), and with organizational topics (such as deadlines, duties and responsibilities, policies and procedures, and quite extensively–with interorganizational group relations).[22] These sessions, which stimulated a 1954 *Personnel* article by Tannenbaum, Kallejian, and Weschler were conducted "with all managers of a given organizational unit present,[23] "The more personally oriented dynamics of such sessions were described in a 1955 Harvard Business review article by the same authors.[24]

Chris Argyris

In 1957, Chris Argyris, then a faculty member at Yale University (later at Harvard), was one of the first to conduct team-building sessions with a CEO and the top executive team. Two of Argyri's early clients were IBM and Exxon. His early research and interventions with a top executive group are reported in his 1962 book *Interpersonal Competence and Organizational Effectiveness*.[25]

In 1950, while working on a Ph. D. at Cornwell University, Argyris visited Bethel as a member of NTL's research staff in order to study T-groups. In his words, "I became fascinated with what I saw, and wanted to become a trainer. Several years later ... I was invited to become a staff member."[26]

Argyris was later to make extensive contributions to theory and research on laboratory training, OD, and organizational learning. One of his several books on OD, *Intervention Theory and Method*, stands as a classic in the field.[27]

Douglas McGregor

Beginning about 1957, Douglas McGregor, as a professor-consultant, working with Union Carbide was one of the first behavioral scientists to address the transfer problem and to talk systematically about and to help implement the application of T-group skills in complex organizations.[28] John Paul Jones, who had come up through industrial relations at Union Carbide, in collaboration with McGregor and with the support of a corporate executive vice president and director, Birny Mason, Jr. (later president of the corporation) established a small internal consulting group. In large part, this group used behavioral science knowledge to help line managers and their subordinates learn how to be more effective in-groups. McGregor's ideas were a dominant force in this consulting group; other behavioral scientists who influenced Jone's thinking were Rensis Likert and Mason Haire. Jone's organization was later called an "organization development group".[29]

Herbert Shepard

During the same year, 1957, introductions by Douglas McGregor led to Herbert Shepard's joining the employee relations department of Esso Standard Oil (now Exxon) as a research associate. Shepard was to have a major impact on the emergence of OD. Although we will focus mainly on Shepard's work at Esso, we also want to note that Shepard was later involved in community development activities and, in 1960, at the Case Institute of Technology, founded the first program devoted to training OD specialists.

In 1958 and 1959 Shepard launched three experiments in organization development at major Esso refineries: Bayonne, New Jersey: Baton Rouge, Louisiana; and Bayway, texas. At Bayonne, he conducted an interview survey that was discussed with top management. The survey was follower by a series of three-day laboratories for all members of management.[30] Paul Buchanan, who had worked earlier at the Naval Ordnance Test Station and more recently had been using a somewhat similar approach in Republic Aviation, collaborated with Shepard at Bayonne and subsequently joined the Esso staff.

Herbert Shepard and Robert Blake

At Baton Rouge, Robert Blake joined Shepard, and the two initiated a series of two–week laboratories attended by all members of "middle" management. At first, they tried to combine the case method with the laboratory method, but their designs soon emphasized T-groups, organizational exercises, and lectures. One innovation in this training program was an emphasis on intergroup as well as interpersonal problems affecting work performance was clearly an organizational effort, between group problem solving had even greater organization development implications because it involved a broader and more complex segment of the organization.

At Baton Rouge, efforts to involve top management failed, and as a result follow-up resources for implementing organization development were not available. By the time the Bayway program started, two fundamental OD lessons had been learned: the requirement for top management's active involvement in and leadership of the program and the need for on-the-job application.

Robert Blake and Jane Mouton

Several influences on Robert Blake up that point were important in the emergence of OD. While at Berea College majoring in psychology and philosophy (later an M.A. University of Virginia, and a Ph. D. University of Texas). Blake was strongly influenced by the works of Korzybshki and the general semanticists and found that "seeing discrete things as representative of a continuous series was much more stimulating and rewarding than just seeing two things as 'opposites.'" This thinking contributed in later years to Blake's conceptualization of the Managerial Grid with Jane Mouton and to their intergroup research on win–lose dynamics, This intergroup research and the subsequent design of their intergroup conflict management workshops were also heavily influenced by Muzafer Sherif's fundamental research on intergroup dynamics.[31] Jane Mouton's influence on Blake's thinking and on the development of the Grid stemmed partly, in her words, "from my undergraduate work (at Texas) in pure mathematics and physics which emphasized the significance of measurement, experimental design, and a scientific approach to phenomena,"[32] (Mouton later attained an M.A. from the University of Virginia and a Ph. D. from the University of Texas).

Richard Beckard

Richard Beckhard worked with McGregor at General Mills in 1959 or 1960, where McGregor was working with Dewey Balsch, vice president of personnel and industrial relations, in an attempt to facilitate "a total organizational culture change program which today might be called quality of work life or OD." Beckard goes on to say, "The issues that were being worked were relationships between workers and supervision; roles of supervision and management at various levels; participative management for real ... This experience was one of the influences on Doug's original paper, 'The Human side of Enterprise' ... and from which the book emerged a year or so later."[33]

Beckard developed one of the first major nondegree training programs in OD, NTL's Program for Specialists in Organizational Training and Development (PSOTD). The first program was an intensive four–week session held in the summer of 1967 at Bethel, Maine, the same year that UCLA launched its Learning Community in OD. Core staff members the first year in the NTL program were Beckard as dean, Warner Burke, and Fritz Steele. Additional resource persons the first year were Herbert Shepard, Sheldon Davis, and Chris Argyris.

Warren Bennis

During his career, Bennis became vice president for academic affairs at State University of New York at Buffalo, and then president of the University of Cincinnati. His associates and mentors, particularly in the earlier years, included Douglas McGregor, Ed Schein, Mason Haire, Abraham Maslow, Carl Rogers, Kenneth Benne, Herb Shepard, Leland Bradford, Peter Drucker, and Robert Chin. He was also influenced by the labor economist George Schultz (later to be Secretary of Labor and Secretary of State). Elton Mayo, and Henry Stack Sullivan. Some of his more notable publications include the book The Planning of Change, written with Kenneth Benne and Robert Chin,[34] and the essay "Democracy Is Inevitable,"[35] co-authored with Philip Slater.

Eva Schindler-Rainman

Probably one of the first persons to be an NTL staff member doing OD work and have been trained almost exclusively in the social work field was Eva Schlinder-Rainman. Schlinder-Rainman was awarded both a masters and doctorate from the University of

Southern California with specialties in group work, organizational behavior, and community organization. While employed as director of personnel and training for the Los Angeles Girl Scouts Council, in the early 1950s she attended one of the first events of the Western Training Laboratory. Her T-group trainers there were Gordon Hearn and Marguerite Vanderworker.

Schindler-Rainman worked with a wide range of clients, both in the United States and internationally. A few of her well-known publications are *The Creative Volunteer Community*,[36] *A Collection of Writings* and *Team Training for Community Change*.[37] (The latter three, were co-authored with Ronald Lipitt.) Schlinder-Rainman's extensive processional training, her collaboration with a number of key mean and women in the early days of NTL and the OD movement, and her early and extensive contribution to the community development movement clearly identify her as one of the pioneers in the laboratory training stem of OD.

The Term Organization Development

It is not entirely clear who coined the term *organization development*, but the term likely emerged more or less simultaneously on two or three places through the works of Robert Blake, Herbert Shepard, Jane Mouton, Douglas McGregor, and Richard Beckhard.[38] The phrase, *development group* had been used earlier by Blake and Mouton in connection with human relations training at the University of Texas, and it appeared in their 1956 document distributed for use in the Baton Rouge Experiment.[39] (The same phrase appeared in a Mouton and Blake article first published in the journal *Group Psychotherapy* in 1957.[40]) The Baton Rouge T-groups run by Shepard and Blake were called *development groups*,[41] and this program of T-groups was called "organization development" to distinguish it from the complementary management development programs already underway.[42]

Thus, the term emerged as a way of distinguishing a different mode of working with organizations and as a way of highlighting its developmental, systemwide, dynamic thrust.

THE SURVEY RESEARCH AND FEEDBACK STEM

Survey research and feedback,[43] a specialized form of action research (see chapter 7) constitutes the second major stem in the history of organization development. The history of this stem revolves around the techniques and approach developed over a period of years by staff members at the Survey Research Center (SRC) of the University of Michigan.

Rensis Likert

The SRC was founded in 1946 after Rensis Likert, director of the Division of Program Surveys of the Federal Bureau of Agricultural Economics, and other key members of the division moved to Michigan. Likert held a Ph. D. in psychology from Columbia, and his dissertation. *A Technique for the Measurement of Attitudes* was the classic study that developed the widely used five-point Likert scale. After completing his degree and teaching at Columbia for a while, Likert worked for the Life Insurance Agency Management Association. There he conducted research on leadership, motivation, moral, and productivity. He then moved to the U.S. Department of Agriculture, where his Division of Program Surveys furthered a more scientific approach to survey research in its work with various federal departments, including the Office of War Information.[44] In 1948 after helping to develop and direct the Survey Research Center, Likert became the director of a new Institute for Social Research, which included both the SRC and the Research Center for group Dynamics. The latter had moved to Michigan from MIT after Lewin's death.

Floyd Mann, Rensis Likert, and Others

Part of the emergence of survey research and feedback was based on refinements made by SRC staff members in survey methodology. Another part was the evolution of feedback methodology.

> The problem of how the company could best use the data from the survey to bring improvement in management and performance. This led to the development and use of the survey–feedback method. Floyd particularly played a key role in this development. He found that when the survey data were reported to a manager (or supervisor) and he or she failed to discuss the results with subordinates and failed to plan with them what the manager and others should do to bring improvement, little change occurred. On the other hand, when the manager discussed the results with subordinates and planned with them what to do to bring improvement, substantial favorable changes occurred.[45]

Another aspect of the Detroit Edison study was the process of feeding back data from an attitude survey to the participating departments in what Mann calls an "interlocking chain of conferences. Additional insights are provided by Baumgartel, who participated in the project and who drew the following conclusions from the Detroit Edison study:"

> The results of this experimental study lend support to the idea that an intensive, group discussion procedure for utilizing the results of an employee questionnaire survey can be an effective tool for introducing positive change in a business organization. It may be that the effectiveness of this method, in comparison to traditional training courses, is that it deals with the system of human relationships as a whole (superior and subordinate can change together) and it deals with each manager, supervisor, and employee in the context of his own job, his own problems, and his own work relationships.[46]

Links between the Laboratory Training Stem and the Survey Feedback Stem

As early as 1940, links occurred between people who were later to be key figures in the laboratory training stem of OD and people who were to be key features in the survey feedback stem. These links, which continued over the years, were undoubtedly of significance in the evolution of both stems. Of particular interest are the links between the Likert and Lewin and between Likert and key figures in the laboratory training stem of OD. As Likert states, "I met Lewin at the APA annual meeting at State College, Pa. I believe in 1940. When he came to Washington during the war, I saw him several times and got to know him and his family quite well".[47]

THE ACTION RESEARCH STEM

In earlier chapters we briefly described action research as a collaborative, client-consultant inquiry. Chapter 7 describes four versions of action research, one of which, participant action research, is used with the most frequency in OD. The laboratory training stem in the history of OD has a heavy component of Action research; the survey feedback stem is the history of a specialized form of action research; and Tavistock projects have had a strong action research thrust, as we will discuss shortly.

THE SOCIOTECHNICAL AND SOCIOCLINICAL STEM

A fourth stem in the history of OD is the evolution of socioclinical and sociotechnical approaches to helping groups and organizations. Parallel to the work of the RCD, the SRC, and the NTL was the work of the Tavistock Clinic in England.

In the latter half of 1960s, 14 individuals from India visited U.S. and studied in NTL, some were supported by IIM-Calcutta and some were self–sponsored, etc (Sinha 1986). They started offering laboratory training to industrial companies and realised soon that facilitators like NTL would be needed in India too. In 1971, by Francis Menezes' proposal, a two-day conference for establishing an association of T-Group facilitators was held in Pune. As a result, the Indian Society for Applied Behavioral Science (ISABS) was established in 1972.

W. R. Bion, Rickman, and Others

The professional staff of the Tavistock Clinic was extensively influenced by such innovations as W0orld War II applications of social psychology to psychiatry, the work of W.R. Bion and John Rickman and others in group therapy, Lewin's notions about the "social field" in which a problem was occurring, and Lewin's theory and experience with action research. Bion, Rickman, and others had been involved with the a six-week "Northfield Experiment" at a military hospital near Birmingham during World War II. In this experiment each soldier was required to join a group that performed some task such as handicraft or map reading as well as discussed feelings, interpersonal relations, and administrative and managerial problems. Insights from this experiment carried over into Bion's theory of group behavior.[48]

Eric Trist

A clear historical and conceptual connection can be made between the group dynamics filed and the sociotechnical approaches to assisting organizations. Tavistock's sociotechnical approach is particularly significant in that it grew out of Eric Trist's 1947 visit to a British coal mine at Haighmoor; his insights as to a relevance of Lewin's work on group dynamics and Bion's work on leaderless groups resulted in a new approach to solving mine problems.[49] Trist was also influenced by the systems concepts of Von Bertalanffy and Andras Angyal.[50]

Trist's subsequent experiments in work design and the use of semiautonomous work teams in coal mining were the forerunners of other work redesign experiments in various industries in Europe, India, Australia, and the United States. In these experiments, terms such as *industrial democracy*, *open systems*, and *sociotechnical systems* were used by Trist and his colleagues, including Fred Emergy.[51] (Emergy's extensive collaboration with Eric Trist includes the development of "Search Conferences", to be discussed later.)

Tavistock-U.S. Links

Tavistock leaders, including Trist and Bion, had frequent contact with Kurt Lewin, Rensis Likert, Chris Argyris, and others in the United States. One product of this collaboration was the decision to publish the journal Human Relations as a joint publication between Tavistock and MIT's Research Center for Group Dynamics.[52] Some Americans prominent in the emergence and evolution of the OD field, for example, Robert Blake, as we noted earlier, and Warren Bennis,[53] studied at Tavistock. Chris Argyris held several seminars with Tavistock leaders in 1954.[54]

SECOND-GENERATION OD

Practitioners and researchers are giving considerable attention to emerging concepts, interventions, and areas of application that might be called second-generation OD. Each, to some extent, overlaps with some or all of the others. Second-generation OD, in particular, has a focus on organizational transformation.

Interest in Organizational Transformation

More and more practitioners and scholars are talking about "organizational transformation." "Amir Levy and Uri Merry give one of the most complete explorations of this topic in their book, *Organizational Transformation.* They define the term as follows: Second-order change (organization transformation) is a multi–dimensional, multi–level, qualitative, dis- continuous, radical organizational change involving a paradigmatic shift.[55]

Increasingly, OD professionals distinguish between the more modest, or evolutionary, efforts toward organization improvement and those that are massive and, in a sense, revolutionary. For example, Nadler and Tushman refer to "transitions" on the one hand, and "frame bending" on the other.[56] Goodstein and Burke contrast "fine tuning" Barczak, Smith, and Wilemon differentiate "adaptive, incremental change" from "large-scale change in the organisation strategy and culture,"[57] Beckhard and Pritchard contrast "incremental" change strategies and "fundamental" change strategies.[58] Organizational transformation is seen as requiring more demands on top leadership, more visioning, more experimenting, more time, and the simultaneous management of many additional variables.

Interest in the Learning Organization

The works of Argyris,[59] Argyris and Schon,[60] and Senge have stimulated considerable interest in the conditions under which individuals, teams, and organizations learn. Argyris, for example, has focused on the defensive routines of organizational members, or "master programs in their heads that tell them how to deal with embarrassment and threat," Basically, according to Argyris, individuals tend to follow these rules:

1. Bypass embarrassment and threat whenever possible.
2. Act as though you are not bypassing them.
3. Don't discuss steps 1 and 2 while they are happening.
4. Don't discuss the undiscussability of the undiscussable.[61]

Workshops with top management teams are designed to tackle simultaneously major tasks such as strategy formulation plus learning how to recognize defensive routines that hinder improvements in communications and the quality of team decision-making.[62]

Senge writes extensively about the importance of systems thinking ("the fifth discipline") in organizations, and about the learning disabilities that plague organizations. One learning disability, for example, is focusing on one's own job exclusively with little sense of responsibility for the collective product. Another is blaming the "enemy out there" for things that are wrong, whether it's another department in the same organization or a competitor overseas.[63] Senge is noted for workshops in which he uses games and exercises to create an awareness of these disabilities and to develop different ways of thinking about complex problems.[64]

Intensified Interest in Teams

A focus on intact work teams and other team configurations has been central to OD since the emergence of the field, but recent years have seen a widening and deepening interest in teams, especially what are called high-performance teams, and self-managed teams, Interest has intensified particularly in self-managed or self-directed teams. This interest had accelerated due to converging pressures on organizations to improve quality, to become more flexible, to reduce layers of management, and to enhance employee morale.[65]

Laboratory training methods have proved highly useful in training team members in effective membership and leadership behaviors, and in training supervisors and managers in the arts of delegation and empowerment. Furthermore, many organizations use team-building approaches to help self-managed teams and cross-functional teams get started. In addition, as self- managed teams have assumed many functions previously performed by management, supervisors and middle managers have used team-building approaches within their own ranks to help conceptualize their own roles.

Interest in Total Quality management

The past decade has seen a mushrooming of interest in total quality management worldwide, and then perhaps some decline in application as both successes and failures have been reported. Applications that have been successful appear to have some ingredients in common with OD efforts.

Ciampa, who acknowledges the pioneering contributions of Joseph Juran, W. Edwards Deming, and Armand Feigenbaum to the development of TQM,[66] provides a clear statement on the relationship between TQM and OD. First, his definition: "Total Quality is typically a countrywide effort seeking to install and make permanent a climate where employees continuously improve their ability to provide on demand products and services that customers will find of particular value."[67] He then goes on to say that one element that separates successful TQ efforts from less successful ones is

> … a particular set of values about the individual and the individual's role in the organization. TQ efforts in these companies encourage true employee involvement, demand teamwork, seek to push decision- making power to lower levels in the company, and reduce barriers between people…. These values are at the core of Organization Development (OD), as well.[68]

Burke also comments on the contribution OD can make TO TQM efforts. Focusing on the OD practitioner, he states: "...the quality movement, to be successful, is highly dependent on effective process—and process is the OD practitioner's most important product."[69]

Interest in Visioning and Future Search

Interventions designed to help organizational members look to the future-visioning are not new to OD, but renewed interest has developed in using interventions to look at trends projected into the future and their organizational implications. Marvin Weisbord, for example, has built on the work and experience of Ronald Lipitt and Edward Lindaman, Ronald Fox, Ronald Lipitt, and Eva Schlinder-Rainman,[70] and Eric Trist and Fred Emery[71] to develop "future search conferences." In a two-or-three-day conference, participants are asked to "(a) build a data base, (b) look at it altogether, (c) interpret what they find, and (d) draw conclusions for action."[72] This last part of the conference asks participants to develop next action steps and a structure for carrying them out, including task forces and specific assignments.[73]

Senge believes that "the origin of the vision is much less important than the process whereby it comes to be shared." He strongly urges that "shared visions" be based on encouraging organizational members to develop and share their own personal visions, and he claims that a vision is not truly shared "until it connects with the personal visions of people throughout the organization." This type of connection obviously requires OD–like processes to implement.

Rediscovering Large Meetings and Getting the "Whole System" in the Room

As described earlier, one contributing factor in the emergence of the IOD movement was the experience of people such as Leland Bradford, Ronald Lipitt, and Richard Beckhard in improving the effectiveness of large meetings. Early on, Beckhard wrote an article entitled "The Confrontation Meeting," which was really about getting the total management group of an organization together in a one-day session to diagnose the state of the system and to make plans for quickly improving conditions.[74] In recent years, Marvin Weisbord and others have written about the importance of OD consultants "getting the whole system in the room." For example, with reference to future search conferences, he advises that such conferences, he advises that such conferences involve all of top management and "people from as many functions and levels as feasible." Again, the final products are action plans and specific assignments to carry the process forward.[75]

Others Directions and Areas of interest

Widespread business and media interest in *reengineering*—called by various names such as *business process reengineering and core process redesign*[76]–has caught the attention of OD practitioners and theorists. OD processes and values appear not to underly most reengineering efforts, and the almost-stampede by business and industry to embrace reengineering raises a number of issues pertaining to the role that OD practitioners should or should not play relative to this phenomenon.

All these areas are fruitful areas for OD theory, research, and practice. However, with the diffusion of OD techniques into so many areas, identifying what is and what is not OD becomes more difficult. Thus, the importance of examining the assumptions and the processes underlying various improvement efforts cannot be overstated—not because OD or the team "OD" is inherently sacred—because the fundamental building blocks of OD as defined in this book are vital ingredients, we believe, to long-term organizational effectiveness and to participant satisfaction and development.

EXTENT OF APPLICATION

Applications have varied, with the total organization involved in many instances, but with only some divisions or plants in others. Further, some efforts have moved ahead rapidly, only to flounder at a later time. In many situations, OD approaches have become an ongoing way of managing with little program visibility and under different terminology. Thus, the extent of application is sometimes difficult to report with any precision.

Business and industrial organizations are by no means the only kinds of institutions involved. Applications can be made, for example, in public school systems; colleges; medical schools; social welfare agencies; police departments; professional associations; governmental units at the local, country, state, and national levels; the White House;[77] various health care delivery systems; churches; Native American tribes; and the U.S. military.

The emergence and growth of the OD Network indicates the widespread application of organization development concepts. The OD Network began in 1964 and by 1998 had a membership of about 34,000 and 46 regional networks. Most members either have major roles in the OD efforts of organizations or are scholar-practitioners in the OD field. Although most Network members reside in the United States, in 1998 the Network included 184 international members, the majority from Canada. Thirty-one countries were represented in addition to the United States.

The first doctoral program devoted to training OD specialists was founded by Herbert Shepard in 1960 at the Case Institute of Technology. Originally called The Organizational Behavior Group, this program is not part of the Department of Organizational Behavior, School of Management, Case Western Reserve University, UCLA also has a program at the doctoral level. Pepperdine offers a Doctor of Education in Organization Change (EdDOC), and Benediction University offers a Ph.D. in Organization Development.

CONCLUDING COMMENTS

Organization development emerged largely from applied behavioral sciences and has four major stems: (1) the invention of the T-group and innovations in the application of laboratory training insights to complex organizations, (2) the invention of survey feedback technology, (3) the emergence of action research, and (4) the evolution of the Tavistock socioclinical approaches.

Key figures in this early history interacted with each other across these stems and were influenced by concepts and experiences, from a wide variety of disciplines and settings.

These disciplines included social psychology, clinical psychology, family group therapy, ethnography, military psychology and psychiatry, the theater, general semantics, social work, systems theory, mathematics and physics, philosophy, psychodrama, client-centered therapy, survey methodology, experimental and action research, human resources management, organizational behavior, general management theory, and large conference management.

The context for applying OD approaches has changed to an increasingly turbulent environment. While practitioners still rely on OD basics, they are giving considerable attention to new concepts, interventions, and areas of application. Among the directions of interest in second-generation OD are organizational transformation, organizational culture, the learning organization, high-performance teams, total quality management, "getting the whole system in the room," future search, and the role of OD practitioners should play in reengineering.

The field of OD is emergent in that a rapidly increasing number of behavioral scientists and practitioners are building on the research and insights of the past as well as rediscovering the utility of some of the earlier insights. These efforts, often under different terminology, are now expanding and include a wide range of organizations, types of institutions, occupational categories and geographical locations.

In the chapters that follow, the assumptions, theory, and techniques of organization development, as well as problems with implementing OD processes, will be examined in considerable depth. We will also speculate on the future viability of OD or OD-like processes.

NOTES

1. See Richard Beckhard, *Organization Development: Strategies and Models* (Reading, MA: Addision-Wesley Publishing Company, 1969), p. 9; Warren G. Bennis, *Organization Development: Its Nature, Origins, and Prospects* (Reading, MA: Addison-Wesley Publishing Company, 1969), p. 2; Richard Schmuck and Matthew Miles, *Organization Development in Schools* (Palo Alto, CA: National Press Books, 1971), p. 2; and Warner Burke and Harvey A. Hornstein, *The Social Technology of Organization Development* (Fairfax, VA: Learning Resources Corp., 1972), p. ix.
2. See Michael Beer, *Organization Change and Development* (Santa Monica, CA: Goodyear Publishing, 1980), p. 10; Peter B. Vaill, "Seven Process Frontiers for Organization Development," in *The Emerging Practice of Organization Development*, Walter Sikes, Allan B. Drexler, and Jack Gant, eds. (La Jolla, CA: Copublished by NTL Institute and University Associates, 1989), p. 261; Jerry I. Porras and Peter J. Robertson, "Organizational Development: Theory, Practice, and Research," in Marvin D. Dunnette and Leaetta M. Hough, eds., *Handbook of Industrial and Organizational Psychology*, 2d ed., vol. 3 (Palo Alto, CA: Consulting Psychologists Press, 1992), p. 272; Thomas G. Cummings and Christopher G. Worley, Organization Development and Change, 5th ed. (St. Paul, MN: West Publishing, 1993), p. 2; W. Warner Burke, *Organization Development: A Process of Learning and Changing*, 2d ed. (Reading, MA: Addison-Wesley Publishing Company, 1994), p. 12.
3. Ralph H. Kilmann, *Beyond The Quick Fix: Managing Five Tracks to Organizational Success* (San Francisco: Jossey-Bass, 1984).
4. Peter M. Senge, *The Fifth Discipline: The Art and Practice of the Learning Organization* (New York: Doubleday/Currency, 1990), p. 3.

5. Chris Argyris, *Strategy, Change, and Defensive Routines* (Boston: Pitman, 1985).
6. A. L. Kroeber and Clyde Kluckhohn, *Culture: A Critical Review of Concepts and Definitions* (New York: Vintage Books, 1952). They examined 164 definitions of culture and arrived at the following synthesis: "*Culture consists of patterns, explicit and implicit, of and for behavior acquired and transmitted by symbols, constituting the distinctive achievement of human groups, including their embodiments in artifacts; the essential core of culture consists of traditional (i.e., historically derived and selected) ideas and especially their attached values; culture systems may, on the one hand, be considered as products of action, on the other as conditioning elements of further action,*" pp. 291, 357, authors' emphasis. Our definition is congruent with their synthesis. See also Ralph H. Kilmann, Mary J. Saxton, Roy Serpa, and Associates, *Gaining Control of the Corporate Culture* (San Francisco: Jossey-Bass Publishers, 1985), p. ix.
7. Edgar H. Schein, "Organizational Culture," *American Psychologist*, 45 (February 1990), p. 111.
8. Porras and Robertson, "Organizational Development: Theory, Practice, and Research," p. 720.
9. Edgar H. Schein, *Process Consultation, Vol. I: Its Role in Organization Development* (Reading, MA: Addision-Wesley Publishing Company, 1988), pp. 5–11.
10. The phrase *group dynamics* was coined by Kurt Lewin in 1939. See Warrent Bennis, address to the Academy of Management, San Diego, California, August 3, 1981.
11. This and the next paragraph are based on Kenneth D. Benne, Leland P. Bradford, Jack R. Gibb, and Ronald O. Lippitt, eds., *The Laboratory Method for Changing and Learning: Theory and Application* (Palo Alto, CA: Science and Behavior Books, 1975), pp. 1–6; and Alfred J. Marrow, *The Practical Theorist: The Life and Work of Kurt Lewin* (New York: Basic Books, 1969), pp. 210–214. For additional history, see Leland P. Bradford, "Biography of an Institution," Journal of Applied Behavioral Science, 3 (April–June 1967), pp. 127–143; and Alvin Zander, "The Study of Group Behavior During Four Decades," *The Journal of Applied Behavioral Science*, 15 (July–September 1979), pp. 272–282. We are indebted to Ronald Lippitt for his correspondence, which helped to clarify this and the following paragraph.
12. Jerrold I. Hirsch, The History of the National Training Laboratories 1947–1986 (New York: Peter Lang publishing, 1987), pp. 17–18; and address by Ronald Lippitt, Academy of Management annual conference, Chicago, Illinois, August 1986. For more on Bradford, see David L. Bradford, "A Biography of Leland P. Bradford," *Journal of Applied Behavioral Science*, 26, no. 1 (1990), viii.
13. See also Nancie Coan, "A History of NTL Institute in Bethel," *NTL Institute News & Views* (February 1991), pp. 11–15.
14. Peter B. Smith, ed., *Small Groups and Personal Change* (London: Methuen & Co. 1980), pp. 8–9.
15. Robert Chin and Kenneth D. Benne, "General Strategies for Effecting Changes in Human Systems," in Warren G. Bennis, Kenneth D. Benne, and Robert Chin, eds., *The Planning of Change*, 2d ed. (New York: Holt, Rinehardt and Winston, 1969), pp. 100–102.
16. Correspondence with Kenneth Benne. Raup was Benne's Ph.D. major professor at Columbia. Benne states that he was also influenced by Edward Lindeman. For more on Benne, see Paul Nash, "Biography of Kenneth D. Benne," *Journal of Applied Behavioral Science*, 28 (June 1992), p. 167.
17. Chin and Benne, op cit., p. 102.
18. See, for example, S. R. Slavson, *An Introduction to Group Therapy* (New York: The Commonwealth Fund, 1943); and S. R. Slavson, *Creative Group Education* (New York: Association press, 1937), especially chapter 1.

19. Edgar H. Schein and Warren G. Bennis, *Personal and Organizational Change Through Group Methods: The Laboratory Approach* (New York: John Wiley & Sons, 1965), p. 35.

20. Based largely on correspondence with Ronald Lippitt. According to Lippitt, as early as 1945 Bradford and Lippitt were conducting "three-level training" at Freedman's Hospital in Washington, D.C., in an effort "to induce interdependent changes in all parts of the same system." Lippitt also reports that Leland Bradford very early was acting on a basic concept of "multiple entry," that is, simultaneously training and working with several groups in the organization.

21. Correspondence with Robert Tannenbaum.

22. Tannenbaum correspondence; memorandum of May 12, 1952, U.S. Naval Ordnance Test Station from E. R. Toporeck to "Office, Division and Branch Heads, Test Department," and "Minutes, Test Department Management Seminar, 5 March 1953."

23. Robert Tannenbaum, Verne Kallejian, and Irving R. Weschler, "Training Managers for Leadership," *Personnel*, 30 (January 1954), p. 3.

24. Verne J. Kallejian, Irving R. Weschler, and Robert Tannenbaum, "Managers in Transition," *Harvard Business Review*, 33 (July–August 1955), pp. 55–64.

25. Correspondence with Chris Argyris; and Chris Argyris, *Interpersonal Competence and Organizational Effectiveness* (Homewood, IL: Richard D. Irwin, 1962).

26. Argyris correspondence.

27. Chris Argyris, *Intervention Theory and Method* (Reading, MA: Addison-Wesley, 1970).

28. See Richard Beckhard, W. Warner Burke, and Fred I. Steele, "The Program for Specialists in Organization Training and Development," p. ii, mimeographed paper (NTL Institute for Applied Behavioral Science, December 1967); and John Paul Jones, "What's Wrong with Work?" in *What's Wrong with Work?* (New York: National Association of Manufacturers, 1967), p. 8. According to correspondence with Rensis Likert, the link between McGregor and John Paul Jones occurred in the summer of 1957. Discussion took place between the two when Jones attended one of the annual two-week seminars at Aspen, Colorado, organized by Hollis Peter of the Foundation for Research on Human Behavior and conducted by Douglas McGregor, Mason Haire, and Rensis Likert.

29. Gilbert Burck, "Union Carbide's Patient Schemers," *Fortune*, 72 (December 1965), pp. 147–149. For McGregor's account, see "Team Building at Union Carbide," in Douglas McGregor, *The Professional Manager* (New York: McGraw-Hill, 1967), pp. 106–110.

30. Much of the historical account in this paragraph and the following three paragraphs is based on correspondence and interviews with Herbert Shepard, with some information added from correspondence with Robert Blake.

31. Blake correspondence.

32. Mouton correspondence.

33. Correspondence with Richard Beckhard.

34. Bennis, *An Invented Life: Reflections on Leadership and Change* pp. 15–29.

35. Warren G. Bennis and Philip Slater, "Democracy Is Inevitable," *Harvard Business Review* (September–October 1990).

36. Eva Schindler-Rainman, *The Creative Volunteer Community: A Collection of Writings by Eva Schindler-Rainman*, D.S.W. (Vancouver, BC: Vancouver Volunteer Centre, 1987).

37. Eva Schindler-Rainman and Ronald Lippitt, *Team Training for Community Change: Concepts, Goals, Strategies and Skills* (Bethesda, MD: Development Publications, 1972). (Third printing, 1993, available through Dr. Eva Schindler-Rainman, 4267 San Rafaei Avenue, Los Angeles, CA 90042.)

38. Interpretations of Blake correspondence, Shepard interview, Beckhard correspondence, and Larry Porter, "OD: Some Questions Some Answers—An Interview with Beckhard and Shepard," *OD Practitioner*, 6 (Autumn 1974), p. 1.

39. Blake correspondence.
40. Jane Srygley Mouton and Robert R. Blake, "University Training in Human Relations Skills," *Selected Readings Series Three: Forces in Learning* (Washington DC: National Training Laboratories, 1961), pp. 88–96, reprinted from *Group Psychotherapy*, 10 (1957), pp. 342–345.
41. Shepard and Blake correspondence.
42. Interview with Herbert Shepard, San Diego, California, August 3, 1981.
43. This history is based largely on correspondence with Rensis Likert and partially on "The Career of Rensis Likert," ISR Newsletter (Winter 1971); and *A Quarter Century of Social Research*, Institute for Social Research (1971). See also Charles Cannell and Robert Kahn, "Some Factors in the Origins and Development of The Institute for Social Research, The University of Michigan," *American Psychologist*, 39 (November 1984), pp. 1256–1266.
44. "Rensis Likert," *ISR newsletter*, p. 6.
45. Likert correspondence. Floyd Mann later became the first director of the Center for Research on the Utilization of Scientific Knowledge (CRUSK) when the center was established by ISR in 1964. See also Floyd C. Mann, "Studying and Creating Change," in Bennis, Benne, and Chin, eds. *Planning of Change*, pp. 605–613.
46. Howard Baumgartel, "Using Employee Questionnaire Results for Improving Organizations: The Survey (Feedback) Experiment," *Kansas Business Review*, 12 (December 1959), pp. 2–6.
47. Likert correspondence.
48. Based on Ibid., 5, 7, 133, 140; and Robert DeBoard, *The Psychoanalysis of Organizations* (London: Tavistock 1978), pp. 35–43.
49. Eric Trist and Marshall Sashkin, "Interview," *Group & Organization Studies*, 5 (June 1980), pp. 150–151; and Kleiner, The Age of Heretics, pp. 63–64.
50. Trist and Sashkin, p. 155. See also William A. Pasmore and Guruder S. Khalsa, "The Contributions of Eric Trist to the Social Engagement of Social Science," *Academy of Management Review*, 18 (July 1993), pp. 546–569.
51. Kleiner, p. 65.
52. Trist and Sashkin, pp. 144–151.
53. Bennis address, Academy of Management, August 3, 1981.
54. Argyris correspondence.
55. Amir Levy and Uni Merry, *Organizational Transformation* (New York: Praeger Publishers, 1986), p. 5.
56. David A. Nadler and Michael L. Tushman, "Organizational Frame Bending: Principles for Managing Reorientation," *The Academy of Management EXECUTIVE*, 3 (August 1989), pp. 194–204.
57. Leonard D. Goodstein and W. Warner Burke, "Creating Successful Organization Change," *Organizational Dynamics*, 19 (Spring 1991), pp. 5–17.
58. Richard Beckhard and Wendy Pritchard, *Changing the Essence* (San Francisco: Jossey-Bass Publishers, 1992), p. 3; and Richard Beckhard, "Choosing and Leading a Fundamental Change," *Academy of Management ODC Newsletter* (Summer 1993), pp. 6–8.
59. Chris Argyris, *Overcoming Organizational Defensive Routines* (Boston: Allyn and Bacon, 1990).
60. Chris Argyris and Donald Schon, *Organizational Learning* (Reading, MA: Addison-Wesley, 1976).
61. Chris Argyris, "Strategy Implementation and Experience in Learning," *Organizational Dynamics*, 18 (Autumn 1989), pp. 8, 9.
62. Ibid., pp. 5–15; and Chris Argyris, "Teaching Smart People How to Learn," *Harvard Business Review*, 69 (May–June 1991), pp. 99–109.

63. Peter M. Senge, *The Fifth Discipline: The Art and Practice of the Learning Organization* (New York: Doubleday/Currency, 1990), pp. 12, 18, 19, 44.

64. John A. Byrne, "Management's New Gurus," *Business Week*, August 31, 1992, pp. 44–52.

65. For more on teams, see Jon R. Katzenbach and Douglas K. Smith, *The Wisdom of Teams* (Boston: Harvard Business School Press, 1993); Richard S. Wellins, William C. Byham, and Jeanne M. Wilson, *Empowered Teams* (San Francisco: Jossey-Bass Publishers, 1991); David Barry, "Managing the Bossless Team: Lessons in Distributed Leadership," *Organizational Dynamics*, 20 (Summer 1991), pp. 31–46; Eric Sundstrom, Kenneth P. De Meuse, and David Futrell, "Work Teams: Applications and Effectiveness," *American Psychologist*, 45 (February 1990), pp. 120–133; Glenn M. Parker, *Team Players and Teamwork* (San Francisco: Jossey-Bass Publishers, 1990); and Larry Hirschhorn, *Managing in the New Team Environment* (Reading, MA: Addison-Wesley Publishing Company, 1991).

66. Dan Ciampa, *Total Quality* (Reading, MA: Addison-Wesley Publishing Company, 1992), p. xxi. See also Marshall Sashkin and Kenneth J. Kiser, *Total Quality Management* (Seabrook, MD: Ducochon Press, 1991).

67. Ciampa, *Total Quality*, p. xxii.

68. Ibid., p. xxiv.

69. W. Warner Burke, *Organization Development: A Process of Learning and Changing* (Reading, MA: Addison-Wesley Publishing Company, 1994), p. 199.

70. Ronald Fox, Ronald Lippitt, and Eva Schindler-Rainman, *The Humanized Future: Some New Images* (LaJolla, CA: University Associates, 1973).

71. Merrelyn Emery, *Searching: For New Directions, in New Ways for New Times* (Canberra: Centre for Continuing Education, Australian National University, 1982).

72. Marvin R. Weisbord, "Future Search: Toward Strategic Integration," in Walter Sikes, Allan Drexler, and Jack Gant, eds., *The Emerging Practice of Organization Development* (Alexandria, VA: NTL Institute for Applied Behavioral Science, and San Diego, CA: University Associates, 1989), p. 171; and Marvin R. Weisbord, "Future Search: Innovative Business Conference," *Planning Review*, 12 (July 1984), pp. 16–20.

73. Marvin R. Weisbord, *Productive Workplaces* (San Francisco: Jossey-Bass Publishers, 1987), pp. 289–292.

74. Richard Beckhard, "The Confrontation Meeting," *Harvard Business Review*, 45 (March–April 1967), pp. 149–155. See also W. Warner Burke and Richard Beckhard, *Conference Planning*, 2d ed. (San Diego: University Associates, 1970).

75. Marvin R. Weisbord, "Toward Third-Wave Managing and Consulting," *Organizational Dynamics*, 15 (Winter 1987), pp. 19–20.

76. Gerard Burke and Joe Peppard, *Examining Business Process Re-Engineering: Current Perspectives and Research Directions* (London: Kogan Page, 1995), p. 25.

77. *The Wall Street Journal*, March 5, 1993, p. B7A.

CHAPTER 3

Values, Assumptions, and Beliefs in OD

A set of values, assumptions, and beliefs constitutes an integral part of organization development, shaping the goals and methods of the field and distinguishing OD from other improvement strategies. Most of these beliefs were formulated early in the development of the field, and they continue to evolve as the field itself evolves. These values and assumptions developed from research and theory by behavioral scientists and from the experiences and observations of practicing managers. Let's begin with some definitions. A *belief* is a proposition about how the world works that the individual accepts as true; it is a cognitive fact for the person. *Values* are also beliefs and are defined as: "beliefs about what is a desirable or a 'good' (e.g., free speech) and what is an undesirable or a 'bad' (e.g., dishonesty).[1] *Assumptions* are beliefs that are regarded as so valuable and obviously correct that they are taken for granted and rarely examined or questioned. Thus, values, assumptions, and beliefs are all cognitive facts or propositions, with values being beliefs about good and bad, and assumptions being strongly held, relatively unexamined beliefs accepted as the truth. Values, assumptions, and beliefs provide structure and stability for people as they attempt to understand the world around them.

OD values tend to be humanistic, optimistic, and democratic. Humanistic values proclaim the importance of the individual; respect and dignity, assume that everyone has intrinsic worth, view all people as having the potential for growth and development. Optimistic values posit that people are basically good, that progress is possible and desirable in human affairs, and that rationality, reason, and goodwill are the tools for making progress. Democratic values assert the sanctity of the individual, the right of people to be free from arbitrary misuse of power, the importance of fair and equitable treatment for all, and the need for justice through the rule of law and due process.

Evidence for the validity of these values and their supporting assumptions comes from many sources—the Hawthorne studies, the human relations movement, the laboratory training movement, the clash between fascism and democracy in World War II, increasing awareness of the dysfunction of bureaucracies, research on the effects of different leadership styles, greater understanding of individual motivation and group dynamics, and the like.

Values and assumptions do not spring full-grown from individuals or societies; they are formed from the collective beliefs of an era—the *zeitgeist*, or spirit of the time. Major ingredients of the zeitgeist that influenced OD values and assumptions are presented here in a brief chronology. As these ingredients accumulated, they were fashioned into a coherent value foundation for the theory and practice of organization development.

EARLY STATEMENTS OF OD VALUES AND ASSUMPTIONS

Values have always been an integral part of OD. We will examine three early statements regarding OD values that had a significant impact on the field. The Bennis and Beckhard quotations come from their books in the Addison-Wesley Six-pack. Tannenbaum and Davis presented their ideas in an article appearing in the *Industrial Management Review*.

Writing in 1969, Warren Bennis proposed that OD practitioners (change agents) share a set of *normative goals* based on their humanistic/democratic philosophy. He listed these normative goals as follows:

1. Improvement in interpersonal competence.
2. A shift in values so that human factors and feelings come to be considered legitimate.
3. Development of increased understanding between and within working groups in order to reduce tensions.
4. Development of more effective "team management," that is, the capacity for functional groups to work more competently.
5. Development of better methods of conflict resolution. Rather than the usual bureaucratic methods which rely mainly on suppression, compromise, and unprincipled power, more rational and open methods of conflict resolution are sought.
6. Development of organic rather than mechanical systems. This is a strong reaction against the idea of organizations as mechanisms which managers "work on," like pushing buttons.[2]

Bennis clarified some of the salient differences between mechanical systems and organic systems. (The earlier work by Tom Burns and G. M. Stalker used the term "mechanistic" in contrast to "mechanical,"[3]) For example, mechanical systems rely on "authority" obedience relationships" while organic systems rely on "mutual confidence and trust." Mechanical systems insist on "strict division of labor and hierarchical supervision" while organic systems foster "multigroup membership and responsibility." Mechanical systems encourage "centralized decision making" while organic systems encourage "wide sharing of responsibility and control."[4]

He then went on to state what he believed to be the central value underlying organization development theory and practice:

> The basic value underlying all organization development theory and practice is that of choice. Through focused attention and through the collection and feedback of relevant data to relevant people, more choices become available and hence better decisions are made.[5]

Another major player in the field was Richard Beckhard. In his 1969 book he described "several assumptions about the nature and functioning of organizations" held by OD practitioners. Here is his list.

1. The basic building blocks of an organization are groups (teams). Therefore, the basic units of change are groups, not individuals.
2. An always-relevant change goal is the reduction of inappropriate competition between parts of the organization and the development of a more collaborative condition.
3. Decision making in a healthy organization is located where the information sources are, rather than in a particular role or level of hierarchy.

4. Organizations, subunits of organizations, and individuals continuously manage their affairs against goals. Controls are interim measurements, not the basis of managerial strategy.
5. One goal of a healthy organization is to develop generally open communication, mutual trust, and confidence between and across levels.
6. "People support what they help create." People affected by a change must be allowed active participation and a sense of ownership in the planning and conduct of the change."[6]

Robert Tannenbaum, professor at UCLA, and Sheldon Davis, director of organization development at TRW Systems, presented their view of OD values in a 1969 article. They asserted that an important shift in values was occurring and that this shift signaled a more appropriate and accurate view of people in organizations. They listed these "values in transition" as follows:

Away from a view of people as essentially bad toward a view of people as basically good.
Away from avoidance of negative evaluation of individual toward confirming them as human beings.
Away from a view of individuals as fixed, toward seeing them as being in process.
Away from resisting and fearing individual differences toward accepting and utilizing them.
Away from utilizing an individual primarily with reference to his or her job description toward viewing an individual as a whole person.
Away from walling off the expression of feelings toward making possible both appropriate expression and effective use.
Away from one maskmanship and game playing toward authentic behavior.
Away from use of status for maintaining power and personal prestige toward use of status for organizationally relevant purposes.
Away from distrusting people toward trusting them.
Away from avoiding facing others with relevant data toward making appropriate confrontation.
Away from avoidance of risk taking toward willingness to risk.
Away from a view of process work as being unproductive effort toward seeing it as essential to effective task accomplishment.
Away from a primary emphasis on competition toward a much greater emphasis on collaboration.[7]

These values and assumptions may not seem profound today, but in the 1950s and 1960s they represented a radical departure from accepted beliefs and assumptions. Beliefs such as trust and respect for the individual, the legitimacy of feelings, open communication, decentralized decision making, participation and contribution by all organization members, collaboration and cooperation, appropriate uses of power, authentic interpersonal relations, and so forth were seldom espoused and rarely implemented in the vast majority of organizations at the time.

IMPLICATIONS OF OD VALUES AND ASSUMPTIONS

Let's examine specific assumptions and their implications for organization leaders and members. We answer the question: What are some of the implications of OD assumptions and values for dealing with individuals, groups, and organizations?

Implications for Dealing with Individuals

Two basic assumptions about individuals in organizations pervade organization development. The first assumption is that most individuals have drives toward personal growth and development if provided an environment that is both supportive and challenging. Most people want to develop their potential. The second assumption is that most people desire to make, and are capable of making, a greater contribution to attaining organization goals than most organizational environments permit. A tremendous amount of constructive energy can be tapped if organizations realize and act on these assumptions. The people doing the work are generally experts on how to do it—and how to do it better. The implications of these two assumptions are straightforward: Ask, listen, support, challenge, encourage risk taking, permit failure, remove obstacles and barriers, give autonomy, give responsibility, set high standards, and reward success.

Implications for Dealing with Groups

Several assumptions relate to the importance of work teams and the collaborative management of team culture. First, one of the most psychologically relevant reference groups for most people is the work group, including peers and boss. What occurs in the work group, at both the formal and informal levels, greatly influences feelings of satisfaction and competence. Second, most people wish to be accepted and to interact cooperatively with at least one small reference group, and usually with more than one group, such as a work group, the family, a church or club group, and so on. Third, most people are capable of making greater contributions to a group's effectiveness and development. Implications of these assumptions are several. *Let teams flourish* because they are often the best way to get work done, and, in addition, are the best way to satisfy social and emotional needs at work. Also, *leaders should invest* in-groups: invest the time required for group development, invest training time and money to increase group members' skills, invest energy and intelligence in creating a positive climate. It is especially important that leaders *adopt a team leadership style*, not a one-on-one leadership style. To do this, leaders need to give important work to teams, not individuals.

Another assumption is that the formal leader cannot perform all the leadership and maintenance functions required for a group to optimize its effectiveness. Hence, group members should assist the leader with the multiple roles required for group effectiveness skills such as group problem solving and decision-making, conflict management, facilitation, and interpersonal communication. And because suppressed feelings and attitudes adversely affect problem solving, personal growth, and job satisfaction, group members should be encouraged to learn to deal effectively with positive and negative feelings. This skill is a trainable one. Dealing appropriately with feelings and attitudes increases the level of interpersonal trust, support, and cooperation within the group.

Finally, the assumption is that attitudinal and motivational problems in organizations require interactive and transactional solutions. Such problems have the greatest chance of constructive solution if all parties in the system alter their mutual relationships. The question becomes not how A can get B to perform better, but *how A and B can work together to modify their interactions toward the goal of B becoming more effective and A and B becoming more mutually effective*. Frequently, the challenge is broader, including *how persons C, D, and E can support these changes*. By implication, this group perspective requires a shift from viewing problems as "within the problem person" to viewing problems and solutions as transactional and as embedded in a system.

Implications for Designing and Running Organizations

Clearly, traditional hierarchical forms of organization—fairly steep pyramid, emphasis on top-down directives, grouping by specialized function, adherence to the chain of command, formalized cross-functional communications, and so on-are obsolete. They cannot meet the needs of the marketplace. Therefore, experimenting with new organization structures and new forms of authority is imperative. In addition, a growing awareness that "win-lose" organizational situations, in which one side wins and the other side loses, are dysfunctional over the long run and highlight the need for a "win-win" attitude. Creating cooperative by rather than competitive organizational dynamics is a primary task of the organization's leaders.

A key assumption in organization development is that the needs and aspirations of human beings are the reasons for organized effort in society. This notion suggests it is good to have a developmental outlook and seek opportunities in which people can experience personal and professional growth. Such an orientation creates a self-fulfilling prophecy. The belief that people are important tends to result in their being important. The belief that people can grow and develop in terms of personal and organizational competency tends to produce that result. By implication, an optimistic, developmental set of assumptions about people is likely to reap rewards beneficial to both the organization and its members.

Finally, it is possible to create organizations that on the one hand are humane, developmental, and empowering, and on the other hand are high performing in terms of productivity, quality of output, and profitability. Evidence for this assumption comes from numerous examples where "putting people first" paid off handsomely in profits and performance. The implication is that people are an organization's most important resource; they are the source of productivity and profits and should be treated with care.

A VALUES STUDY

A values survey given to OD practitioners suggests that, in practice, professionals in the OD field attempt to operationalize the values described in these statements of the late 1960s. The authors of the survey randomly selected 1,000 OD practitioners from the rosters of the OD Network and the OD Division of the American Society of Training and Development, sent them a brief survey, and received 289 responses in return. The survey addressed three broad areas: (1) What attracted you to OD? (2) Which values do you believe are associated with OD work today? (3) Which values do you think should be associated with OD work today?

In answer to the first question, the five most frequent response categories in order of frequency were: A desire to... (1) create change, (2) positively impact people and organizations, (3) enhance the effectiveness and profitability of organizations, (4) learn and grow, and (5) exercise power and influence.

To answer the two value questions, respondents rated 31 value statements on a five-point scale from 1 ("of little importance") to 5 ("extremely important"). For the question asking which values respondents believe are associated with OD work today, the top five values were (1) increasing effectiveness and efficiency, (2) creating openness in communication, (3) empowering employees to act, (4) enhancing productivity, and (5) promoting organizational participation. For the question concerning which values respondents think should be associated with OD work today, the five values considered most important were (1) empowering employees to act, (2) creating openness in communication, (3) facilitating ownership of process and outcome, (4) promoting a culture of collaboration, and (5) promoting inquiry and continuous learning.[8]

Still, values are never static; they change over time. The rapid technological, societal, and organizational changes taking place assure that tomorrow will bring new definitions of what is "true" and new beliefs about what is "good" as behavioral scientists and managers continue to develop better understanding of authority structures, organizing structures, and ways to optimize human potential.

ILLUSTRATION OF OD VALUES IN AN INDIAN PHARMACEUTICAL ORGANIZATION

A leading Indian pharma company has adopted the following values of openness, confrontation, trust, authenticity, proactiveness, autonomy, collaboration and experimentation in order to ensure a culture of trust and openness. These vital values form the OCTAPACE culture in a company necessary for initiating Organisation Development activities and interventions. These values are interpreted as follows in the Sales and Marketing function of the same company:

OCTAPACE SITUATIONS IN SALES/MARKETING FUNCTION

Openness

1. Informing the superiors in advance about shortfall in targets to be achieved.
2. Representatives' feedback to the Product Management Team on effectiveness of strategies deployed.
3. Informing Distribution function on outstanding/expiry of products.

Confront – The Problem

1. Discussing with the Distribution function the non-availability of physical stocks.
2. Defending the productwise target based on the potential of the market.

3. Appealing the R and D for cost reduction of the products in comparison to competitors' pricing strategies.

Trust

1. Restricting improper utilization of information and data available on the product marketing strategies.
2. Appreciating the suggestions made by the representative/any other person regarding relevant product improvement, strategic change etc.
3. Expecting the delivery of the products as per the schedule agreed.
4. Sales Managers following up on actions/problems as reported by the field force.

Authenticity

1. Sales managers establishing Procedures/Sop's for Doctors.
2. Avoiding false or exaggerated sales forecast or production planning for new products.
3. Consistent application of criteria for selecting High Fliers/Doctors for investments.
4. Implementing in-clinic performance as per the guidance of the superiors.

Proaction

1. Preparing a focused Doctors' list for a new product to be launched.
2. Preparing contingency plans to maintain sales targets to be achieved, counter variation.
3. Initiating action to reduce expiry/breakage costs.
4. Recommending strategies to aggressively increase the market share.

Autonomy

1. Allowing line managers to take decisions on investment on Doctors within the framework of the policy.
2. Respecting the rejection of new combination of molecules by Medical Department.
3. Making *realistic* targets based on last year *performance* supported by *market*.
4. Improving quality of inputs/resources to the field by Market Planning Team.

Collaboration

1. Departmental Heads identifying *developmental* needs of the field force with emphasis on training.
2. Providing necessary inputs to the sales administration for quicker settlements of the grievances of the field employees.
3. Following Joint Accountability with the employees of the concerned departmental goals to remove fear of losing points in the final appraisal.
4. Joint field working with representatives.

Experimentation

1. Encourage newer marketing strategies for new products.
2. Identify suitable training/developmental programme for Sales/Market personnel, planning and administering it to them.
3. Deploying newer methods for capturing the fieldwide effectiveness of Medical Sales Representatives.

CONCLUDING COMMENT

The field of organisation development rests on a foundation of values and assumptions about people and organizations. These beliefs help to define what OD is and guide its implementation. This discussion was intended to articulate an appreciation of OD values and explain where they come from. These values were considered revolutionary when they emerged in the 1950s, but are widely accepted today.

NOTES

1. David Krech, Richard S. Crutchfield, and Egerton Ballachey, *Individual in Society* (New York: McGraw-Hill, 1962), p. 102.
2. Bennis, *Organization Development: Its Nature, Origins, and Prospects*, p. 15.
3. Tom Burns and G. M. Stalker, *The Management of Innovation* (London: Tavistock, 1961), pp. 119–125.
4. Bennis, p. 15.
5. Ibid. p. 17.
6. Beckhard, *Organization Development: Strategies and Models*, pp. 26–27.
7. Robert Tannenbaum and Sheldon A. Davis, "Values, Man, and Organizations," *Industrial Management Review*, 10 (Winter 1969), pp. 67–83.
8. Robert F. Hurley, Allan H. Church, W. Warner Burke, and Donald F. Van Eynde, "Tension, Change and Values in OD," *OD Practitioner*, 24 (September 1992), pp. 1–5.

CHAPTER 4

Foundations of Organization Development

This chapter describes the foundations of organization development theory and practice, art and science, which form the knowledge base upon which OD is constructed. Leaders and OD practitioners use this knowledge base to plan and implement effective change programs. In this discussion you will learn *what* OD practitioners think and *how* they think as they engage in the complicated task of improving organizational functioning.

The knowledge base of OD is extensive and is constantly growing. Here we describe what we believe are the most important underpinnings for the field. We will examine the following concepts:

Models and theories of planned change

Systems theory

Participation and empowerment

Teams and teamwork

Parallel learning structures

A normative-reeducative strategy of changing

Applied behavioral science

Action research

MODELS AND THEORIES OF PLANNED CHANGE

Organizational development is planned change in an organization context. The development of models of planned change facilitated the development of OD. Models and theories depict, in words or pictures, the important features of some phenomenon, describe those features as variables, and specify the relationships among the variables. Planned change theories are rudimentary as far as explaining relationships among variables, but pretty good for identifying the important variables involved. Several recent theories show great promise for increasing our understanding of what happens and how it happens in planned change. Here we provide a framework for thinking about planned change by exploring several models from the literature.

Kurt Lewin and Friends

Kurt Lewin introduced two ideas about change that have been influential since the 1940s[1]. The first idea states that what is occurring at any point in time is a *resultant* in a field of opposing forces. That is, the status quo—whatever is happening right now—is the result of forces pushing in opposing directions. For example, we can think of the production level of a manufacturing plant as a resultant *equilibrium point* in a field of forces, with some forces pushing toward higher levels of production and some forces pushing toward lower levels of production. The production level tends to remain fairly constant because the field of forces remains fairly constant. Likewise, we can think of the level of morale in that plant as a resultant equilibrium point. Although morale may get a little better or a little worse on occasion, it generally hovers around some *equilibrium point* that is the resultant in a field of forces, some forces pushing toward higher morale, and some pushing towards lower morale. With a technique called the force-field analysis, we can identify the major forces that make up the field of forces and then develop action plans for moving the equilibrium point in one direction or the other. This concept is useful for thinking about the dynamics of change situations.

Lewin's second idea was a model of the change process itself. He suggested that change is a three-stage process: *unfreezing* the old behavior (or situation), *moving* to a new level of behavior, and *refreezing* the behavior at the new level. Change entails moving from one equilibrium point to another. Take the example of a man who smokes cigarettes and wants to quit. The three-stage model says he must first unfreeze the old behavior of smoking, that is, believe that cigarette smoking is bad for him and that he should stop smoking. Next, he must move, that is, change his behavior from being a smoker to being a nonsmoker. Finally, the nonsmoking behavior must become permanent—not smoking becomes the new

---

Table 4-1 A Three-Stage Model of the Change Process

Stage 1. *Unfreezing:* Creating motivation and readiness to change through.
  a. Disconfirmation or lack of confirmation.
  b. Creation of guilt or anxiety.
  c. Provision of psychological safety.

Stage 2. *Changing through Cognitive Restructuring:* Helping the client to see things, judge things, feel things, and react to things differently based on a new point of view obtained through.
  a. Identifying with a new role model, mentor, etc.
  b. Scanning the environment for new relevant information.

Stage 3. *Refreezing:* Helping the client to integrate the new point of view into:
  a. The total personality and self-concept.
  b. Significant relationships.

Source: Edgar H. Schein, *Process Consultation*, vol.II (Table 6-1), p.93.© 1987 by Addison-Wesley Publishing Company, Inc. Reprinted by permission of the publisher.

equilibrium point. Refreezing the desired behavior requires establishing a new field of forces to support the new behavior.

Lewin's three-stage model is a powerful tool for understanding change situations. Edgar Schein took this excellent idea and improved it by specifying the psychological mechanisms involved in each stage.[2]

In stage 1, *unfreezing,* disconfirmation creates pain and discomfort, which cause guilt and anxiety, which motivate the person to change. But unless the person feels comfortable with dropping the old behaviors and acquiring new ones, change will not occur. That is, the person must develop a sense of psychological safety on order to replace the old behaviors with new behaviors.

In stage 2, *moving,* the person undergoes cognitive restructuring. The person acquires information and evidence showing that the change is desirable and possible. This motivating evidence showing that the change is desirable and possible. This motivating evidence is gained by, for example, identifying with ex-smokers and learning about the health risks of smoking.

The primary task in stage 3, *refreezing,* is to integrate the new behaviors into the person's personally and attitudes. That is, stabilizing the changes requires testing to see if they fit—fit with the individual, and fit with the individual's social surroundings. The phrase *significant relationships* refers to important people in the person's social environment—do these significant others approve of the changes?

Another modification of Lewin's model was proposed by Ronald Lippitt, Jeanne Watson, and Bruce Westley. They expanded the three-stage model into a seven-stage model representing the consulting process. Their seven stages are as follows:

Phase 1. Developing a need for change. This phase corresponds to Lewin's unfreezing phase.

Phase 2. Establishing a change relationship. In this phase a client system in need of help and a change agent from outside the system establish a working relationship.

Phase 3. Clarifying or diagnosing the client system's problem.

Phase 4. Examining alternative routes and goals; establishing goals and intentions of action.

Phase 5. Transforming intentions into actual change efforts. Phases 3, 4 and 5 correspond to Lewin's *moving* phase.

Phase 6. Generalizing and stabilizing change. This phase corresponds to Lewin's *refreezing* phase.

Phase 7. Achieving a terminal relationship, that is, terminating the client-consultant relationship.[3]

This seven-stage model lays out the logical steps involved in OD consulting. Similar models have been developed by Kolb and Frohman and by Burke.[4] These "road maps" are useful for thinking about change.

The Burke-Litwin Model of Organizational Change

The next model to be examined is the Burke-Litwin model of individual and organizational performance, developed by Warner Burke and George Litwin.[5] This model shows how to create *first-order* and *second-order change* (which the authors call "transactional change" and "transformational change"). In *first-order change,* some features of the organization change but the fundamental nature of the organization remains the same. First-order change goes by many different labels: transactional, evolutionary, adaptive, incremental, or continuous change. In *second-order change,* the nature of the organization is fundamentally and substantially altered—the organization is transformed. Second-order change goes by many different labels: transformational, revolutionary, radical, or discontinuous change. OD programs are directed toward both first and second-order change, with an increasing emphasis on second-order, transformational change.

The model distinguishes between organizational climate and organizational culture. *Organizational climate* is defined as people's perceptions and attitudes about the organization—whether it is a good or bad place to work, friendly or unfriendly, hardworking or easy-going, and so forth. These perceptions are relatively easy to change because they are built on employees' reactions to current managerial and organizational practices. On the other hand, *organizational culture* is defined as deep-seated assumptions, values, and beliefs that are enduring, often unconscious, and difficult to change. Changing culture is much more difficult than changing climate. The premise of the Burke-Litwin model is this: *OD interventions directed toward structure, management practices, and systems (policies and procedures) result in first-order change; interventions directed toward mission and strategy, leadership, and organization culture result in second-order change.*

The model also makes a distinction between transactional and transformational leadership styles. These two concepts come from leadership research which found that some leaders are capable of obtaining extraordinary performance from followers while other leaders are not.[6] *Transformational leaders* are "leaders who inspire followers to transcend their own self-interest for the good of the organization and who are capable of having a profound and extraordinary effect on their followers." Transformational leadership embodies inspiration which leads to new heights of performance. *Transactional leaders* are "leaders who guide or motivate their followers in the direction of established goals by clarifying role and task requirements."[7] Transactional leadership embodies a fair exchange between leader and follower that leads to "normal" performance. Transactional leadership is sufficient for causing first-order change. Transformational leadership is required for causing second-order change.

Now let's look at the Burke-Litwin model. We will do so in several steps. Figure 4-1 shows the factors involved in *first-order* (transactional) change. Changing structure, management practices, and systems cause changes in work unit *climate,* which changes motivation and, in turn, individual and organizational performance. Transactional leadership is required to make this change in organizational climate.

On the other hand, if we want to cause *second-order* (transformational) change, we must change mission and strategy, leadership styles, and organization culture, as shown in Figure 4-2. Interventions directed toward these factors transform the organization and cause a permanent change in organization culture, which produces changes in individual and organizational performance.

Putting Figures 4-1 and 4-2 together yields the full Burke-Litwin model shown in Figure 4-3. The top half of Figure 4-3 displays the factors involved in transformational change. These factors are powerful enough to *change the culture* fundamentally. The bottom half of Figure 4-3 displays the factors involved in transactional change. These factors are able to *change the climate.*

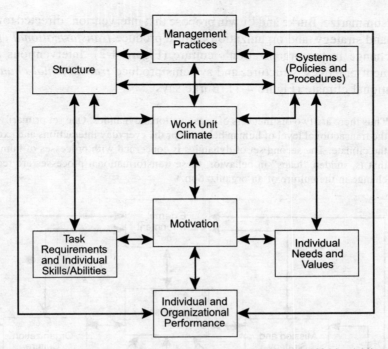

Source: W. Warner Burke, *Organization Development*, 2d ed. (Figure 7.3), p.131 © 1994 by Addison-Wesley Publishing Company, Inc. Reprinted by permission of the publisher.

FIGURE 4-1   The Transactional Factors Involved in First-Order Change

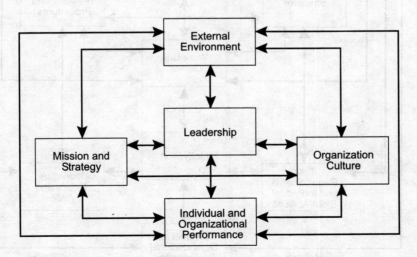

Source: W. Warner Burke, *Organization Development*, 2d ed. (Figure 7.2), p.130 © 1994 by Addison-Wesley Publishing Company, Inc. Reprinted by permission of the publisher.

FIGURE 4-2   The Transformational Factors Involved in Second-Order Change

To summarize, Burke and Litwin propose that interventions directed toward leadership, mission and strategy, and organization culture produce *transformational change* or fundamental change in the organization's culture (Figure 4-2). Interventions directed toward management practices, structure, and systems produce *transactional change* or change in organizational climate (Figure 4-1). Burke says:

> Thus there are two distinct sets of organizational dynamics. One set primarily is associated with the transactional level of human behavior or the everyday interactions and exchanges that create the climate. The second set of dynamics is concerned with processes of human transformation; that is, sudden "leaps" in behavior; these transformational processes are required for genuine change in the culture of an organization.[8]

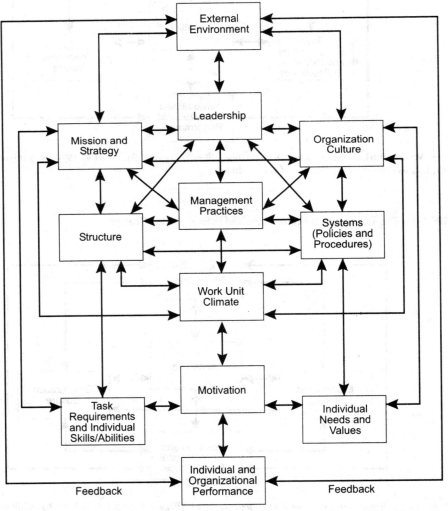

Source: W. Warner Burke, *Organization Development*, 2d ed. (Figure 7.1), p.128 © 1994 by Addison-Wesley Publishing Company, Inc. Reprinted by permission of the publisher.

FIGURE 4-3 The Burke-Litwin Model of Organizational Performance and Change

We consider the Burke-Litwin model to be a significant advance in thinking about planned change. The OD practitioner sizes up the change situation, determines the kind of change required (transactional or transformational), and then targets interventions toward factors of the organization that produce the desired change. Research by Burke and his students suggests the model performs as intended.[9]

SYSTEMS THEORY

A second foundation of organization development is systems theory, which views organizations as open systems in active exchange with their environments. This section explains systems theory, describes the characteristics OD systems, and shows how systems theory enhances the practice of OD.

Ludwig von Bertalanffy first articulated the principles of general systems theory in 1950, and Kartz and Kahn were the first to apply open systems theory to organizations in 1966.[10] Systems theory is one of the most powerful conceptual tools available for understanding the dynamics of organizations and organizational change. Fagen defines system as "a set of objects together with relationships between the objects and between their attributes,"[11] Von Bertalanffy refers to a system of "elements standing in interaction.[12] Kast and Rosenzweig define *system* as "an organized, unitary whole composed of two or more interdependent parts, components, or subsystems, and delineated by identifiable boundaries from its environmental suprasystem." Hanna says: "A system is an arrangement of interrelated parts. The words *arrangement* and *interrelated* describe interdependent elements forming an entity that is the system. Thus, when taking a systems approach, one begins by identifying the individual parts and then seeks to understand the nature of their collective interaction."[14] To summarize, *system* denotes interdependency, interconnectedness among elements in a set that constitutes an identifiable whole or gestalt.

The Nature of Systems

The nature, dynamics, and characteristics of open systems are well known. Organizations are open systems. Therefore, studying open systems leads to a good understanding of organizations. Here we examine the characteristics of open systems drawing on expositions by Katz and Kahn and Hanna.[15]

All open systems are *input-throughout-output* mechanisms. Systems take *inputs* from the environment in the form of energy, information, money, people, raw materials, and so on. They do something to the inputs via *throughput, conversion,* or *transformation* processes that change the inputs; and they export products to the environment in the form of *outputs*. Each of these three system processes must work well if the system is to be effective and survive. Figure 4-4 shows a system in a diagrammatic form.

Every system is delineated by a boundary. What is inside the boundary is the system, and what is outside the boundary is the environment. A good rule of thumb for drawing the boundary is that more energy exchange occurs *within* the boundary than *across* the boundary. Boundaries of open systems are *permeable*, in that they permit exchange of information, resources, and energy between system and environment.

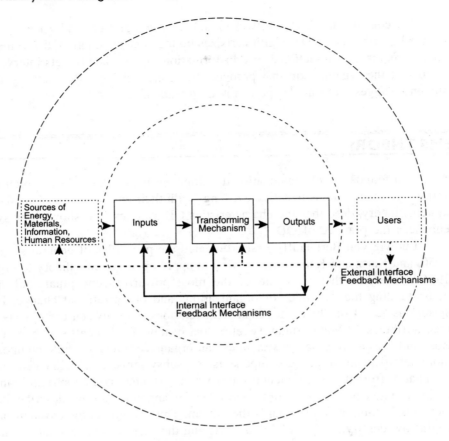

FIGURE 4-4 A System in Interaction with Its Environment

Open systems have *purposes and goals*, the reasons for their existence. These purposes must align with purposes or needs in the environment. For example, the organization's purposes will be reflected in its outputs, and if the environment does not want these outputs, the organization will cease to exist.

The law of entropy states that all systems "run down" and disintegrate unless they reverse the entropic process by importing more energy than they use. Organizations achieve *negative entropy* when they are able to exchange their outputs for enough inputs to keep the system from running down.

Information is important in systems in several ways. Feedback is information from the environment about system performance. Systems require two kinds of feedback, negative and positive. Hanna writes: "Negative feedback measures whether or not the output is on course with the purpose and goals. It is also known as *deviation-correcting* feedback.... Positive feedback measures whether or not the purpose and goals are aligned with environmental needs. It is sometimes called deviation-amplifying feedback.[16] For example, if a rocket ship traveling to the moon strays off it trajectory, it received information to that effect in the form of negative feedback, and makes a course correction. If the mission (target) changes, however, that information is called positive feedback, and the system adjusts to a new goal, say, "return to earth."

Here is another example of negative and positive feedback, say your company makes buggy whips, and the production plan calls for 100 buggy whips per month. Negative feedback tells you if you are on track with your scheduled production output. Positive feedback comes from the environment; it will signal whether the environment needs and/ or wants buggy whips. Hanna states: "The usefulness of the two concepts is that they demonstrate that it is not enough to merely measure our outputs versus the intended targets. Survival of the system is equally influenced by whether or not the target themselves are appropriate."[17]

Systems are bombarded by all kinds of information: some is useful, but most is not useful. Systems "code" useful information and incorporate it, while screening out other information. For example, organizations in the fast-food industry pay a lot of attention to information about their industry—nutrition, eating fads, competitors, and the like. By the same token, they usually ignore information about other industries such as electronics, mining, aerospace, and so on.

Another characteristic of open systems is *steady state* or *dynamic homeostasis*. Systems achieve a steady state or equilibrium point and seek to maintain this equilibrium against disruptive forces, either internal or external. As Katz and Kahn say: "*The basic principle is the preservation of the character of the system.*[18] Also, systems tend to get more elaborated, differentiated, specialized, and complex over time; this process is called *differentiation*. With increased differentiation, increased *integration* and *coordination* are necessary. Another characteristic of systems is *equifinality*, the principle that there are multiple ways to arrive at a particular outcome or state–systems have multiple ways to arrive at a particular outcome or state-systems have multiple paths to goals. *Subsystems* exist within larger systems. These subsystems can be arranged into a *hierarchy of systems* moving from less important to more important.

The characteristic of open systems explain many phenomena we observe in organizations. Why do organizations resist change? A desire to preserve the charter of the system, the steady state and dynamic homeostasis. Why does Plan A fail and fail again, then succeed? Equifinality. Why do organizations become increasingly bureaucratic and complex? Differentiation, with its attendant integration and coordination. Why do businesses go bankrupt? Inability to create negative entropy. Why did the American automobile industry fail to react to the Japanese challenge of small cars? Lack of appropriate coding processes and adequate positive feedback mechanisms.

Congruence among System Elements

Let's look at an example that shows how systems thinking is applied in OD. David Nadler and associates at Delta Consulting Group developed the *congruence model* for understanding organizational dynamics and change (see Figure 4-5). This model depicts the organization as an input-throughout-output system.[19]

The three major *input factors* are (1) the *environment*, which imposes constraints and opportunities about what the organization can and can not do; (2) *resources* available to the organization, such as capital, people, knowledge, and technology; and (3) *history*, which consists of memories of past successes, failures, important events, and critical decisions that still influence behavior today. *Outputs* are performance at the total organization level, unit/group level, and individual level. Elements of the *organization* per se are labeled *strategy*,

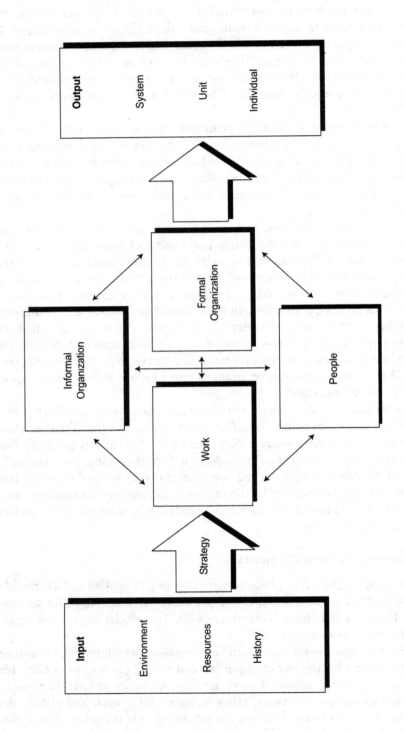

Source: David A. Nadler, Champions of Change, p.41. Reproduced by permission of Jossey-Bass Inc., Publishers.© 1998.

FIGURE 4-5 The Congruence Model Showing the Organization as a System

what the organization is trying to accomplish and how it plans to do it; work, the tasks people perform to create products and service markets; *people*, which includes formal structures, processes, and systems for performing the work; *formal organisation*, which includes formal structures, processes, and systems for performing the work; and *informal organization*, which includes the organization's culture, informal rules and understandings, and how things *really* work (versus how they are *supposed* to work as defined by the formal organization).

The congruence model's value is an analytical tool for (1) assessing the characteristics and functioning if each of the elements, and (2) evaluating the "goodness of fit" or how well the elements "go together." The premise is that alignment (harmony, fit) must be present among the system's components for the organization to produce satisfactory outputs. For example, if people don't have the skills and knowledge required to do the work, performance will suffer. If the strategy calls for entrepreneurial quickness and risk-taking and the formal organization is bureaucratic and highly centralized, performance will suffer. If the organization's culture (informal organization) praises individual accomplishments and the work requires teamwork and collaboration, performance will suffer.

You can use this model to analyze organizations with which you are familiar. In a company that is performing poorly, which components are "not functioning correctly," and which elements are "not functioning correctly," and which elements are poorly aligned? In companies showing outstanding performance, what is it about each element that causes that part of the system to function well, and what are the characteristics of each element that cause all of them to fit together smoothly? The congruence is an excellent diagnostic tool. Systems models are essential for the practice of OD.

Sociotechnical Systems Theory and Open Systems Planning

Two major variations open systems theory—sociotechnical systems theory (STS) and open systems planning (OSP)—play an especially important role in organization development. We will discuss these briefly.

Sociotechnical systems theory was developed by Eric Trist, Fred Emery, and others at the Tavistock Institute in the 1950s. The thesis of STS is that all organizations comprise two interdependent systems, a social system and a technical system, and that changes in one system affect the other system. To achieve high productivity and employee satisfaction, organizations must optimize both systems. STS is the principal conceptual foundation for efforts in work redesign and organization restructuring, two active segments of OD today.

A number of design principles have been developed to implement sociotechnical systems theory. Principles such as optimizing the social and technical systems, forming autonomous work groups, training group members in multiple skills, giving information and feedback to the people doing the work, and identifying core tasks help STS consultants structure organizations and tasks for maximum effectiveness and efficiency. High-performance organizations almost always use principles from sociotechnical systems theory, especially autonomous work groups (self-regulated teams or self-directed teams), multiskilled teams, controlling variance at the source, and information to the point of action, that is, to the workers during the job. Excellent reviews of STS theory, principles, and practice appear in works by Pasmore, Pava, Cummings, Hanna, and Bushe and Shani.[20]

Open systems planning entails (1) scanning the environment to determine the expectations and stakeholders; (2) developing scenarios of possible futures, both realistic (likely to happen if the organization continues on its current course) and ideal (what the organization would like to see happen); and (3) developing action plans to ensure that a desirable future occurs. Most OD practitioners engaged in redesign projects use a combination of sociotechnical systems theory and open systems planning. For example, this combination is often used in designing high–performance organizations.

Open Systems Thinking

Open systems thinking is required for creating learning organizations, according to Peter Senge. Learning organizations can cope effectively with rapidly changing environmental demands. Senge believes five disciplines must be mastered to create a learning organization: personal mastery, mental models, building shared vision, team learning, and systems thinking. Of all these disciplines, the fifth discipline, systems thinking, is the most important.

In conclusion, system theory pervades the theory and practice of organization development, from diagnosis to intervention to evaluation. Viewing organizations from this perspective has several consequences. First, issues, events, forces and incidents are not viewed as isolated phenomena, but seen in relation to other issues, events, and forces. Second, because, most phenomena have more than one cause, a systems approach encourages analysis of events in terms of multiple causation rather than single causation. Third, changing one part of a system influences other parts; therefore, OD practitioners expect multiple effects, not single effects, from other activities. Fourth, according to field theory (Kurt Lewin), the forces in the field at the time of the event are the relevant forces for analysis. This idea moves the practitioner away from analyzing historical events and toward examining contemporary events and forces. And fifth, to change a system, one changes the system, not just its component parts.

PARTICIPATION AND EMPOWERMENT

One of the most important foundations of organization development is a participation/empowerment model. Participation in OD programs is not restricted to elites or the top people; it is extended throughout the organization. Increased participation and empowerment have always been central goals and fundamental values of the field. These pillars of OD practice are validated by both research and practice.

To empower is to give someone power, which is done by giving individuals the authority to make decisions, to contribute their ideas, to exert influence, and to be responsible. Participation is an especially effective form of empowerment. Participation enhances empowerment, and empowerment in turn enhances performance and individual well-being.

OD interventions are deliberately designed to increase involvement and participation by organization leaders and members. For example, autonomous work groups, quality circles, team building, survey feedback, quality of work life programs, search conferences, and the culture audit are all predicated on the belief that increased participation will lead to better solutions. Rules of thumb such as "Involve all those who are part of the problem or part of the solution," and "Have decisions made by those who are closest to the problem," direct leaders to push decision making lower in the organization, treat those closest to the problem as the relevant experts, and give more power to more people. OD interventions are basically methods for increasing participation. The entire field of OD is about empowerment.

The Leadership Challenge by Kouze and Posner is an excellent manual on empowerment.[21] For many years, Kouze and Posner conducted leadership seminars in which, among other things, they asked participants to describe a "personal best" leadership situation from their own experience. Analysis of hundreds of these "personal best" leadership stories led to identifying five leadership practices and ten behavioral commitments exhibited by successful, empowering leaders. The five practices, with two behavioral commitments, are the following:

Challenging the process

Search for opportunities

Experiment and take risk

Inspiring a shared vision

Envision the future

Enlist others

Enabling others to act

Foster collaboration

Strengthen others

Modeling the way

Set the example

Plan small wins

Encouraging the heart

Recognize individual contributions

Celebrate accomplishments.[22]

We have used this book and the "personal best" exercise, and find this to be an excellent way to start people thinking about empowerment in practical, specific, behavioral terms.

Empowerment is an important ingredient in high-performance organizations. Lawler's research, reported in *The Ultimate Advantage* and *From the Ground Up*, documents the efficacy of involvement and empowerment, especially when empowered employees are formed into empowered teams.[23]

Finally, the concept of "open-book management" as a possible way to run a business is receiving a great deal of attention in management circles today.[24] Open-book management pushes the idea of empowerment to the extreme, usually with excellent financial results. Conceived by Jack Stack, president and CEO of Springfield Remanufacturing Company, this approach encourages every employee of a company to think like an owner of the business, and then start to act like one. Open-book management rests on several simple principles: (1) every employee in an open-book company sees—and learns to understand—

the company's financials, along with all the other numbers that are critical to tracking the business's performance; (2) employees assume that, whatever else they do, part of their job is to move those numbers in the right direction; and (3) employees have a direct stake in the company's success.[25] Participation/empowerment works.

TEAMS AND TEAMWORK

A fundamental belief in organization development is that work teams are the building blocks of organizations. A second fundamental belief is that teams must manage their culture, processes, systems, and relationships if they are to be effective. Theory, research, and practice attest to the central role teams play in organizational success. Teams and teamwork are part of the foundation of organization development

The previous discussion focused on empowerment and concluded that the act of empowering individuals greatly increased their performance and satisfaction. The message of this section is that putting those empowered individuals into teams creates extraordinary effects on performance and satisfaction.

Teams are important for a number of reasons. First, much individual behavior is rooted in the sociocultural norms and values of the work team. If the team, as a team, changes those norms and values, the effects on individual behavior are immediate and lasting. Second, many tasks are so complex they cannot be performed by individuals; people must work together to accomplish them. Third, teams create synergy, that is, the sum of the efforts of team members is far greater than the sum of the individual efforts of people wowing alone. Synergy is a principal reason teams are so important. Fourth, teams satisfy people's need for social interaction, status, recognition, and respect-nurture human nature. In this section, we examine the potential of teams and teamwork, and explore ways to realize that potential.

A number of OD interventions are specifically designed to improve team performance. Examples are team building, intergroup teambuilding, process consultation, quality circles, parallel learning structures, sociotechnical systems programs, Grid OD, and techniques such as role analysis technique, role negotiation, and responsibility charting. These interventions apply to formal work teams as well as startup teams, cross-functional teams, temporary teams, and the like

Team-building activities are now a way of life for many organizations. Teams periodically hold team-building meetings, people are trained as group leaders and group facilitators. Organizations using autonomous work groups or self-directed teams devote considerable time and effort to ensure that team members possess the skills to be effective in groups. The net effect is that teams perform at increasingly higher levels, that they achieve synergy, and that teamwork becomes more satisfying for team members.

An emerging development is the application of technology to improve team performance. Groupware is the generic term for electronic and nonelectric tools designed to help teams, especially business teams, function better. To our knowledge, the book, *Leading Business Teams*, by Johansen, Sibbet, Benson, Martin, Mittman, and Saffo is the first complete exposition on this subject.[26] These authors describe the gamut of tools available—telephones, computers, electronic mail, voice mail, audio teleconferencing, copyboards, local area networks (LANs), and the like—and show how they can be used separately or in combination to help teams get the job done.

The authors also explain how to design a team room—a room filled with tools, gadgets, and furniture to help teams be more effective. A key goal is to help teams make better decisions; therefore, this room provides a variety of decision-support tools, including computer workstations. Experimentation with groupware is certain to increase in the future. (We were relieved to discover that flip charts and magic markers were included in the team room.)

We have used groupware and find it highly effective; it speeds up decision making, allows anonymous contributions, focuses attention on one issue at a time, facilitates setting priorities, enhances consensus building, and provides quick feedback regarding the group's progress.[27] Group can improve a group's performance on both simple and complex tasks.

Teams have always been an important foundation of OD, but there is a growing awareness of the teams' unique ability to create synergy, respond quickly and flexibly to problems, find new ways to get the job done, and satisfy social needs in the work place.

PARALLEL LEARNING STRUCTURES

Parallel learning structures, specially created organizational structures for planning and guiding change programs, constitute another important foundation of organization development. Dale and Zand introduced this concept in 1974 under the label *collateral organization* and defined it as "a supplemental organization coexisting with the usual, formal organization."[28] The purpose of the collateral organization is to deal with "ill-structured" problems the formal organization is unable to resolve. Considerable experimentation with collateral organizations occurred in the 1970s and 1980s.

Gervase Bushe and Abraham (Rami) Shani summarized and extended the work on this connect in their comprehensive treatment titled *Parallel Learning Structures*.[29] We will use the terms *parallel learning structures* and *parallel structures* to refer to this structural intervention. Parallel learning structures are a mechanism to facilitate innovation in large bureaucratic organizations where the forces of inertia, hierarchical communication patterns, and standard ways of addressing problems inhibit learning, innovation, and change. In essence, parallel structures are a vehicle for *learning* how to change the system, and then *leading* the change process.

Bushe and Shani decree the idea as follows: "We offer the term 'parallel learning structure' as a generic label to cover interventions where: (a) a 'structure' (that is, a specific division and coordination of labor) is created that (b) operates 'parallel' (that is, tandem or side-by-side) with the formal hierarchy and structure and (c) has the purpose of increasing an organization's 'learning' (that is, the creation and/or implementation of new thoughts and behaviors by employees)."[30] In its most basic form, a parallel learning structure consists of a steering committee and a number of working groups that study what changes are needed, make recommendations for improvement, and monitoring the change efforts. Additional refinements include having a steering committee plus idea groups, action groups, or implementation groups, with the groups serving specific functions designated by the steering committee. The parallel structure should be a microcosm of the larger organization, that is, it should have representatives from all parts of the organization. One or more top executives should be members of the steering committee to give the parallel structure authority, legitimacy, and clout.

Parallel structures help people break free of the normal constraints imposed by the organization, engage in genuine inquiry and experimentation, and initiate needed changes. We believe parallel learning structures are a foundation of OD because they are prevalent in so many different OD programs. The quality of work life programs of the 1970s and 1980s used parallel structures composed of union leaders, managers, and employees. Most sociotechnical systems redesign efforts and open systems planning programs use parallel structures. High performance organizations often use parallel structures to coordinate self-directed teams. At Ford Motor Company, a steering committee and working teams were used to coordinate the employee involvement teams. Parallel learning structures are often the best way to initiate change in large bureaucratic organizations, especially when the change involves a fundamental shift in the organization's methods of work and/or culture. Bushe and Shani recount a number of examples from a variety of settings where this intervention was used to great advantage.

A NORMATIVE-REEDUCATIVE STRATEGY OF CHANGING

Organization development involves change, and it rests on a particular strategy for change that had implications for practitioners and organization members alike. Chin and Benne describe three types of strategies for changing.[31] The first type of empirical-rational self-interest, and will change if and when they come to realize change is advantageous to them. The second group of strategies is normative-reeducative strategies, based on the assumptions that norms form the basis for behavior, and change comes through reeducation in which old norms are discarded and supplanted by new ones. The third set of strategies is the power-coercive strategies, based on the assumption that change is compliance of those who have less power with the desires of those who have less power with the desires of those who have more power. Evaluated against these three change strategies, OD clearly falls within the normative-reeducative and the empirical-rational strategies. Chin and Benne indicate the nature of the normative-reeducative strategy as follows:

> A second group of strategies we call normative-reeducative. These strategies build upon assumptions about human motivation different from those underlying the first. The rationality and intelligence of men are not denied. Patterns of action and practice are supported by sociocultural norms and by commitments on the part of the individuals to these norms. Sociocultural norms are supported by the attitude and value systems of individuals—normative outlooks which undergird their commitments. Change in a pattern of practice or action, according to this view, will occur only as the persons involved are brought to change their normative orientations to old patterns and develop commitments to new ones. And changes in normative orientations involve changes in attitudes, values, skills, and significant relationships, not just changes in knowledge, information, or intellectual rationales for action and practice.[32]

An illustration may clarify these three strategies of changing. Suppose that the Salk polio vaccine has just been invented, tested, and cleared for public use, and that you are in charge of disseminating it to the public. The procedures you use would depend upon the strategy of changing you believed in. if you exposed the empirical-rational strategy, then you would assume that all rational, self-interested people (and that is just about everyone) would use the vaccine if only they had information about its availability and its efficacy. Your plan, therefore, would be to disseminate the information, and as a consequence everyone would take the vaccine because it would be in his or her best interest.

On the other hand, if you believed in a normative-reeducative strategy of changing, you would do additional things. While you do not disregard people's intelligence, rationality, and self-interest, you also believe that many behaviors are rooted in sociocultural norms, values, and beliefs that must be changed if people are to accept and use the vaccine. Some of these beliefs might be that "all new drugs are dangerous until they have been on the market for ten years"; "My neighbor, Mrs. Jones, isn't going to use the vaccine, and neither am I since she's always right about these things"; "Well, no one in my family has ever had polio, so I'm not afraid of getting it and don't need to be vaccinated." You would mount both an education campaign about the new drug and a reeducation campaign to change possible people's norms and values.

If you believed in a power-coercive strategy of changing, your task would be straightforward: You would pass a law stating that all persons must get vaccinated, and you would enforce compliance with the law. If you had the power to pass the law and power to enforce the law, people would take the vaccine.

The point here is that different strategies are available for effecting change, and OD is based primarily on a normative-reeducative strategy and secondarily on a rational-empirical strategy. Chin and Buena suggest that a normative-reeducative strategy has the following implications for the practice of OD. The client system members define what changes and improvements they want to make, rather than the OD practitioner; the practitioner intervenes in a collaborative way with the clients, and together they define problems and seek solutions. Anything hindering effective problem solving is brought to light and publicly examined; that is, doubts, anxieties, and negative feelings are surfaced for "working through." Solutions to problems are not a priori assigned to greater technical information but may reside in values, attitudes, relationships and customary ways of doing things.[33] The norms to be changed and the form of reeducation are decided by the client system members. These implications give clients considerable control over the situation; they impel a collaborative effort rather than a "doing something to" effort, and they give more options to both the clients and the practitioner.

Because norms are socially accepted beliefs held by groups about appropriate and inappropriate behaviors, norms can best be changed by focusing on the group, not the individual.

Norms help determine individual behavior and a normative-reeducative strategy of changing pervades the practice of OD.

APPLIED BEHAVIORAL SCIENCE

This foundation of OD relates to the primary knowledge base of the field, behavioral science knowledge. OD is the *application* of behavioral science knowledge, practices, and skills on ongoing systems in collaboration with system members. Although human behavior in organizations is far from an exact science, lawful patterns of events produce effectiveness and ineffectiveness. OD practitioners know about these patterns through research and theory. The aim of this discussion is to look briefly at how behavioral science knowledge becomes *applied* behavioral science knowledge.

A conventional distinction is made between (1) "pure" or basic science, the object of which is knowledge for its own sake, and (2) "technology" applied science, or practice, the object of which is knowledge to solve practical, pressing problems.[34] OD emphasizes the latter, applied science or practice. Greenwood discusses the activities of the practitioner

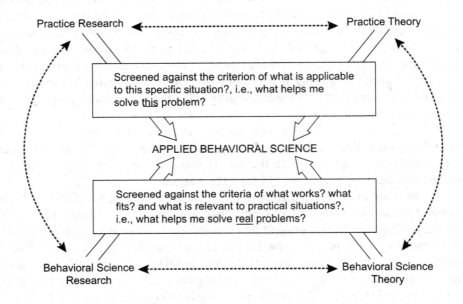

FIGURE 4-6 Composition of Applied Behavioral Science

as follows: "The problem that confronts a practitioner is customarily a state of disequilibrium that requires rectification. The practitioner examines the problem situation, on the basis of which he or she prescribes a solution that, hopefully, reestablishes the equilibrium, thereby solving the problem. This process is customarily referred to as diagnosis and treatment.[35] Both diagnosis and treatment consist of observing a situation and, on the basis of selected variables, placing it in a classification scheme or typology. The diagnostic typology allows the practitioner to know what category of situation he or she has examined; the treatment typology allows the practitioner to know what remedial efforts to apply to correct the problem.

From this "practice theory," the OD practitioner works; first diagnosing the situation, then selecting and implementing treatments based on the diagnosis, and finally evaluating the effects of the treatments.

Organization development is both a result of applied behavioral science and a form of applied behavioral science; perhaps more accurately, it is a program of applying behavioral science to organization. Figure 5-6 shows some of the inputs to applied behavioral science. The two bottom inputs, behavioral science research and behavioral science theory, represent contributions from pure or basic science; the two top inputs, practice research and practice theory, represent contributions from applied science.

The following are some examples of contributions from these four sources that are relevant for organization development.

CONTRIBUTIONS FROM BEHAVIORAL SCIENCE THEORY

The importance of social norms in determining perceptions, motivations, and behaviors (Sherif)

The role of an exchange theory of behavior that postulates that people tend to exchange approximately equivalent units to maintain a balance between what is given and received (Gouldner, Homans)

The importance of the existing total field of forces in determining and predicting behavior (Lewin)

The relevance of role theory in accounting for stability and change in behavior (G. H. Mead)

The possibilities inherent in views of motivation different from those provided by older theories (McGregor, Herzberg, Maslow)

The importance of individual goal setting for increasing productivity and improving performance (Locke)

The place of social cognitive theory, general theories of learning, effects of reward and punishment, attitude change theories, and so on in understanding organizational behavior (Bandura, Skinner, McGuire)[36]

CONTRIBUTIONS FROM BEHAVIORAL SCIENCE RESEARCH

Studies on the causes, conditions, and consequences of induced competition on behavioral within and between groups (Sheriff and Blake and Mouton)

Results on the effects of cooperative and competitive group goal structures on behavior within groups (Deutsch)

Studies on the effects of organizational and managerial climate on leadership style (Fleishman)

Studies on the variables relevant for organizational health (Likert)

Studies showing the importance of the social system in relation to the technical system (Trist and Bamforth)

Studies on different communication networks (Leavitt), causes and consequences of conformity (Asch), group problem solving (Kelley and Thibaut), and group dynamics (Cartwright and Zander)[37]

CONTRIBUTIONS FROM PRACTICE THEORY

Implications from the theory and practice of the laboratory training method (Bradford, Benne, and Gibb)

Implications from theories of group development (Bion and Bennis and Shepard)

New dimensions in the helping relationship and specifically the client–consultant relationship (Rogers)

Codification of the practice of management (Drucker)

New ideas about the education process (Dewey)

The concept of "management by objectives" (Drucker, McGregor)

Implications of social learning theory and behavior modeling for supervisor training (Goldstein and Sorcher)

Explorations in intervention theory and method (Argyris)

Developments in consultation typologies and theory (Blake and Mouton)

Implications and applications from theories of planned change (Lipitt, Watson, and Westley; Bennis, Benne, and Chin)[38]

CONTRIBUTIONS FROM PRACTICE RESEARCH

Studies showing that feeding back survey research data can bring about organization change (Mann, Likert, Baumgartel)

Results indicating the importance of the informal work group on individual and group performance (Roethlisberger and Dickson)

Results showing the efficacy of grid organization development in large organizations (Blake, Mouton, Barnes, and Greiner)

Results documenting improved organizational performance and improved organization climate stemming from a long-term OD effort in a manufacturing firm (Marrow, Bowers, and Seashore)

Results showing the ability of behavior modeling training to improve supervisory human relations skills (Latham and Saari) and organizational effectiveness (Porras)

Results from the action research studies in chapter 7 showing how to change organizational practices.[39]

This list of contributions is not meant to be exhaustive, but only to show some of the sources and kinds of information/knowledge OD practitioners, as applied behavioral scientists, bring to the organizational setting. In fact, most of the citations listed throughout this book represent contributions to the behavioral science theory and research, or practice theory and research underlying OD.

ACTION RESEARCH

The action research model—a data-based, problem-solving method that replicates the steps involved in the scientific method of inquiry underlies most OD activities. Action research involves three processes; data collection, feedback of the data to the client system members, and action planning based on the data.[40] Action research is especially well suited for planned change programs.

Action research is a method that combines *learning* and *doing*—learning about the dynamics of organizational change, and doing or implementing change efforts.

CONCLUDING COMMENTS

These foundations of organization development form the theoretical and practice underpinnings of the field. Taken separately, each is a powerful conceptual tool for thinking about and implementing change. Taken collectively, they constitute the beginning of a theory of organization development and change that has enormous potential for improving organizational performance and individual development.

NOTES

1. See Kurt Lewin, *Field Theory in Social Science* (New York: Harper, 1951).

2. Edgar Schein, *Process Consultation: Lessons for Managers and Consultants*, vol. 2 (Reading, MA: Addison-Wesley Publishing Company, 1987). This discussion is based on pp. 92–114. Table 5-1 is taken from p. 93.

3. R. Lippitt, J. Watson, and B. Westley, *Dynamics of Planned Change* (New York: Harcourt and Brace, 1958).

4. See, for example, D. Kolb and A. Frohman, "An Organization Development Approach to Consulting," *Sloan Management Review*, 12, no. 1 (1970), pp. 51–65. Also, W. Warner Burke, *Organization Development: A Process of Learning and Changing* (Reading, MA: Addison-Wesley Publishing Company, 1994).

5. See Warner Burke, *Organization Development*, chap. 7.

6. The leadership research can be found in James M. Burns, *Leadership* (New York: Harper & Row, 1978); B. M. Bass, *Leadership and Performance Beyond Expectations* (New York: The Free Press, 1985); and N. M. Tichy and M. A. Devanna, *The Transformational Leader* (New York: Wiley and Sons, 1986).

7. These definitions are from Stephen P. Robbins, *Organizational Behavior*, 4th ed. (Englewood Cliffs, N.J.: Prentice Hall, 1989), p. 329.

8. W. Warner Burke, *Organization Development*, pp. 126–127.

9. See, for example, W. W. Burke and P. Jackson, "Making the Smith Kline Beecham Merger Work," in *Human Resource Management*, 30 (1991), pp. 69–87. See also W. M. Bernstein and W. W. Burke, "Modeling Organizational Meaning Systems," in R. W. Woodman and W. A. Pasmore, eds., *Research in Organizational Change and Development* (Greenwich, CT: JAI Press, 1989), pp. 117–159.

10. Ludwig von Bertalanffy, "The Theory of Open Systems in Physics and Biology," *Science*, 111 (1950), pp. 23–28. D. Katz and R. L. Kahn, *The Social Psychology of Organizations* (New York: Wiley, 1966). A second edition appeared in 1978.

11. See A. D. Hall and R. E. Fagen, "Definition of a System," *General Systems*, Yearbook of the Society for the Advancement of General Systems Theory, 1 (1956), pp. 18–28.

12. L. von Bertalanffy, "General System Theory," *General Systems*, Yearbook of the Society for the Advancement of General Systems Theory, 1 (1956) pp. 1–10.

13. Fremont E. Kast and James E. Rosenzweig, *Organization and Management: A Systems Approach*, 4th ed. (New York: McGraw-Hill, 1985), p. 15.

14. David P. Hanna, *Designing Organizations for High Performance* (Reading, MA: Addison-Wesley Publishing Company, 1988), p. 8.

15. This discussion follows the descriptions of Katz and Kahn, *The Social Psychology of Organizations* 2d ed., pp. 18–34; and Hanna, *Designing Organizations for High Performance*, pp. 1–31.

16. Hanna, pp. 14–15.

17. Ibid., p. 16.

18. Katz and Kahn, p. 27.

19. David A. Nadler, *Champions of Change* (San Francisco: Jossey-Bass Publishers, 1998), pp. 21–43. The congruence model is found on p. 41.

20. See W. A. Pasmore, *Designing Effective Organizations: The Sociotechnical Systems Perspective* (New York: Wiley, 1988); C. Pava, "Redesigning Sociotechnical Systems Design: Concepts and Methods for the 1990s," *Journal of Applied Behavioral Science*, 22 (1986), pp. 201–221; T. G. Cummings, "Future Directions of Sociotechnical Systems Theory and Research," *Journal of Applied Behavioral Science*, 22 (1986), pp. 355–360; D. P. Hanna,

Designing Organizations for High Performance; and G. R. Bushe and A. B. Shani, *Parallel Learning Structures* (Reading, MA: Addison-Wesley Publishing Company, 1991).

21. James M. Kouzes and Barry Z. Posner, *The Leadership Challenge* (San Francisco: Jossey-Bass Publishers, 1990).
22. Ibid., p. 14.
23. Edward E. Lawler III, *The Ultimate Advantage* (San Francisco: Jossey-Bass Publishers, 1992), and From the Ground Up (San Francisco: Jossey-Bass Publishers, 1996).
24. See Jack Stack, *The Great Game of Business* (New York: Currency Doubleday, 1992). See also John Case, *Open-Book Management* (New York: Harper Collins Publishers, Inc., 1995).
25. Case, *Open-Book Management*, chapter 3.
26. Robert Johansen, David Sibbet, Suzyn Benson, Alexia Martin, Robert Mittman, and Paul Saffo, *Leading Business Teams* (Reading, MA: Addison-Wesley Publishing Company, 1991).
27. We have worked with Enterprise Solutions, Inc., a Seattle, Washington, company specializing in facilitating executive decision making. Group problem solving and decision making are greatly enhanced through the use of their proprietary software and computer network.
28. Dale Zand, "Collateral Organization: A New Change Strategy," *Journal of Applied Behavioral Science*, 10 (1974), pp. 63–89. This quotation is from p. 64.
29. Bushe and Shani, *Parallel Learning Structures*.
30. Ibid., p. 9.
31. Robert Chin and Kenneth D. Benne, "General Strategies for Effecting Changes in Human Systems," in W. G. Bennis, K. D. Benne, R. Chin, and K. E. Corey, eds., *The Planning of Change*, 3rd ed. (New York: Holt, Rinehart, and Winston, 1976), pp. 22–45.
32. Ibid., p. 23.
33. Based on a discussion in Chin and Benne, "General Strategies," pp. 32–33.
34. Warner Burke, *Organization Development*, p. 151.
35. Ernest Greenwood, "The Practice of Science and the Science of Practice," in Bennis, Benne, and Chin, eds., *The Planning of Change*, 1961, p. 78.
36. These citations, listed in order of mention in the text, are: (1) M. Sherif, *The Psychology of Social Norms* (New York: Harper & Bros., 1936). (2) A. W. Gouldner, "The Norm of Reciprocity: A Preliminary Statement," *American Sociological Review*, 25 (April 1960), pp. 161–178. (3) C. G. Homans, *The Human Group* (New York: Harcourt, Brace & World, 1950). (4) K. Lewin, *Field Theory in Social Science* (New York: Harper & Bros., 1951). (5) G. H. Mead, *Mind, Self, and Society* (Chicago: University of Chicago Press, 1934). (6) D. M. McGregor, *The Human Side of Enterprise* (New York: McGraw-Hill, 1960). (7) F. B. Herzberg, B. Mausner, and B. Snyderman, *The Motivation to Work* (New York: John Wiley, 1959). (8) A. Maslow, *Motivation and Personality* (New York: Harper & Row, 1964). (9) E. A. Locke, "Toward a Theory of Task Motivation and Incentives," *Organizational Behavior and Human Performance*, 3 (1968), pp. 157–189. (10) A. Bandura, *Social Foundations of Thought and Action: A Social Cognitive Theory* (Englewood Cliffs, NJ: Prentice Hall, 1986). (11) B. F. Skinner, About *Behaviorism* (New York: Alfred A. Knopf, 1974). (12) W. J. McGuire, "The Nature of Attitudes and Attitude Change," in G. Lindzey and E. Aronson, eds., *Handbook of Social Psychology*, 2d ed., vol. 3 (Reading, MA: Addison-Wesley Publishing Company, 1969), pp. 136–314.
37. These citations, listed in order of mention in the text, are: (1) M. Sherif, O. J. Harvey, B. J. White, W. R. Hood, and C. Sherif, *Intergroup Conflict and Cooperation: The Robbers Cave Experiment* (Norman, OK: University Book Exchange, 1961). (2) R. R. Blake, "Conformity, Resistance, and Conversion," in I. A. Berg and B. M. Bass, eds., *Conformity and Deviation* (New York: Harper & Row, 1961), pp. 1–37. (3) M. Deutsch, "A Theory of Cooperation and Competition," *Human Relations*, 2, no. 2 (1949), pp. 129–152. (4) E. A. Fleishman, "Leadership Climate, Human Relations Training and Supervisory Behavior," *Personnel Psychology*,

6 (Summer 1953), pp. 205–222. (5) R. Likert, *New Patterns of Management* (New York: McGraw-Hill, 1961). (6) E. L. Trist and K. W. Bamforth, "Some Social and Psychological Consequences of the Longwall Method of Coal-Getting," *Human Relations*, 4, no. 1 (1951), pp. 1–38. (7) H. J. Leavitt, "Some Consequences of Certain Communication Patterns on Group Performance," *Journal of Abnormal and Social Psychology*, 46 (January 1951), pp. 38–50. (8) S. Asch, "Studies of Independence and Conformity: A Minority of One Against a Unanimous Majority," *Psychological Monographs*, 7, no. 9 (1956). (9) H. H. Kelley and J. W. Thibaut, "Group Problem Solving," in G. Lindzey and E. Aronson, eds., *Handbook of Social Psychology*, 2d ed., vol. 4 (Reading, MA: Addison-Wesley Publishing Company, 1969), pp. 1–101. (10) D. Cartwright and A. Zander, *Group Dynamics*, 2d ed. (New York: Harper & Row, 1960).

37. These citations, listed in order of mention in the text, are: (1) L. P. Bradford, J. R. Gibb, and K. D. Benne, eds., *T-Group Theory and Laboratory Method* (New York: John Wiley, 1964). (2) W. R. Bion, *Experiences in Groups* (New York: Basic Books, 1961). (3) W. G. Bennis and H. A. Shepard, "A Theory of Group Development," *Human Relations*, 9, no. 4 (1956), pp. 415–438. (4) C. R. Rogers, *Client-Centered Therapy* (Boston: Houghton Mifflin, 1951). (5) P. F. Drucker, *The Practice of Management* (New York: Harper & Row, 1954). (6) J. Dewey, *How We Think*, (rev. ed.) (New York: Heath, 1933). (7) P. F. Drucker, *The Practice of Management* (New York: Harper & Row, 1954). (8) D. M. McGregor, *The Human Side of Enterprise* (New York: McGraw-Hill, 1960). (9) A. P. Goldstein and M. Sorcher, *Changing Supervisor Behavior* (New York: Pergamon Press, 1974). (10) C. Argyris, *Intervention Theory and Method: A Behavioral Science View* (Reading, MA: Addison-Wesley Publishing Company, 1970). (11) R. R. Blake and J. S. Mouton, *Consultation* (Reading, MA: Addison-Wesley Publishing Company, 1976). (12) R. Lippitt, J. Watson, and B. Westley, *The Dynamics of Planned Change* (New York: Harcourt, Brace & World, 1958). (13) W. G. Bennis, K. D. Benne, and R. Chin, eds., *The Planning of Change* (New York: Holt, Rinehart and Winston, 1961).

39. These citations, listed in order of mention in the text, are: (1) F. C. Mann, "Studying and Creating Change," in W. G. Bennis, K. D. Benne, and R. Chin, eds., *The Planning of Change* (New York: Holt, Rinehart and Winston, 1961), pp. 605–613. (2) R. Likert, *New Patterns of Management* (New York: McGraw-Hill, 1961). (3) H. Baumgartel, "Using Employee Questionnaire Results for Improving Organizations: The Survey 'Feedback' Experiment," *Kansas Business Review*, 12 (December 1959), pp. 2–6. (4) F. J. Roethlisberger and W. J. Dickson, *Management and the Worker* (Cambridge, MA: Harvard University Press, 1939). (5) R. R. Blake, J. S. Mouton, L. B. Barnes, and L. E. Greiner, "Breakthrough in Organization Development," *Harvard Business Review*, 42 (November–December 1964), pp. 133–155. (6) A. J. Marrow, D. G. Bowers, and S. E. Seashore, *Management by Participation* (New York: Harper & Row, 1967). (7) G. P. Latham and L. M. Saari, "The Application of Social Learning Theory to Training Supervisors Through Behavior Modeling," *Journal of Applied Psychology*, 64 (1979), pp. 239–246. (8) J. I. Porras, K. Hargis, K. J. Patterson, D. G. Maxfield, N. Roberts, and R. J. Bies, "Modeling-Based Organizational Development: A Longitudinal Assessment," *The Journal of Applied Behavioral Science*, 18, no. 4 (1982), pp. 433–446.

40. Richard Beckhard, *Organizational Development: Strategies and Models* (Reading, MA: Addison-Wesley Publishing Company, 1969), p. 28.

CHAPTER 5

Managing the OD Process

In this chapter we examine what leaders, organization members, and OD practitioners do as they implement and manage organization programs. By now you know that *diagnosis* forms a foundation for *intervening*, and that intervening involves *implementing various change-inducing action programs*. Thinking about how to manage this process is the focus of the present discussion. First we take an in-depth look at diagnosis. Then we examine the considerations that go into selecting and implementing interventions. Finally, we present guidelines for the overall management of OD programs.

DIAGNOSIS

All OD programs have three basic components: *diagnosis, action,* and *program management.* The diagnostic component represents a continuous collection of data about the total system, its subunits, it processes, and its culture. The action component consists of all activities and interventions designed to improve the organization's functioning. The program management component encompasses all activities designed to ensure success of the program. (In fact, all three components are interventions into the organization members. They are separated here for analysis purposes.) Figure 5-1 shows what we mean when we describe the OD process in terms of diagnosis, action, and program management components.

The first step is to diagnose the state of the system, focusing on the client's major concerns. What are its strengths? What are its problem areas? What are its unrealized opportunities? Is there a discrepancy between the vision of the desired future and the current situation? The diagnosis identifies strengths, opportunities, and problem areas. Action plans are developed in step 2 to correct problems, seize opportunities, and maintain areas of strength. These action plans are OD interventions specifically tailored to address issues at the individual, group, intergroup, or organizational levels, as well as issues related to selected processes. Step 3 consists of fact-finding about the results of the actions. Did the actions have the desired effects? Is the problem solved or the opportunities achieved? If the answer is yes, organization members move on to new and different problems and opportunities; if the answer is no, the members initiate new action plans and interventions to resolve the issue (step 4). When problems remain unsolved after an initial attack, steps 3 and 4 usually entail redefining the problem areas. Steps 5, 6, 7, and so on may be required for some problems and opportunities, but further steps are just iterations of the basic sequence of diagnosis-action-evaluation-action. Again, this process looks logical and linear in Figure 5-1, but in practice is more complicated.

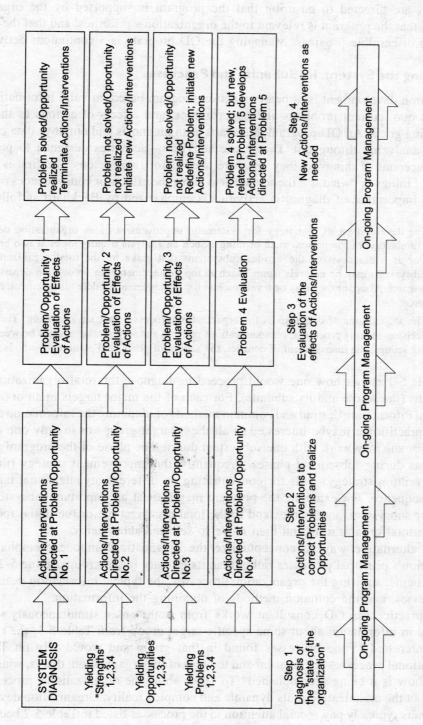

FIGURE 5-1 Components of the OD Process: Diagnosis, Action, Program Management

During the entire sequence, managing the OD process itself requires attention. Energy and effort are directed to ensuring that the program is supported by the organization members, that the program is relevant to the organization's priorities, and that the program is making discernible progress. Managing the OD program is a continuous activity.

Diagnosing the System, Its Subunits and Processes

Organization development is at heart an action program based on valid information about the status quo, current problems and opportunities, and effects of actions as they relate to achieving goals. An OD program thus starts with diagnosis and employs data collecting and data analyzing throughout. Diagnostic activities—activities designed to provide an accurate account of things as they are—are needed for two reasons: the first is to know the state of things or "what is"; the second is to know the effects or consequences of actions.

The importance of diagnostic activities is emphasized by Beckhard as follows:

> The development of a strategy for systematic improvement of an organization demands an examination of the present state of things. Such an analysis usually looks at two broad areas. One is a diagnosis of the various subsystems that make up the total organization. These subsystems may be natural "teams" such as top management, the production department, or a research group; or they may be levels such as top management, middle management, or the work force.
>
> The second area of diagnosis is the organization processes that are occurring. These include decision-making processes, communications patterns and styles, relationships between interfacing groups, the management of conflict, the setting of goals, and planning methods.[1]

Table 5-1 shows how one would proceed to diagnose the total organization and its subsystems (the whole and its subunits). For each of the major targets in an organization, the typical information desired and common methods of obtaining the information are given. The OD practitioner maybe interested in all these target groups or in only one or two of them; he or she may work with one subsystem during one phase of the program and other subsystems during subsequent phases. Frequently, the improvement strategy (the overall OD intervention strategy) calls for concentrating on different organizational targets in a planned sequence. For example, the program may start at an important subsystem, move to another subsystem, and then extend to the total organization; or the initial focus could be on the total organization and then move to selected subsystems.

An alternative way to conceptualize the diagnostic component emphasizes the organization's principal processes rather than its primary target groups. Table 5-2 presents such a scheme, showing the organization processes, the typical information desired about the processes, and the common methods of obtaining the information.

In practice the OD consultant works from both tables simultaneously. Although interested in information about some specific target group from Table 5-1, the consultant is also interested in the processes found in that group and would rely on Table 5-2. Organizational processes are the *what* and the *how* of the organization, that is, what is going on? and how is it being accomplished? To know about the organization's processes is to know about the organization in its dynamic and complex reality. Organization development practitioners typically pay special attention to the processes listed in Table 5-2 because they are central for effective organization functioning and because significant organizational

TABLE 5-1 Diagnosing Organizational Subsystems

Diagnostic Targets	*Explanation and Identifying Examples*
The total organization (having a common "charter" or mission and a common authority structure)	The total system is the entity analyzed. Diagnosis also includes extrasystem (environmental) organizations, groups, or forces, such as customers, suppliers, and governmental regulations. Examples: a manufacturing firm, a hospital, a school system, a department store chain, a church denomination.
Large complex and heterogeneous subsystems	This target group refers to major units within a larger organization—divisions, subsidiary companies, "European operations," and functional departments such as marketing, manufacturing, and human resources.
Small, simple, and relatively homogeneous subsystems	These are typically formal work groups or teams. They may be permanent groups, temporary task forces, or newly constituted groups (e.g., the group charged with the "start-up" of a new operation, or the group formed by an acquisition or merger). Examples are the top-management team, managers and key subordinates, task force teams, the workforce in an office, the teachers in a single school.
What are the norms of the organization? What is the organization's culture? What are the attitudes and feelings toward such things as compensation, organization goals, supervision, and top management? What is the organization climate—open vs. closed, authoritarian vs. democratic, cooperative vs. competitive? How well do key organizational processes function? How effective are the organization's "sensing mechanisms" to monitor internal and external demands? Are organization goals and strategy understood and accepted? What is the organization's performance?	Questionnaire surveys are most popular with large organizations. Interviews, both group and individual, are useful for getting detailed information. Panels of representative members surveyed periodically are useful to chart changes over time. Examination of organizational records—rules, regulations, policies, symbols of office and/or status, etc., yields insight into the organization's culture and functioning. Diagnostic meetings held at various levels yield a great amount of information in a short time period. Focus groups give valuable information.
All of the preceding, plus: How does this subsystem view the whole and vice versa? What are the unique demands on	If the subsystems are large or widely dispersed, questionnaire survey techniques are recommended. Interviews, observa-

Typical Information Sought	*Common Methods of Diagnosis*
this subsystem? Are organization structures and processes related to the unique demands? What are the major problems confronting this subsystem and its subunits? Are the subsystem's goals compatible with organization goals? Do conflicting role demands and functional identity get in the way of effective subsystem performance? The key issues are "part-whole" relationships and alignment.	tions, and organization records are good sources of information about performance and problems. Interviews of "liaisons" between "part" and "whole" are valuable.
Questions on culture, climate, attitudes, and feelings are relevant here, plus: What are the major problems of the team? How can team effectiveness be improved? What do people do that gets in the way of others? Are member/leader relations those that are desired? Do individuals know how their jobs relate to group and organizational goals? Are the group's processes effective? Is good use made of group and individual resources?	Typical methods include the following: individual interviews, followed by a group meeting to review the interview data; questionnaires; observation of staff meetings and other day-to-day operations; and a formal group meeting for self-diagnosis.
Interface or intergroup subsystems	These consist of subsets of the total system that contain members of two subsystems, such as a matrix organizational structure requiring an individual or a group to have two reporting lines. But more often this target consists of members of one subsystem having common problems and responsibilities with members of another subsystem such as production and maintenance overlaps, marketing and production overlaps.
Dyads and/or triads	Superior/subordinate pairs, interdependent peers, linking pins—i.e., persons who have multiple group memberships—all these are subsystems worthy of analysis.
Individuals	All individuals within the organization.
Roles	A role is a set of behaviors enacted by a person as a result of occupying a certain position within the organization. All per-

Diagnostic Targets	*Explanation and Identifying Esamples*
	sons in the organization have roles requiring certain behaviors: administrative assistants, supervisors, accountants, scientists, custodians, executives, sales representatives.
Between-organization systems constituting a suprasystem—this is the arena of transorganizational OD.	An example is the system of law and order in a region, including local, county, state, federal police or investigative and enforcement agencies, courts, prisons, parole agencies, prosecuting officers and grand juries. Most such suprasystems are so complex that change efforts tend to focus on a pair or a trio of subparts.
How does each subsystem see the other? What problems do the two groups have in working together? How do the subsystems get in each other's way? How can they collaborate to improve the performance of both groups? Are goals, subgoals, areas of authority and responsibility clear? What is the nature of the climate between the groups? What do the members want it to be?	Confrontation meetings between both groups are often the method for data gathering and planning corrective actions. Organization mirroring meetings are used when three or more groups are involved. Interviews of each subsystem followed by a "sharing the data" meeting or observation of interactions can be used. Flowcharting critical processes is useful.
What is the quality of the relationship? Do the parties have the necessary skills for task accomplishment? Are they collaborative or competitive? Are they effective as a subsystem? Are they supportive of each other?	Separate interviews followed by a meeting of the parties to view any discrepancies in the interview data are often used. Checking their perceptions of each other through confrontation situations may be useful. Observation is an important way to assess the dynamic quality of the interaction.
Do people perform according to the organization's expectations? How do they view their place and performance? Do certain kinds of problems typically arise? Do people meet standards and norms of the organization? Do they need particular knowledge, skills, or ability? What career development opportunities do they have/want/need? What pain are they experiencing?	Interviews, information from diagnostic meetings, or problems identified by the human resources department are sources of information. Self-assessment is another source.

Typical Information Sought	Common Methods of Diagnosis
Should the role behaviors be added to, subtracted from, or changed? Is the role defined adequately? What is the "fit" between person and role? Should the role performer be given special skills and knowledge? Is this the right person for this role?	Usually information comes from observations, interviews, role analysis technique, a team approach to "management by objectives." Career planning activities yield this information as an output.
How do key people in each segment of the suprasystem view the whole and the subparts? Are there frictions or incongruities between subparts? Are there high-performing and low-performing subunits? Why?	Organizational mirroring, or developing lists of how each group sees each other, is a common method of joint diagnosis. Questionnaires and interviews are useful. Flowcharting critical processes is useful.

problems often stem from them. Carefully examining the two tables gives a good sense of the inner workings of an OD program—its thrusts, emphasis, and mechanics.

These tables are intended as tools for diagnosing organizations, their processes, and their subunits. For example, say the vice president of a large heterogeneous division composed of several different businesses with multiple manufacturing and marketing organizations is worried about decreasing profitability. The vice president needs answers to Table 5-1 questions concerning the total organization and large subsystems, as well as questions from Table 5-2 about organizational processes such as goal setting, decision-making, technology, and strategic management. The diagnostic phase of an OD effort sponsored by the vice president would produce the answers.

Continual diagnosis is thus necessary in any planned change effort. Such diverse activities as getting rich, managing your time, and losing weight, for example, all begin with an *audit* of "what is"—the status quo—and then require continual monitoring of the changing status quo over time. Comparing "what is" with "what should be" reveals the gap between actual and desired conditions. Action plans are then developed to close the gap; and the effects (consequences) of these actions are continuously monitored to measure progress toward the goal.[2] Diagnosis is therefore basic to all goal-seeking activities.

Organization development continuously generates system data. In this regard, Argyris states that the consultant ("interventionist:" in his terms) has three "primary intervention tasks": (1) to help the client system generate valid data; (2) to enable the client system to have free, informed choice; and (3) to help the client system generate internal commitment to the choices made.[3] Argyris says: "One condition that seems so basic as to be defined axiomatic is the generation of *valid information*. Without valid information, it would be difficult for the client to learn and for the interventionist for help ... valid information is that which describes the factors, plus their interrelationships, that create the problem for the client system."[4]

TABLE 5-2 Diagnosing Organizational Processes	
Organizational Process	*Identifying Remarks and Explanation*
Communications patterns, styles and flows	Who talks to whom, about what? Who initiates? Is communication two-way or one-way? Is it top-down, down-up, lateral? Does information get to the right places in a timely manner?
Goal setting	Setting task objectives and determining criteria to measure accomplishment of the objectives should take place at all organizational levels.
Decision making, problem solving, and action planning	Evaluating alternatives and choosing a plan of action are integral and central functions for organizations. They include getting the necessary information, establishing priorities, evaluating alternatives, and implementing an alternative.
Conflict resolution and management	Conflict—interpersonal and intergroup—frequently exists in organizations. Does the organization have effective ways of dealing with conflict?
Managing interface relations	Interfaces represent these situations where two or more groups (subsystems) face common problems or overlapping responsibility. This is most often seen when two separate groups are interdependently related in achieving an objective but have separate accountability.
Superior-subordinate relations	Formal authority in organizations requires that some people lead and others follow: these situations are often a source of organizational problems.
Technological and engineering systems	All organizations rely on multiple technologies—for production and operations, for information processing, for planning, for marketing, etc., to produce goods and services.
Is communication directed upward, downward, laterally? Are communications filtered? Why? How? Do communications patterns "fit" the jobs to be accom-	Observations, especially in meetings; questionnaires for large organizations; interviews and discussions with group members—all these methods may be

Typical Information Sought	*Common Methods of Diagnosis*
plished? What is the "climate" of communications? Is communication open or closed?	used. Analysis of videotaped sessions is especially useful.
Do people set goals? Who participates? Do they possess the necessary skills for effective goal setting? Are they able to set long-range and short-range objectives? Are goals achieved?	Questionnaires, interviews, and observation are ways to assess goal-setting ability of individuals and groups within the organization.
Who makes decisions? Are they effective? Are all available sources used? Are additional decision-making skills needed? Are additional problem-solving skills needed? Are organization members satisfied with problem-solving and decision-making processes?	Observation of problem-solving meetings at various organizational levels is particularly valuable in diagnosing this process. Analysis of videotaped sessions is useful. Organizational records are valuable sources.
Where does conflict exist? Who are the involved parties? How is it being managed? What are the system norms for dealing with conflict? Does the reward system promote conflict?	Interviews, third-party observations, and observation meetings are common methods to use.
What is the nature of the relations between two groups? Are goals clear? Is responsibility clear? What major problems do the two groups face? What structural conditions promote/inhibit effective interface management?	Interviews, third-party observations, and observation of group meetings are common methods for diagnosing these processes.
What are the prevailing leadership styles? What problems arise between superiors and subordinates?	Questionnaires show overall leadership climate and norms. Interviews and questionnaires reveal desired leadership behaviors.
Are the technologies adequate for satisfactory performance? What is the state of the art and how does this organization's technology compare with that? Are changes in technology needed?	Generally this area is not within the expertise of the OD consultant. He or she must then seek help from "experts" either inside the organization or outside. Interviews and group discussions focused on technology are among the best ways to determine the adequacy of technological systems. Sometimes outside experts conduct an audit and make recommendations; sometimes inside experts do.

Diagnostic Targets	Explanation and Identifying Esamples
Strategic management and long-range planning Vision/Mission formulation	Monitoring the environment, adding and deleting "products," predicting future events, and making decisions that affect the long-term viability of the organization must occur for the organization to remain competitive and effective. Vision and mission establish the framework for strategy.
Organizational learning	Learning from past successes and failures, from present "blind spots" and from all organizational members is essential to remain competitive, vital, and to develop new paradigms.

[a]Peter M. Senge, *The Fifth Discipline: The Art and Practice of the Learning Organization* (New York: Doubleday/Currency, 1990), pp. 12, 18–19, 44.
[b]Edgar Schein, "Organization Development and the Study of Organizational Culture," *Academy of Management Newsletter* (Summer 1990), pp. 3–5.
[c]Chris Argyris, "Teaching Smart People How to Learn," *Harvard Business Review*, 69 (May–June 1991), pp. 99–109.
[d]Peter M. Senge, *The Fifth Discipline*, pp. 237–238.

Granted that diagnosis is a sine qua non of effective organization development, two issues remain. First, it is the diagnosis systematically planned and structured in advance so that it follows a category system and structured question format, or is the diagnosis more emergent—following the data wherever they may lead? Second, what diagnostic categories will be used? Practice varies widely on these two dimensions. We tend to be in the middle of the "structured in advance-emergent" continuum. We have some structured questions but follow up on leads as they develop in the course of the diagnosis. We also tend to use the diagnostic categories of Tables 5-1 and 5-2 because we focus on system and subsystem cultures and processes.

Furthermore, in an OD program, although the *results* of diagnostic activities are important, *how the information is collected and what is done with the information* is also important. The OD practitioner and the organization members actively collaborate about such issues as what target groups to diagnose, how the diagnosis is best accomplished, which processes to analyze, what to do with the information, and how to use the information to aid action planning. Usually information is collected through a variety of methods—interviews, observations, questionnaires, and organization records. Information is treated as the property of those persons who generated it, and the data serve as the foundation for planning actions. This format is basically an action research model. Therefore, the diagnostic and action components are intimately related in organization development.

Typical Information Sought	*Common Methods of Diagnostics*
Who is responsible for "looking ahead" and for making long-range decisions? Do they have adequate tools and support? Have recent long-range decisions been effective? What is the nature of current and future environmen-tal demands? What are the unique strengths and com-petencies of the organization? What are the threats to the organization? Is mission clear? Widely shared?	Interviews of key policy makers, group discussions, and examination of historical records give insights to this dimension.
What are our strengths, problem areas? What observations, ideas, suggestions are available from all organizational members? Does our present behavior square with what we espouse? What are the "learning disabilities" (Sengea) of this organization? Are the present paradigms changing? What will the new paradigms be like? Are we recording our philosophy, our learnings, our progress?	Interviews, questionnaires, group methods of diagnosis; examination of assumptions and culture (Scheinb); games and exercises to create awareness of organizational learning disabilities; examination of defensive routines (Argyris,c Senged); visioning, including environment analysis.

The Six–Box Model

Another diagnostic tool is Marvin Weisbord's six-box model, a diagnostic framework published in 1976, and still widely used by OD practitioners.[5] This model tells practitioners where to look and what to look for in diagnosing organizational problems. As shown in Figure 5-2, Weisbord identifies six critical areas—purposes, structure, rewards, helpful mechanisms, relationships, and leadership—where things must go right if the organization is to be successful. Practitioners use this model as a cognitive map systematically examining the processes and activities of each box, looking for signs of trouble.

Assume an organization has problems with one of the products. These problems will have their causes in dysfunctional processes located in one or more of the six boxes. The problems could be caused by ill-advised structures, poor leadership, unclear purposes or purposes at variance with the product, lack of helpful mechanisms, and so on. The six-box model is a simple but powerful diagnostic tool.

According to Weisbord, the consultant must attend to both the *formal* and *informal* aspects of each box. The formal system defines the official way things are supposed to happen; the informal system is the way things really happen. For example, the formal reporting relationships and organization of tasks and people prescribed in the structure box may not reflect the real structural arrangements found in the informal system. The practitioner needs answers to two questions; First, are the arrangements and processes called for by the *formal* system *correct* for each box? Second, are the arrangements and

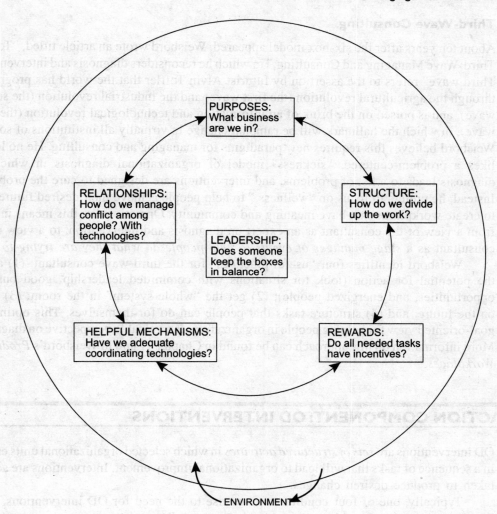

PURPOSES:
What business
are we in?

RELATIONSHIPS:
How do we manage
conflict among
people? With
technologies?

STRUCTURE:
How do we divide
up the work?

LEADERSHIP:
Does someone keep the boxes
in balance?

HELPFUL MECHANISMS:
Have we adequate
coordinating technologies?

REWARDS:
Do all needed tasks
have incentives?

ENVIRONMENT

Source: Marvin R. Weisbord, "Organizational Diagnosis: Six Places to Look With or Without a Theory." *Group and Organizational Studies*, 1 (1976), pp. 430–447. Reprinted by permission.

FIGURE 5-2 The Six-Box Organizational Model

processes developed by the *informal* system *correct* for each box. Commonly, one finds that formal arrangements are inappropriate, but the informal system works around the deficiencies by developing methods to correct them. By the same token, one may also find that the formal system is correctly designed, but the informal system is not following those correct procedures, and consequently performance suffers. The formal/informal distinction, that is, what's supposed to happen versus what is really happening, is a powerful element of OD practice theory and one of the secrets to understanding organizational dynamics. Weisbord recommends a thorough diagnosis, looking at multiple boxes, before choosing interventions.

Third-Wave Consulting

About ten years after the six-box model appeared, Weisbord wrote an article titled, "Toward Third-Wave Managing and Consulting," in which he reconsiders diagnosis and intervention.[6] Third wave" refers to the assertion by futurist Alvin Toffler that the world has progressed through the agricultural revolution (the first wave) and the industrial revolution (the second wave), and is poised on the brink of an information and technological revolution (the third wave), in which the hallmark will be rampant change in virtually all institutions of society. Weisbord believes this requires new paradigms for managing and consulting. He no longer likes a problem-centered, "sickness" model of organizational diagnosis in which the diagnosis leads to a list of problems, and interventions are designed to cure the problems. Instead, he prefers to focus on "wellness," to help people achieve their desired futures and to create workplaces that have meaning and community. Operationally, this means moving from a view of the consultant as an expert on diagnosis and intervention, to a view of the consultant as a *stage manager of events to help people do what they are trying to do.*

Weisbord identifies four "useful practices" for the third-wave consultant: (1) assess the potential for action (look for situations with committed leadership, good business opportunities, and energized people); (2) get the "whole system" in the room; (3) focus on the future; and (4) structure tasks that people can do for themselves. This optimistic, goal-oriented view for helping people in organizations is a valuable perspective on diagnosis. More information on this approach can be found in Chapter 11 and in Weisbord's *Productive Workplaces.*[7]

THE ACTION COMPONENT: OD INTERVENTIONS

OD interventions are *sets of structured activities* in which selected organizational units engage in a sequence of tasks that will lead to organizational improvement. Interventions are actions taken to produce desired changes.

Typically, one of four conditions gives rise to the need for OD interventions. First, the organization has a problem; something is "broken" Corrective actions—interventions—are implemented to "fix" the problem. Second, the organization sees an unrealized opportunity; something it wants is beyond its reach. Enabling actions—interventions—are developed to seize the opportunity. Third, features of the organization are out of alignment; parts of the organization are working at cross-purposes. Alignment activities—interventions—are developed to get things back "in sync." Fourth, the vision guiding the organizations changes; yesterday's vision is no longer good enough. Actions to build the necessary structures, processes, and culture to support the new vision—interventions—are developed to make the new vision a reality. In summary, the interventions are planned sets of actions to change situations the organization members want to change.

The range of OD interventions is quite extensive. Interventions have been developed to solve most problems related to the human side of organizations. An inventory of OD interventions is given in chapters 9 through 13.

The Nature of OD Interventions

To intervene in the client system is to interpose activities so that the intervention activities are done *in addition* to the normal activities or are done *instead of* the normal activities. For example, an "in addition to" intervention would be a staff group including a "process critique" at the end of each staff meeting. This activity simply means that a few minutes are set aside to look at "how we worked"—the process—during the meeting. Critiquing "how we worked" can enable the group to correct deficient processes and become more effective in its deliberations. An example of an "instead of" intervention shop with its user-clients to determine how clients view the services provided and how they want services improved. In this case, instead of the normal activities of begging, cajoling, or coercing the user-clients to use the staff services, a problem-solving workshop called the organization mirror is convened in which the clients give feedback to the service group. This option establishes a dialogue between service providers and service users. Such a meeting would probably not be a normal activity in the organization.

A well-designed OD program unfolds according to a game plan, called the *overall OD strategy*. This strategy may be planned in advance or may emerge as events dictate. The strategy is based on answers to such questions as: What are the overall change/improvement goals of the program? What parts of the organization are most ready and receptive to the OD program? What are the key leverage points (individuals and groups) in the organization? What are the most pressing problems of the client organization? What resources are available for the program in terms of client time and energy and internal and external facilitators? Answers to these questions lead the practitioner to develop a game plan for where to intervene in the system, what to do, how to sequence interventions, and so forth.

Planning actions, executing actions, and evaluating the consequences of actions are integral to organization development. This emphasis on action planning and action taking is a powerful feature of OD, and, in some respects, is a distinguishing one. In many traditional educational and training activities, learning and action taking are then taken back to the organization with the learner being admonished to practice what he or she has learned, that is, to take actions. Most OD interventions minimize this artificial separation in many ways. First, many intervention activities have two goals: an educational goal and an accomplishing-a-task goal. Second, OD problem-solving interventions tend to focus on real problems central to the organization's needs. Third, OD interventions use several learning models, not just one. Let us examine these three points in greater detail.

The dual aspect of OD interventions can be clarified with an illustration. Let us say that the top executives of an organization spend three days in a workshop in which they do the following things: (1) explore the need for a long-range strategic plan for the organization; (2) learn how to formulate such a strategy by analyzing other strategies, determining the strategic variables, being shown a sequence of steps for preparing a comprehensive plan, and so forth; and (3) actually make a three-year strategic plan for the organization.[8] This intervention combines the dual features of learning and action: the executives learned about strategic planning, and they then generated a strategy. In some OD interventions, the "learning aspect" predominates, and in others, the "action aspect" predominates; but both aspects are present in most interventions.

Organization development interventions tend to focus on real problems rather than hypothetical problems. Developing the skills and knowledge to solve real problems as they arise in their "natural state" minimizes the educational problem of "transfer of learning" from one situation to another (although the problem of generalization, that is, knowing the appropriate times and places to apply this particular set of skills and knowledge, is still present).

An additional feature of working on real problems, in OD interventions is that the real set of individuals involved in the problem is the group the problem solvers work with. For example, in a human relations class, if a manager were having trouble understanding and working with minority employees, he or she would perhaps "role play" the situation with the instructor or fellow students. In OD, the manager would probably interact with the minority employees with whom he or she was having difficulties—but would do so in carefully structured activities that have a high profitability of learning for both parties of being a "success experience" for both parties.

Organization development programs rely on several learning models. For example, "if learning how to" do something precedes "doing" it, then we have a traditional approach to learning familiar to most people. If the "doing" precedes the "learning how to," then we have a "deficiency" model of learning in which the learning comes primarily critiquing the actions after the fact to see how they could have been done differently and, presumably, better. Both models are viable learning modes, and both are used extensively in organization development.

Action programs in OD are closely linked with explicit goals and objectives. Careful attention is given to translating goals into observable, explicit, and measurable actions, and equal care is given to ensuring that actions are relevant to and instrumental for attaining goals. Questions such as the following thus become an integral part of organizational life: How does this action relate to the goal we established? What are the action implications of that goal for me and my group? When we say we want to achieve a certain goal, what do we really mean by that, in measurable terms? Given several alternative forms of action, which one seems most appropriate to achieve the goal we have set?

Diagnosis, action taking, and goal setting are all linked in OD programs. Diagnostic activities precede action programs, that is, fact-finding provides a foundation for action. Actions are continuously evaluated for whether they are attainable and whether they can be translated into action programs. Organization development is a continuous process of setting goals, collecting data about the status quo, planning and taking actions based on hypotheses and on the data, and evaluating the effects of action through additional data collection.

Analyzing Discrepancies

A useful model for thinking about diagnosis and intervention could be termed *discrepancy analysis*—examining the discrepancies or gaps between what is happening and what should be happening, and the discrepancies between where one is and where one wants to be. Discrepancies, therefore, define both problems and goals. Discrepancies require *study* (diagnosis and planning) and action to eliminate the gaps. We believe that a good part of OD is problem solving, hence, discrepancy analysis. Action research describes an iterative problem-solving process that is essentially discrepancy analysis linked to action taking. Any manager's primary task essentially discrepancy analysis—the study of problems and opportunities (goals) or the study of the discrepancies between where one wants to be. Organization development provides technologies for studying and closing gaps.

This simple but powerful analytical model is presented clearly by Charles Kepner and Benjamin Tregoe in *The Rational Manager* and *The New Rational Manager*.[9] Kepner and Tregoe state, "The problem analyzer has an expected standard of performance, a 'should' against which to compare actual performance."[10] According to these authors, a problem is a gap; problem solving is discovering the cause of the gap; decision-making is discovering a solution—a set of actions—to close the gap.

In *The New Science of Management Decision*, Herbert Simon also proposed a discrepancy model of problem[11] is a deviation from an expected standard and a cause of a problem is a *change* of some sort. His model is one of analyzing gaps. Kepner and Tregoe call Simon's book "the best statement of problem-solving theory to be found in the literature on the subject."[12]

Goals also represent gaps—gaps between where we are and where we want to be. Goal setting is the process of *imposing* a gap; goal accomplishment is made possible by taking actions to close the gap.

Organization development is more than just problem solving and goal seeking, but a large part of any OD program is devoted to these two critical activities. Discrepancy analysis is a fruitful way to conceptualize problems and goals.

THE PROGRAM MANAGEMENT COMPONENT

Just as OD practitioners apply behavioral science principles and practices to improve organizational functioning and individual development, then apply these same principles and practices as they manage OD programs. They attend equally to task and process. They consider system ramifications of the program, involve organization members in planning and execution, use an action research model, create feedback loops to ensure relevance and timeliness, and so forth. Managing the OD program effectively means the difference between success and failure. The aim of this section is to provide guidelines to help ensure success in managing OD programs. Specifically, we examine the phases in OD programs, several change management models, and a procedure for creating parallel learning structures.

Phases of OD Programs

OD programs follow a logical progression of events—a series of phases that unfolds over time. An important part of managing an OD program well is to execute each phase well. Warner Burke describes the following phases of OD programs:

1. Entry
2. Contracting
3. Diagnosis
4. Feedback
5. Planning change
6. Intervention
7. Evaluation.[13]

Entry represents the initial contact between consultant and client; exploring the situation that led the client to seek a consultant; and determining whether the problem or opportunity, the client, and the consultant constitute a good match. *Contracting* involves establishing mutual expectations reaching agreement on expenditures of time, money, resources, and energy; and generally clarifying what each party expects to get from the other and give to the other. *Diagnosis* is the fact–finding phase, which produces a picture of the situation through interviews, observations, questionnaires, examination of organization documents and information, and the like. Burke observes that the diagnostic phase has two steps—gathering information, and the like. *Feedback* represents returning the analyzed information to the client system; the clients exploring the information for understanding, clarification, and accuracy; and the clients owning the data, their picture of the situation, and their problems and opportunities. *Planning change* involves the clients deciding what action steps to take based on the information they have just learned. Alternative possibilities are explored and critiqued; plans for action are selected and developed. *Intervention* implements sets of actions designed to correct the problems or seize the opportunities. *Evaluation* represents assessing the effects of the program: Was it successful? What changes occurred? What were the causal mechanisms? Are we satisfied with the results?

These phases are straightforward and logical in description, but in practice they often overlap a great deal and look more like an evolving process than a linear progression. The most important point is that each phase builds the foundation for subsequent phases; therefore, each phase must be executed with care and precision. For example, if expectations are not clear in the contracting phase, this mismatch will surface later in unmet expectations and dissatisfaction. Or, if the analysis of the data during the diagnosis phase is incorrect, interventions may not be appropriate.

A Model for Managing Change

Another way to think about managing OD programs is to ask the question: What are the key ingredients in successful change efforts? Cummings and Worley identify five sets of activities required for effective change management (1) motivating change, (2) creating a vision, (3) developing political support, (4) managing the transition, and (5) sustaining momentum.[14] These activities are shown in Figure 5-3.

The first step is getting people to want to change, to believe change is necessary, and to commit to abandoning the status quo for an uncertain future. Cummings and Worley suggest three methods for *creating readiness to change*: sensitize people about the pressures for change, that is, why change must occur; show discrepancies between the current (undesirable) state of affairs and the future (more desirable) state of affairs and communicate positive, realistic expectations for the advantages of the change. One of the greatest motivators for change is *pain*—things aren't working, profits and market share are dropping, survival is in doubt—these conditions increase readiness for change.

The next set of activities, *overcoming resistance to change*, is achieved through three methods: dealing empathetically with feelings of loss and anxiety, providing extensive communication about the change effort and how it is proceeding, and encouraging participation by organization members in planning and executing the change. As Cummings and Worley write: "one of the oldest and most effective strategies for overcoming resistance is to involve organizational members directly in planning and implementing change."[15]

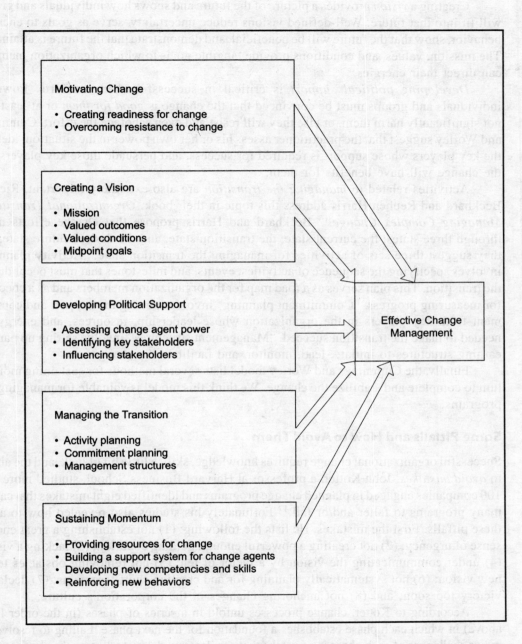

Motivating Change

• Creating readiness for change
• Overcoming resistance to change

Creating a Vision

• Mission
• Valued outcomes
• Valued conditions
• Midpoint goals

Developing Political Support

• Assessing change agent power
• Identifying key stakeholders
• Influencing stakeholders

Effective Change
Management

Managing the Transition

• Activity planning
• Commitment planning
• Management structures

Sustaining Momentum

• Providing resources for change
• Building a support system for change agents
• Developing new competencies and skills
• Reinforcing new behaviors

FIGURE 5-3 Activities Contributing to Effective Change Management

Creating a *vision* provides a picture of the future and shows how individuals and groups will fit into that future. Well-defined visions reduce uncertainty, serve as goals to energize behavior, show that the future will be beneficial, and demonstrate that the future is attainable. The mission, values, and conditions provide tangible goals to which organization members can direct their energies.

Developing political support is critical in successful change efforts. Powerful individuals and groups must be convinced that the change is *good for them* or at least will not significantly harm them, or else they will resist and even sabotage the effort. Cummings and Worley suggest that the practitioner assess his or her own power in the situation, identify the key players whose support is required for success, and persuade those key players that the change will have benefits for them.

Activities related to *managing the transition* are also extremely important. Richard Beckhard and Reuben Harris address this topic in their book. *Organizational Transitions: Managing Complex Change.*[16] Beckhard and Harris propose that change efforts move through three states: the current state, the transition state, and the desired future state, and they suggest three sets of activities for managing the transition state. "Activity planning" involves specifying the sequence of activities, events, and milestones that must occur during the transition. This plan serves as a road map for the organization members and as a checklist for measuring progress. "Commitment planning" involves getting the support and commitment from key players in the organization whose leadership, resources, and energy are needed to make the transition succeed. "Management structures" involve setting up parallel earning structures to initiate, lead, monitor, and facilitate the change.

Finally, the Cummings and Worley model lists several methods for sustaining momentum to complete and stabilize the change. We think this model is valuable for managing OD programs.

Some Pitfalls and How to Avoid Them

Successful organizational change requires knowledge, skill, a little bit of luck, and the ability to *avoid mistakes*. John Kotter, a professor at Harvard Business School, studied more than 100 companies engaged in planned change programs and identified eight mistakes that caused many programs to falter and/or fail.[17] Fortunately his studies also revealed how to avoid these pitfalls. First the mistakes. He lists the following: (1) not establishing a great enough sense of urgency; (2) not creating a powerful enough guiding coalition; (3) lacking a vision; (4) under communicating the vision by a factor of ten; (5) not removing obstacles to the new vision; (6) not systematically planning for and creating short-term wins; (7) declaring victory too soon; and (8) not anchoring changes in the corporation's culture.

According to Kotter, change processes unfold in a series of phases (in the order listed above) in which each phase establishes a foundation for the next phase. Failing to resolve the major challenges of each phase is a mistake that can damage, delay, or destroy the change effort. To ensure successful change, Kotter advises implementing the eight steps shown in Table 5-3. These eight steps tell the change agent what to do in each phase and how to do it.

Anyone who has attempted to implement organizational change recognizes the truth in Kotter's observations. His advice for avoiding the pitfalls is sound.

TABLE 5-3 Eight Steps for Successful Organizational Transformation

Eight Steps to Transforming Your Organization

1. Establishing a sense of urgency
    *   Examining market and competitive realities
    *   Identifying and discussing crises, potential crises, or major opportunities
2. Forming a powerful guiding coalition
    *   Assembling a group with enough power to lead the change effort
    *   Encouraging the group to work together as a team
3. Creating a vision
    *   Creating a vision to help direct the change effort
    *   Developing strategies for achieving that vision
4. Communicating the vision
    *   Using every vehicle possible to communicate the new vision and strategies
    *   Teaching new behaviors by the example of the guiding coalition
5. Empowering others to act on the vision
    *   Getting rid of obstacles to change
    *   Changing systems or structures that seriously undermine the vision
    *   Encouraging risk taking and nontraditional ideas, activities, and actions
6. Planning for and creating short-term wins
    *   Planning for visible performance improvements
    *   Creating those improvements
    *   Recognizing and rewarding employees involved in the improvements
7. Consolidating improvements and producing still more change
    *   Using increased credibility to change systems, structures, and policies that don't fit the vision
    *   Hiring, promoting, and developing employees who can implement the vision
    *   Reinvigorating the process with new projects, themes, and change agents.
8. Institutionalizing new approaches
    *   Articulating the connections between the new behaviors and corporate success
    *   Developing the means to ensure leadership development and succession.

Reprinted by permission of Harvard Business Review. [An Exhibit] From "Leading Change: Why Transformation Efforts Fail," by John P. Kotter, March–April 1995, p. 61. Copyright © 1995 by the President and Fellows of Harvard College; all rights reserved.

Creating Parallel Learning Structures

Earlier we discussed the role of parallel learning structures as devices for introducing and managing change in large bureaucratic organizations. Change programs in large-scale systems almost always use parallel structures. Bushe and Shani developed what they call the *generic parallel learning structure intervention process*, shown in Table 5-4.[18]

Phases 1 and 2 focus on establishing the need for change, building readiness and commitment, and creating an infrastructure that has sufficient political support and executive leadership to sustain the change program. The steering committee includes members from a cross section of the organization and is headed by one or more top executives. Phase 3 communicates openly what is happening and why. Phase 4 solicits widespread involvement from organization members; this participation increases ownership of the change and

TABLE 5-4	The Generic Parallel Learning Structure Intervention Process
Phase 1:	Initial Definition of Purpose and Scope
Phase 2:	Formation of a Steering Committee
	• Reexamining the need for change
	• Creating a vision statement
	• Defining boundaries, strategies, expectations, and rewards
Phase 3:	Communicating to Organization Members
Phase 4:	Formation and Development of Study Groups
	• Selecting and developing internal facilitators
	• Selecting study group members
	• Study group development
	• Establishing working procedures and norms
Phase 5:	The Inquiry Process
Phase 6:	Identifying Potential Changes
Phase 7:	Experimental Implementation of Proposed Changes
Phase 8:	Systemwide Diffusion and Evaluation

Source: Gervase R. Bushe and A. B. Shani, *Parallel Learning Structures* (Table 7.1), p. 125. Copyright © 1991 by Addison-Wesley Publishing Company, Inc. Reprinted by permission of the publisher.

increases the number of good ideas available. Phases 5,6, and 7 represent extensive study, data collection, targeting high-priority problems, and experimenting to find solutions to problems. Solutions (changes) that work are then diffused throughout the organization. This model is presented here to show the flow of events and the things to consider when managing large-scale OD programs.

Summary of Program Management Issues

These ideas about managing OD programs describe some of the important factors OD practitioners take into account as they implement change efforts. Program management is complex, dynamic, difficult, and great fun. The challenges are many, but the sense of accomplishment is great for practitioners, leaders, and organizational members alike as successes build upon successes and the organization realizes its goals.

CONCLUDING COMMENTS

Three components—diagnosis, intervention, and program management—critical to all organization development programs have been explored in this chapter. Each is important in its own right; all are vital to success. The more people learn about these three components, the more effective they will become in their organizational improvement efforts. Organization development is a complex blend of art, science, and craft gained through the study and mastery of these three components.

NOTES

1. Richard Beckhard, *Organization Development: Strategies and Models* (Reading, MA: Addison-Wesley Publishing Company, 1969), p. 26.

2. This "actual condition" versus "ideal condition" discrepancy model is an integral feature of Kurt Lewin's force-field analysis, and appears, in fact, to be basic to all human goal-seeking and problem-solving activities. See K. Lewin, *Field Theory in Social Science* (New York: Harper & Row, 1951). See also George A. Miller, Eugene Galanter, and Karl H. Pribram, *Plans and the Structure of Behavior* (New York: Holt, Rinehart and Winston, 1960).

3. Chris Argyris, *Intervention Theory and Method: A Behavioral Science View* (Reading, MA: Addison-Wesley Publishing Company, 1970).

4. Ibid., pp. 16–17.

5. Marvin R. Weisbord, "Organizational Diagnosis: Six Places to Look for Trouble With or Without a Theory," *Group & Organization Studies* (December 1976), pp. 430–447.

6. Marvin R. Weisbord, "Toward Third-Wave Managing and Consulting," *Organizational Dynamics* (1987), pp. 5–24. See also Alvin Toffler, *The Third Wave* (New York: Bantam Books, 1980).

7. Marvin R. Weisbord, *Productive Workplaces* (San Francisco: Jossey-Bass Publishers, 1987).

8. Actually, in a real strategic planning session, steps 1 and 2 might take place during the first session, with that session concluding with homework assignments to the team in order to generate the necessary information for the strategic plan. Then, in a second session, step 3 would be finalized.

9. Charles H. Kepner and Benjamin B. Tregoe, *The Rational Manager* (New York: McGraw-Hill, 1965). A revised edition appeared in 1981 titled *The New Rational Manager*. These books are highly recommended for OD practitioners.

10. Kepner and Tregoe, *The Rational Manager*, p. 44.

11. Herbert A. Simon, *The New Science of Management Decision* (New York: Harper & Row, 1960).

12. Kepner and Tregoe, *The Rational Manager*, p. 252.

13. W. W. Burke, *Organization Development: A Process of Learning and Changing* (Reading, MA: Addison-Wesley Publishing Company, 1994), see chapter 4.

14. T. G. Cummings and C. G. Worley, *Organization Development and Change* (St. Paul, MN: West Publishing Company, 1993), see chapter 8.

15. Ibid., p. 148.

16. `R. Beckhard and R. T. Harris, *Organizational Transitions: Managing Complex Change*, 2d ed. (Reading, MA: Addison-Wesley Publishing Company, 1987).

17. John P. Kotter, "Leading Change: Why Transformation Efforts Fail," *Harvard Business Review* (March–April 1995), pp. 59–67.

18. G. R. Bushe and A. B. Shani, *Parallel Learning Structures* (Reading, MA: Addison-Wesley Publishing Company, 1991), see chapter 7.

CHAPTER 6

Action Research and Organizational Development

A ction research attempts to meet the dual goals of making action more effective and building a body of scientific knowledge around that action. Action in this context refers to programs and interventions designed to solve problems and improve conditions. Kurt Lewin, as a consummate applied social scientist and motivated by an interest in eradicating the problems of society, proposed action research as a new methodology for behavioral science. Lewin believed that *research on action programs*, especially social change programs, was imperative if progress were to be made in solving social problems. Action research, he thought, would address several needs simultaneously; the pressing need for greater knowledge about the causes and dynamics of social ills; the need to understand the laws of social change; the need for greater collaboration and joint inquiry between scientists and practitioners; the need for "richer" data about real-world problems; the need to discover workable, practical solutions to problems; and the need to discover general laws explaining complex social phenomena.[1]

Action research is a cornerstone of organization development, underlying both the theory and practice of the field. In this chapter, we first examine action research from two perspectives, as a process and as a problem-solving approach. We also give some examples of action research in OD.

ACTION RESEARCH: A PROCESS AND AN APPROACH

Action research may be described as a *process*, that is, as an ongoing series of events and actions. It may be defined as follows:

> Action research is the process of systematically collecting research data about an ongoing system relative to some objective, goal, or need of that system; feeding these data back into the system; taking actions by altering selected variables within the system based both on the data and on hypotheses; and evaluating the results of actions by collecting more data.

This definition characterizes action research in terms of the activities comprising the process. First, the researcher takes a static picture of an organization. On the basis of "what exists," hunches and hypotheses suggest actions; these actions typically entail manipulating variables in the system that are under the action researcher's control, which often means doing something differently from the way it has always been done.

French shows how action research can be used as a generic process in organization development (see Figure 6-1). This process is iterative and cyclical.[2] He clarifies the model as follows:

> The key aspects of the model are diagnosis, data gathering, feedback to the client group, data discussion and work by the client group, action planning, and action. The sequence tends to be cyclical, with the focus on new or advanced problems as the client group learns to work more effectively together.[3]

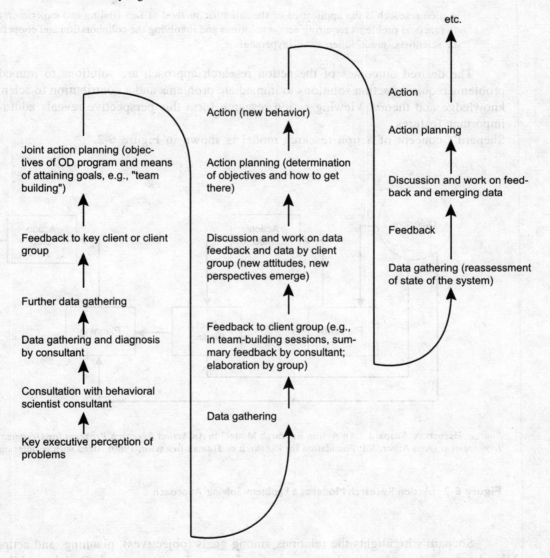

etc.

Action

Action planning

Discussion and work on feedback and emerging data

Feedback

Data gathering (reassessment of state of the system)

Action (new behavior)

Action planning (determination of objectives and how to get there)

Discussion and work on data feedback and data by client group (new attitudes, new perspectives emerge)

Feedback to client group (e.g., in team-building sessions, summary feedback by consultant; elaboration by group)

Data gathering

Joint action planning (objectives of OD program and means of attaining goals, e.g., "team building")

Feedback to key client or client group

Further data gathering

Data gathering and diagnosis by consultant

Consultation with behavioral scientist consultant

Key executive perception of problems

Figure 6-1   An Action Research Model for Organization Development

Action research is a process in two different ways. It is a sequence of events and activities *within each iteration* (data collection, feedback, and taking action based on the data); and it is a cycle of *iterations* of these activities, sometimes treating the same problem several times and then moving to different problems.

Action research may also be described as *an approach to problem solving*, thus suggesting its usefulness as a model, guide, or paradigm. Used in this way, action research may be defined as follows:

> Action research is the application of the scientific method of fact-finding and experimentation to practical problems requiring action solutions and involving the collaboration and cooperation of scientists, practitioners, and laypersons.

The desired outcomes of the action research approach are solutions to immediate problems requiring action solutions to immediate problems and a contribution to scientific knowledge and theory. Viewing action research form this perspective reveals additional important features.

Shepard's concept of action research model is shown in Figure 6-2.

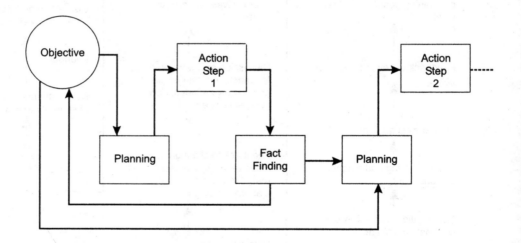

Source: Herbert A. Shepard, "An Action Research Model" in *An Action Research Program for Organization Improvement* (Ann Arbor, MI: Foundation for Research on Human Behavior, 1960). Used with permission.

Figure 6-2 Action Research Model as a Problem-Solving Approach

Shepard's highlights the relations among goals (objectives), planning, and action in his diagram—a point we think is an important feature of action research. Both he and French emphasize the action research is research inextricably linked to action; it is research with a purpose, that is, to guide present and future action.

In an action research approach, the role of the consultant/change agent takes on a special form, as shown by Shepard:

The role is to help the manager plan his actions and design his fact-finding procedures in such a way that he can learn from them, to serve such ends as becoming a more skillful manager, setting more realistic objectives, discovering better ways of organizing. In this sense, the staffs concerned with follow-up research consultants. Their task is to help managers formulate management problems as experiments.[4]

In viewing action research as an approach to problem solving we note the following features: the normative nature of this model, the centrality of the objectives, and the different role requirements of the consultant/change agent vis-a-vis the clients. Three additional features deserve discussion: first, the elements of the action research model that link it to the scientific method of inquiry; second, the collaborative relation among scientists, practitioners, and laypersons that often is a component of action research; and third, the increased richness of knowledge derived from action research programs.

An example applying action research to a typical organizational problem might be helpful. Suppose that the problem is unproductive staff meetings—they are poorly attended, members express low commitment and involvement in them, and they are generally agreed to be unproductive. Suppose also that you are the manager in charge of both the meetings and the staff and that you desire to make the meetings more vital and productive. Following the action research model, the first step is to gather data about the status quo. Assume the data have been gathered and that the data suggest the meetings are generally disliked and regarded as unproductive. The next step is to search for causes of the problem and to generate one or more hypotheses from which you produce the consequences that will allow you to test the hypotheses. Say you come up with the following four hypotheses. Note that an action research hypothesis consists of two aspects: a goal and an action or procedure for achieving that goal.

1. Staff meetings will be more productive if I solicit and use agenda topics from the staff rather than have the agenda made up just by me.
2. Staff meetings will be more productive if I rotate the chair of the meeting among the staff rather than my always being chairperson.
3. Staff meetings will be more productive if we hold them once a week instead of twice a week.
4. I have always run the staff meetings in a brisk "all-business no-nonsense" fashion; perhaps if I encourage more discussion and am more open about how I am reacting to what is being said, then staff meetings will be more productive.

Each of these action research hypotheses has a goal, (better staff meeting productivity), and each has an action or procedure, for achieving the goal. Additional work would be done to clarify and specify the goal and the actions, and then the hypotheses would be systematically tested (implemented) one at a time and, through data collection, evaluated for their effects.

Another distinguishing feature of action research is collaboration between individuals inside the system—clients and individuals outside the system—change agents or researchers. Almost all authors stress the collaborative nature of action research, states with some seeing it as the primary reason for the model's efficacy.[5] A widely used belief states that people support what they have helped to create. Such a belief, highly congruent with the collaborative aspect of action research, impels practitioners and researchers to cooperate extensively with client system members. This point of view implies that the client system members and the researcher should jointly define the methods used for data collection, identify the hypotheses relevant to the situations, and evaluate the consequences of actions. This collaborative ingredient is found in both action research and organization development.

As scientists and laypersons work together to understand and change a problematic condition, their joint inquiry typically yields rich data and insights about the phenomenon. The problem is real, not hypothetical; the actors know more about the situation than the outsiders do; and the actors have a vested interest in getting the facts since they will benefit from the solution. As Shani and Bushe observe: "It is the development of high-quality relations between action researchers and organizational members that creates access to important information that otherwise might not be available to outsiders."[6] As Deutsch observes, this characteristic of action research appealed to Kurt Lewin:

> In addition to the value that action research might have for social agencies, Lewin felt that linking research to social action might give the social scientist access to basic social processes, which he would otherwise be unable to study. Furthermore, Lewin's orientation to dynamics in individual and group psychology led him to the conclusion that change studies are necessary to reveal underlying processes. Since the social scientist is rarely in the position to create social change on is own initiative, he has much to gain through co-operation with social agencies that attempt to produce social and community change.[7]

The richness of the data available in action research adds to the value of action research as a problem-solving approach.

EXAMPLES OF ACTION RESEARCH IN ORGANIZATION DEVELOPMENT

The natures of organizational development and of action research are quite similar. They are both variants of applied behavioral science; they are both action oriented; they are both data based; they both call for close collaboration between insider and outsider; and they are both problem-solving social interventions. Because of these characteristics, we believe a sound organization development program rests on an action research model.

Several examples show how action research can be used in organization development. Gavin conducted a comprehensive survey feedback program in a mining company of approximately 400 employees in the southwestern United States.[8] In several respects the OD program was a success—it was well received by the hourly employees and many key managers; it solved many immediate problems; and it led to numerous long-term organizational changes that increased the effectiveness of the mine. And in several respects it was a failure—some managers grew to distrust the consultants, which led to increasingly ьtrained relations between higher management and the consultant team, which led to the premature termination of the program. But Gavin and his doctoral students had conceptualized the project from the beginning as an action research project, not just an OD effort using survey feedback methodology. Therefore, they simultaneously studied the effects of the OD program, their own intervention's processes and dynamics and the changing client-consultant relations over time. The result was a rich case study yielding vital information about both research and practice.

Another example of action research is provided by Santalainen and Hunt, who used a massive OD program in a Finnish banking group to gain knowledge about how the program was used differently by high - and low-performing banks.[9] A comprehensive, multidimensional OD program was implemented in the 80 largest banks of the 270-bank system. The program was called *results management* (Re Ma) and focused on teaching banks' top teams better strategic planning and operational planning methods, better ways to define desired results, consensus decision making, and better ways to meet the needs and values of employees. Although all banks received the same training, they had wider latitude in implementing the program. What makes this action research interesting is that Santalainen and Hunt researched the results of the OD program itself and at the same time gained knowledge on organizational dynamics in general, specifically, high and low performance.

The 18 highest-performing and 18 lowest-performing banks out of the total of 80 were examined to see how they had used the learning from the OD program. A the end of three years the high-performing banks had made more strategic changes and fewer operational changes; the low-performing banks had made more operational changes and fewer strategic changes. At the end of six years, the high-performing banks had made more "deep-seated" (fundamental and significant) changes than the low-performing banks. This action research had high payoff-knowledge about the results of the OD intervention, and knowledge about the ingredients of high and low performance. This particular program was an excellent blend of action and research.

Action research is also found in sociotechnical systems programs. Most sociotechnical systems theory change projects are conceptualized as action research—research precedes action, and research follows action as OD practitioners and organizational members collaborate to discover what should be done and how. The same is true for open systems planning efforts and parallel learning structure interventions.

INDIAN CASE STUDY

In the Indian scenario, the action research model has been used since long to carry out research in the existing system and then develop interventions to improve the efficacy of the systems in the organisation. One such example is the ECC Construction Group of Larsen and Toubro. This group is one of the largest construction organisations in India rendering comprehensive engineering services in civil, mechanical and electrical fields within the country and abroad. The company was incorporated in 1944 in the name of Engineering Construction Corporation Limited, a wholly owned subsidiary of Larsen and Toubro Limited. From a modest beginning, the company had a gradual and consistent growth. The company started rendering comprehensive services in civil, mechanical and electrical fields after being merged with the Project Execution Department of L & T. The seventies offered opportunities overseas also and ECC now has its share of businesses in Abu Dhabi, Iraq, and Sri Lanka, to mention a few examples. In 1982, a decision was taken for business reasons to merge ECC with L & T and government clearance was finally obtained in March 1984 and the company was renamed as Larsen and Toubro Limited, ECC Group. Its headquarters are located in Madras. It has regional offices in Bombay, Delhi, Chennai, and Kolkata and the overseas Group located in Bombay.

GENESIS OF OD IN THE COMPANY

In the midst of phenomenal growth in business, the company faced a stiff competitive environment in Indian and international markets. Under these circumstances, the need was felt to enhance the organisational effectiveness and to gear up the organisation in its totality to meet new challenges. When an organisation grows, any informality present is replaced by a stricter code and so the culture of the organisation also undergoes a change.

In this new situation, a need to revamp the organisation structure and reporting-relationship was felt by the top management during 1979. An external consultant was engaged to study the organisation structure and make appropriate recommendations related to changes in the organisation structure and design needs to be made after considering all relevant issues regarding scale of activity, dispersal in terms of location, resources available, etc.

The consultant carried out an in-depth study discussing with a cross section of staff on an individual basis with the purpose of gaining an understanding of the relative roles, responsibilities, their interactions with other key personnel. Committees were formed and a preliminary report was prepared indicating widespread changes in the organisation. It was also suggested that OD interventions could be considered for the following reasons:

1. To aid the process of change in culture—from the culture of a well knit compact group to the culture of a large group aspiring for greater heights.
2. While striving for greater results, to develop and maintain organizational health.
3. To sharpen role effectiveness and possibly build teams at some strategic points, although a good team spirit is discernible throughout the organisation.

THE OD PROCESS: A DIAGNOSTIC STUDY

This process of OD intervention in the organisation got triggered off in early 1983 by an organisational diagnostic study to understand the organisational efficiency, efficacy and motivational levels. An external OD consultant was engaged for a diagnostic study and he had the following important functions to carry along with him in his task:

a. Implanting function—To supplement and implant internal expertise.
b. Alternative generating function—To generate several alternatives out of which the organisation can select one or more.
c. Process facilitating function—To act as a process consultant and to perceive various realities and develop roles as the OD programme proceeds.
d. Resource building function—To provide help in generating internal resources by building the necessary expertise as he works with the organisation.
e. Self liquidating function—To generally withdraw from the organisation after building the internal expertise and resources, thus liquidating his role and indispensability.

The OD Consultant went into an in-depth study of the organisation by conducting a series of discussions with and administering questionnaires to a cross-section of the employees of the Company. The results were presented to the senior executives identified for active participation in OD group meetings. This phase was followed by various exercises in identifying crucial issues by the members of the OD group.

CONCLUDING COMMENTS

Two philosophical and pragmatic values underlie action research. The first is that programs designed to solve real problems should be based on valid public data generated collaboratively by clients and consultants. This belief calls for actions to be based on diagnostic research—an action-should-follow-research mode of thinking. Or, to state it another way, diagnose the problem situation and base actions on that diagnosis. The second value is that action in the real world should be accompanied by research on that action in order to build a cumulative body of knowledge and theory of the effects of various actions directed to solving real-world problems—*a research-should-follow-action* mode of thinking. Only if we systematically evaluate (do research on) actions can we know the real effects of these actions. And only if we systematically build a body of knowledge can we build better social science theories.

Thus actions to solve real-world problems offer a unique opportunity for both the scientist-researcher and the administrator-layperson if they approach the problem from the standpoint of the action research model: the administrator's problems will be solved, and the scientists quest for theory and empirical validation of theory will be furthered. The applied behavioral science discipline of organization development is fertile ground for action research projects.

NOTES

1. Kurt Lewin, "Frontiers in Group Dynamics," *Human Relations*, 1, no. 2 (1947), pp. 143–153.
2. Wendell French, "Organization Development Objectives, Assumptions, and Strategies," *California Management Review*, 12 (Winter 1969), pp. 23–34.
3. Ibid., p. 26.
4. Herbert A. Shepard, "An Action Research Model," in *An Action Research Program for Organization Improvement* (Ann Arbor: The Foundation for Research on Human Behavior, University of Michigan, 1960), pp. 33–34.
5. In this regard, the work of Collier (cited later in this chapter), Corey, and Lippitt (cited later) indicates a heavy emphasis on the importance of collaboration between all the individuals affected by a change project of this nature. In an article on action research and OD, client-consultant collaboration is cited as one of the basic processes of the action research model. Mark A. Frohman, Marshall Sashkin, and Michael J. Kavanagh, "Action-Research as Applied to Organization Development," *Organization and Administrative Sciences*, 7, nos. 1 and 2 (Spring–Summer 1976), pp. 129–161.
6. Abraham B. Shani and Gervase R. Bushe, "Visionary Action Research: A Consultation Process Perspective," *Consultation*, 6, no. 1 (Spring 1987) p. 8.
7. Deutsch, "Field Theory in Social Psychology," in *The Handbook of Social Psychology*, Gardner Lindzey and Elliott Aronson, eds., vol. 1, pp. 465–466.
8. James F. Gavin, "Survey Feedback: The Perspectives of Science and Practice," *Group and Organization Studies*, 9, no. 1 (March 1984), pp. 29–70.

9. Timo J. Santalainen and J. G. Hunt, "Change Differences from an Action Research, Results-Oriented OD Program in High- and Low-Performing Finnish Banks," *Group & Organization Studies*, 13, no. 4 (December 1988), pp. 413–440.

10. See Frohman, Sashkin, and Kavanagh, "Action-Research as Applied to Organization Development," pp. 129–161. Also Michael Peters and Viviane Robinson, "The Origins and Status of Action Research," *The Journal of Applied Behavioral Science*, 20, no. 2 (1984), pp. 113–124.

CHAPTER 7

An Overview of OD Interventions

OD Interventions are sets of structured activities in which selected organizational units (target groups or individuals) engage in a task or a sequence of tasks with the goals of organizational improvement and individual development. Interventions constitute the action thrust of organization development. The OD practitioner, a professional versed in the theory and practice of OD, brings four sets of attributes to the organizational setting: a set of values; a set of assumptions about people, organizations and inter-personal relationships; a set of goals for the practitioner and the organization and its members; and a set of structured activities that are the means for achieving the values, assumptions, and goals. These activities are what we mean by the word interventions.

Work gets done in organization development when organization leaders and members systematically address problems and opportunities; usually guided by an OD practitioner. Practitioners have created an array of interventions to help organization members address specific problems effectively. Interventions such as team building, survey feedback, role analysis, and intergroup conflict resolution were developed during the early years of organization development. Interventions such as quality of work life (QWL), work redesign using sociotechnical systems theory (STS), collateral organization (also known as parallel learning structures), and strategic planning methods were developed as the field continued to evolve. Today we have interventions aimed at developing self-directed teams, high-performance work systems, and self-designing organizations, as well as large-scale systems change models to help organizations adapt and survive. OD interventions address a wide range of specific problems and opportunities. But OD is much more than just reaching into the "kit bag" and executing an intervention. OD is a complete strategy for change that encompasses theory, practice methods, and values. Interventions are just one component of the OD formula.

Practice methods refer to *how* practitioners ply their craft to cause organizational change. Principles, rules of thumb, and practical knowledge have accumulated so that a practice theory exists to tell practitioners what to do and how to do it to effect change in human systems. For example, people often resist change and lapse back into old habits after a change. Practice theory tells how to deal with these situations. The secrets to success in OD programs lie in the practice theory. Advances lie in behavioral science theory, practice theory, and the range and scope of interventions have significantly increased the power of OD as a strategy for change.

In this and the next several chapters we discuss OD interventions and describe the most important ones. Knowing the OD interventions and the rationale for their use shows you how change takes place in OD programs because interventions are the vehicles for causing change. In this overview chapter we classify what interventions are, examine some rules of thumb for implementing interventions, and then explore different ways to classify interventions.

CLASSIFYING OD INTERVENTIONS

The inventory of OD interventions is quite extensive. We will explore several classification schemes here to help you understand how interventions "clump" together in terms of (1) the objectives of the interventions and (2) the targets of the interventions. Becoming familiar with how interventions relate to one another is useful for planning the overall OD strategy.

As we see it, the following are the major "families" of OD interventions.

1. *Diagnostic Activities.* Fact-finding activities designed to ascertain the state of the system, the status of a problem, the "way things are." Available methods range from projective devices such as "build a collage that represents your place in this organization" to the more traditional data collection methods of interviews, questionnaires, surveys, meetings, and examining organizational records.

2. *Team-Building Activities.* Activities designed to enhance the effective operation of system teams. These activities focus on task issues such as the way things are done, the skills and resources needed to accomplish tasks, the quality of relationship among the team members or between members and the leader, and how well the team gets its job done. In addition, one must consider different kinds of teams, such as formal work teams, temporary tasks force teams, newly constituted teams, and cross-functional teams.

3. *Intergroup Activities.* Activities designed to improve the effectiveness of interdependent groups—groups that must work together to produce a common output. They focus on joint activities and the output of the group as considered as a single system rather than as two subsystems. When two groups are involved, the activities are designated intergroup or interface activities; when more than two groups are involved, the activities are called organizational mirroring.

4. *Survey Feedback Activities.* Activities that rely on questionnaire surveys to generate information that is then used to identify problems and opportunities. Groups analyze the data regarding their performance and design action plans to correct problems.

5. *Education and Training Activities.* Activities designed to improve individuals' skills, abilities, and knowledge. Several activities are available and several approaches possible. For example, the individual can be educated in isolation from his or her own work group (say, in a T-group consisting of strangers), or one can be educated in relation to the work group (say, when a work team learns how better to manage interpersonal conflict). The activities may be directed toward technical skills required for performing tasks or may be directed toward improving interpersonal competence. The activities may be directed toward leadership issues, responsibilities and functions of group members, decision-making, problem solving, goal setting and planning, and so forth.

6. *Technostructural or Structural Activities*. Activities designed to improve the effectiveness of organizational structures and job designs. The activities may take the form of (a) experimenting with new organization structures and evaluating their effectiveness in terms of specific goals or (b) devising new ways to bring technical resources to bear on problems. In chapter 11 we discuss these activities and label them "structural interventions" defined as "the broad class of interventions or change efforts aimed at improving organization effectiveness through changes in the task, structural, and technological subsystems." Included in these activities are job enrichment, management by objectives, sociotechnical systems, collateral organizations, and physical settings interventions.

7. *Process Consultation Activities*. Activities that "help the client to perceive, understand, and act upon process events which occur in the client's environment."[1] These activities perhaps more accurately describe an approach, a consulting mode in which the client gains insight into the human processes in organizations and learn skills in diagnosing and managing them. Primary emphasis is on processes such as communications, leader and member roles in groups, problem solving and decision making, group norms and group growth, leadership and authority, and intergroup cooperation and competition.

8. *Grid Organization Development Activities*. Activities developed by Robert Blake and Jane Mouton, which constitute a six-phase change model involving the total organization. Internal resources are developed to conduct most of the programs, which may take from three to five years to complete. The model starts with upgrading individual managers' skills and leadership abilities, moves to team improvement activities, then to intergroup relations activities. Later phases include corporate planning for improvement, developing implementation tactics, and finally, an evaluation phase assessing change in the organization culture and looking toward future directions.

9. *Third-Party Peacemaking Activities*. Activities conducted by a skilled consultant (the third party, designed to "help two members of an organization manage their interpersonal conflict. These activities are based on confrontation tactics and an understanding of the processes involved in conflict and conflict resolution.

10. *Coaching and Counseling Activities*. Activities that entail the consultant or other organization members working with individuals to help (a) define learning goals, (b) learn how others see their behavior, and (c) learn new behaviors to help them better achieve their goals. A central feature of this activity is nonevaluative feedback others give to an individual. A second feature is the second exploration of alternative behaviors.

11. *Life- and Career-Planning Activities*. Activities that enable individuals to focus on their life and career objectives and how to go about achieving them. Structured activities include producing life and career inventories, discussing goals and objectives, and assessing capabilities, needed additional training, and areas of strength and deficiency.

12. *Planning and Goal-Setting Activities*. Activities that include theory and experience in planning and goal setting, problem-solving models, planning paradigms, ideal organization versus real organization "discrepancy" models, and the like. The goal is to improve these skills at the levels of the individual, group, and total organization.

13. *Strategic Management Activities*. Activities that help key policy makers to reflect systematically on the organization's basic mission and goals and environmental demands, threats, and opportunities, and to engage in long-range action planning of both a reactive and proactive nature. These activities direct attention in two important

Target Group	Interventions Designed to Improve Effectiveness
Individuals	Life- and career-planning activities Coaching and counseling T-group (sensitivity training) Education and training to increase skills, knowledge in the areas of technical task needs, relationship skills, process skills, decision making, problem solving, planning, goal-setting skills Grid OD phase 1 Work redesign Gestalt OD Behavior modeling
Dyads/Triads	Process consultation Third-party peacemaking Role negotiation technique Gestalt OD
Teams and Groups	Team building — Task directed — Process directed Gestalt OD Grid OD phase 2 Interdependency exercise Appreciative inquiry Responsibility charting Process consultation Role negotiation Role analysis technique "Startup" team-building activities Education in decision making, problem solving, planning, goal setting in group settings Team MBO Appreciations and concerns exercise Sociotechnical systems (STS) Visioning Quality of work life (QWL) programs Quality circles Force-field analysis Self-managed teams
Intergroup Relations	Intergroup activities — Process directed — Task directed Organizational mirroring Partnering Process consultation Third-party peacemaking at group level Grid OD phase 3 Survey feedback
Total Organization	Sociotechnical systems (STS) Parallel learning structures MBO (participation forms) Cultural analysis Confrontation meetings Visioning Strategic planning/strategic management activities Real-time strategic change Grid OD phases 4, 5, 6 Interdependency exercise Survey feedback Appreciative inquiry Search conferences Quality of work life (QWL) programs Total quality management (TQM) Physical settings Large-scale systems change

FIGURE 7-1 Typology of OD Interventions Based on Target Groups

directions: outside the organization to a consideration of the environment, and away from the present to the future.

14. *Organizational Transformation Activities.* Activities that involve large-scale system changes; activities designed to fundamentally change the nature of the organization. Almost everything about the organization is changed—structure, management philosophy, reward systems, the design of work, mission, values, and cultures. Total quality programs are transformational: so are programs to create high-performance organizations or high-performance work systems. Sociotechnical systems theory and open systems planning provide the basis for such activities.

Each of these families of interventions includes many activities. They involve both conceptual material and actual experience with the phenomenon being studied. Some families are directed toward specific targets, problems, or processes. For example, team-building activities are specific to work teams, while life-planning activities are directed to individuals, although these latter activities take place in-group settings. Some interventions are *problem* specific: examples are the third-party peacemaking activities and the goal-setting activities. Some activities are *process* specific: an example is intergroup activities that explore the processes involved in managing interfaces.

Another way to classify OD interventions is by the primary target of the intervention, for example, individuals, dyads and triads, teams and groups, intergroup relations, and the total organization. Figure 7-1 shows this classification scheme. Some interventions have multiple targets and multiple uses, and thus appear in several places in the figure.

These classification schemes are intended to help you understand the range and uses of OD interventions.

THINKING ABOUT OD INTERVENTIONS

First, behind every program is an overall game plan or *intervention strategy*. This plan integrates the problem or opportunity to be addressed, the desired outcomes of the programs, and the sequencing and timing of the various interventions. Intervention strategies are based on diagnosis and the goals desired by the client system. Let's say the clients want to redesign the way work is done at a production facility, changing from an assembly-line arrangement of individualized simple tasks to complex tasks performed by self-managed teams. This desired redesign requires diagnosis to determine whether the work is amenable to such a system, to test the employees' willingness to undertake such a change, to calculate the time and effort required to make the change, and to assess the probable benefits. Sociotechnical systems theory would likely be the guiding model for the program, which would entail dozens of significant changes and different interventions—training, education, parallel structures, employee involvement, modified reward systems and management philosophy, and so forth. A series of activities designed to move the system in step-wise fashion from the current state to a new state would be laid out against a time line of several years. This overall strategy would be the road map for the change program. The key questions are: What are we trying to accomplish? What activities/interventions will help us get there? What is the proper timing and sequencing of the interventions? What have we learned from the diagnosis about readiness to change, barriers and obstacles, key stakeholders, and sources of energy and leadership?

Second, some ways to structure activities to promote learning and change are "better"; and some are "worse." The following points help practitioners structure activities in "better" ways:

1. Structure the activity to include the relevant people, the people affected by the problem or the opportunity. For example, if the goal is improved team effectiveness, have the whole team engage in the activities. If the goal is improved relations between two separate work groups, have both work groups present. If the goal is to build linkages with some special group, say, the industrial relations people, have them there along with the people from the home group. If the goal is better customer service, include customers in the activity. Preplanning the group composition is necessary for properly structuring the activity.

2. Structure the activity so that it is (a) problem oriented or opportunity oriented, and (b) oriented to the problems and opportunities generated by the clients themselves. Solving problems and capitalizing on opportunities are involving, interesting, and enjoyable tasks for most people, whether due to a desire for competence or mastery (as suggested by White[2]), or a desire to achieve (as suggested by McClelland[3]), especially when the issues have been defined by the client. When clients are solving issues that they have stated have highest priority, the activity has built-in support and a high payoff.

3. Structure the activity so that the goal is clear and the way to reach the goal is clear. Few things are as demotivating as not knowing what one is working toward and not knowing how what one is doing contributes to goal attainment. Both these points are part of structuring the activity properly. (Parenthetically, the goals will be important for the individuals if point 2 is followed.)

4. Structure the activity to ensure a high probability of success. Implicit in this point is the warning that the practitioners' and clients' expectations should be realistic. But more than that, manageable attainable objectives once achieved produce feelings of success, competence, and potency for the people involved. This sense of achievement, in turn, raises aspiration levels and feelings of self- and group-worth. The task can still be hard, complicated, taxing—but it should be attainable. And if participants fail to accomplish the goal, the reasons should be examined so this can be avoided in the future.

5. Structure the activity so that it contains both experience-based learning and conceptual learning. New learnings gained through experience become a permanent part of the individual's repertoire when augmented with conceptual material that puts the experience into a broader framework of theory and behavior. Relating the experience to conceptual models and other experiences helps the learning become integrated for the individual.

6. Structure the climate of the activity so that individuals are "freed up" rather than anxious or defensive. That is, set the climate of interventions so that people expect "to learn together" and "to look at practices in an experimenting way so that we can build better procedures."

7. Structure the activity so that the participants learn both how to solve a particular problem and "learn how to learn." Such structure often means scheduling time for reflecting on the activity and teasing out learnings; it may mean devoting as much as half the activity to one focus and half to the other.

8. Structure the activity so that individuals learn about both task and process. The task is what the group is working on, that is, the stated agenda items. The term process refers to how the group's processes and dynamics, individual styles of interacting and behaving, and so on. Learning to be skilful in both of these areas is a powerful asset.

9. Structure the activity so that individuals are engaged as whole persons, not segmented persons. It means calling into play role demands, thoughts, beliefs, feelings, and strivings. Integrating disparate parts of individuals in an organizational world that commonly divides roles, feelings, and thoughts enhances the individual's ability to learn and grow.

These points developed form practice theory, and implementing them causes interventions to be more effective.

A third set of considerations concerns choosing and sequencing intervention activities. Michael Beer suggests the following guidelines:

> These decision rules can help a change agent focus on the relevant issues in making decisions about how to integrate a variety of interventions. They are rules for managing the implementation process.

1. *Maximize diagnostic data.* In general, interventions that will provide data needed to make subsequent intervention decisions should come first. This is particularly true when change agents do not know much about the situation. Violation of this rule can lead to choosing inappropriate interventions.

2. *Maximize effectiveness.* Interventions should be sequenced so that early interventions enhance the effectiveness of subsequent interventions. For example, interventions that develop readiness, knowledge, or skills required by other interventions should come first. Violation of this rule (leapfrogging) can result in interventions that do not achieve their objectives, regression, and the need to start a new sequence of interventions.

3. *Maximize efficiency.* Interventions should be sequenced to conserve organizational resources such as time, energy, and money. Violation of this rule will result in overlapping interventions or in interventions that are not needed by certain people or parts of the organization.

4. *Maximize speed.* Interventions should be sequenced to maximize the speed with which ultimate organizational improvement is attained. Violation of this rule occurs when progress is slower than is necessary to conform to all the other rules.

5. *Maximize relevance.* Interventions that management sees at most relevant problems should come first. In general, this means interventions that will have an impact on the organization's performance or task come before interventions that will have an impact on individuals or culture. Violation of this rule will result in loss of motivation to continue with organization development.

6. *Minimize psychological and organizational strain.* A sequence of interventions should be chosen that is least likely to create dysfunctional effects such as anxiety, insecurity, distrust, dashed expectations, psychological damage to people, and unanticipated and unwanted effects on organizational performance. Violating this rule will lower people's sense of competence and confidence and their commitment to organizational improvement.[4]

Good advice. Paying attention to these guidelines helps ensure success. Disregard of these rules has caused many an OD program to flounder.

Fourth, different interventions have different dynamics; they do different things because they are based on different causal mechanisms. It's important to know the underlying causal mechanisms of interventions to ensure the intervention fits the desired outcomes. Robert Blake and Jane Mouton identified the following types of interventions based on the underlying causal mechanisms:

1. *Discrepancy intervention*, which calls attention to a contradiction in action or attitudes that then, leads to exploration.
2. *Theory intervention*, where behavioral science knowledge and theory are used to explain present behavior and assumptions underlying the behavior.
3. *Procedural intervention*, which represents a critiquing of how something is being done to determine whether the best methods are being used.
4. *Relationship intervention*, which focuses attention on interpersonal relationships (particularly those where there are strong negative feelings) and surfaces the issues for exploration and possible resolution.
5. *Experimentation intervention*, in which two different action plans are tested for their consequences before a final decision on one is made.
6. *Dilemma intervention*, in which an imposed or emergent dilemma is used to force close examination of the possible choices involved and the assumptions underlying them.
7. *Perspective intervention*, which draws attention away from immediate actions and demands and allows a look at historical background, context, and future objectives in order to assess whether or not the actions are "still on target."
8. *Organization structure intervention*, which calls for examination and evaluation of structural causes for organizational ineffectiveness.
9. *Cultural intervention*, which examines traditional, precedents, and practices—the fabric of the organization's culture—in a direct, focused approach.[5]

These different kinds of interventions provide a range of ways for the OD practitioner to intervene in the client system. They also explain the underlying dynamics of interventions.

Blake and Mouton have continued to refine the nature of interventions and proposed a theory and typology for the entire consultation field.[6] The typology, called the Consulcube, is a 100-cell cube depicting virtually all consultation situations. The cube is built on three dimensions. The first is what the consultant *does*, that is, which of five basic types of interventions the consultant uses—*acceptant* (the consultant gives the client a sense of worth, value, acceptance, and support); *catalytic* (the consultant helps the client generate data and information to restructure the client's perceptions); *confrontation* (the consultant points out value discrepancies in the client's beliefs and actions); prescription (the consultant tells the client what to do to solve the problem): and theories and principles (the consultant teaches the client relevant behavioral science theory so the client can learn to diagnose and solve his or her own problems).

The second dimension is the *focal issues* causing the client's problems. Blake and Mouton identify four focal issue categories: power/authority, morale/cohesion, norms/standards of conduct, and goals/objectives.

The third dimension of the cube is the unit of change that is the target of the consultation. Five units are proposed: individual, group, intergroup, organization, and larger social systems such as a community or even a society.

Five kinds of interventions, four different focal issues, and five different units of change thus encompass the range of consultation possibilities. Blake and Mouton's Consulcube represents a major contribution to developing a theory of consultation and intervention.

As we said, interventions do different things; they *cause different things to happen.* One intervention's major result may be increasing interaction and communication between parties. Another intervention's major result may be increasing feedback, or increasing accountability. These *differential* results are often exactly what is needed to produce change in the particular situation. For example, a situation requiring increased accountability will benefit more from an intervention that directly increases accountability than an intervention that increases interaction and communication. The following list shows some of the results one can expect from OD interventions.

1. *Feedback.* It refers to learning new data about oneself, others, group processes, or organizational dynamics—data that did not previously take active account of and that reflects an objective picture of the real world. Awareness of this new information may lead to change if the feedback is not too threatening. Feedback is prominent in interventions such as process consultation, organizational mirroring, sensitivity training, coaching and counseling, and survey feedback.

2. *Awareness of Changing Sociocultural Norms or Dysfunctional Current Norms.* Often people modify their behavior, attitudes, and values when they become aware of changes in the norms influencing their behavior. This awareness has change potential because the individual will adjust his or her behavior to bring it in line with the new norms. One's awareness that "this is a new ball game" or that "we're now playing with a new set of rules" causes changes in individual behavior. Also, awareness of dysfunctional current norms serves as incentive to change. When people sense a discrepancy between the outcomes, their present norms are causing and the outcomes they want, they are led to change. This causal mechanism probably operates in team building, intergroup team-building activities, culture analysis, Grid OD, and sociotechnical systems programs.

3. *Increased Interaction and Communication.* Increasing interaction and communication between individuals and groups causes changes in attitudes and behavior. Homans, for example, suggests that increased interaction leads to increased positive sentiments.[7] Individuals and groups in isolation tend to develop "tunnel vision" or "autism," according to Murphy.[8] Increasing communication counteracts this tendency, Increased communication allows one to check one's perceptions to see if they are socially validated and shared. This mechanism underlies almost all OD interventions. The rule of thumb is: Get people talking and interacting in new, constructive ways and good things will result.

4. *Confrontation.* This term refers to surfacing and examining differences in beliefs, feelings, attitudes, values, or norms to remove obstacles to effective interaction. Conformation is a process that seeks to discern real differences that are "getting in the way," to uncover those issues, and to work on them in a constructive way. Many obstacles to growth and learning exist, and they continue to exist when they are not actively examined. Confrontation underlies conflict resolution interventions such as intergroup team building, third-party peacemaking, and role negotiation.

5. *Education.* Education activities upgrade (a) knowledge and concepts, (b) beliefs and attitudes, and (c) skills. In organization development education activities increase these three components in several content areas: task achievement, social relationships, organizational dynamics and processes, and processes for managing change. Education is the primary mechanism operating in behavior modeling, force-field analysis, life- and career-planning, self-directed teams, and T-groups.

6. *Participation.* Increasing the number of people involved in problem solving goal setting, and generating new ideas increases the quality and acceptance of decisions, increases job satisfaction, and promotes employee well-being. Participation activities are found in quality circles, collateral organizations, quality of work life (QWL) programs, team building, search conferences, survey feedback, and Beckhard's Confrontation Meeting. Participation plays a role in most OD interventions.

7. *Increased Accountability.* Activities that clarify people's responsibilities and that monitor performance related to those responsibilities increase accountability. Both features must be present for accountability to enhance performance. OD interventions that increase accountability are the role analysis technique, responsibility charting, Gestalt OD, life-and career-planning, quality circles, MBO, self-managed teams, and partnering.

8. *Increased Energy and Optimism.* Activities that energize and motivate people through visions of new possibilities contribute toward a future that is desirable, worthwhile, and attainable. Increased energy and optimism are direct results of interventions such as appreciative inquiry, visioning, "getting the whole system in the room," quality of work life programs, search conferences, total quality programs, self-managed teams, and so forth.

These ideas are only some aspects to consider when planning OD programs and choosing and implementing OD interventions. One learns this practice theory through experience, reading, workshops, mentors, and reflecting on successes and failures.

CONCLUDING COMMENTS

This overview of OD interventions—the action component of organization development—presents some of the thinking that goes into planning and implementing OD interventions. Leaders and practitioners are encouraged to learn the full range of interventions so that change efforts will be relevant, timely, properly structured, and ultimately successful.

NOTES

1. E. H. Schein, *Process Consultation*, Vol. I (Reading, MA: Addison-Wesley, 1988).
2. R. W. White, "Motivation Reconsidered: The Concept of Competence," *Psychological Review*, 66 (1959), pp. 297–334.
3. D. C. McClelland, J. W. Atkinson, R. A. Clark, and E. L. Lowell, *The Achievement Motive* (New York: Appleton-Century-Crofts, 1953).
4. From Michael Beer, *Organization Change and Development* (Glenview, IL: Scott, Foresman and Company, 1980). Copyright © 1980 by Scott, Foresman and Company. Reprinted by permission.

5. Robert R. Blake and Jane S. Mouton, *The Managerial Grid* (Houston: Gulf, 1964), pp. 281–283. There is also *The Managerial Grid III* (1985) and *The Managerial Grid IV* (1990).
6. Robert R. Blake and Jane S. Mouton, Consultation (Reading, MA: Addison-Wesley, 1976). See also *Consultation*, 2d ed. (1983).
7. George C. Homans, *The Human Group* (New York: Harcourt, Brace & Co., 1950).
8. Gardner Murphy, "The Freeing of Intelligence," *Psychological Bulletin*, 42 (1945), pp. 1–19.

CHAPTER 8

Team Interventions

In chapters 8 through 13 will examine in detail many of the interventions that are used in contemporary OD efforts. These interventions are techniques and methods designed to change the culture of the organization, move it from "where it is" to where organizational members want it to be, and generally enable them to improve their practices so that they may better accomplish individual, team, and organizational goals. The broad nature of these interventions and a preliminary look at the different types of methods have already been presented. In this chapter we present descriptions, goals and mechanics of the various technical tools directed toward improving the performance of ongoing work teams—from office or plant floor to board rooms—as well as temporary team configurations.

TEAMS AND WORK GROUPS: STRATEGIC UNITS OF ORGANIZATION

Collaborative management of the work team culture is a fundamental emphasis of organization development programs. The reality is that much of the organization's work is accomplished directly or indirectly through teams; work team culture exerts a significant influence on individual behavior. In large part, the techniques and the theory for understanding and improving team processes come from the laboratory training movement coupled with research in the area of group dynamics. An appreciation of the importance of the work team as a determinant of individual behavior has come from cultural anthropology, sociology, organization theory, and social psychology.

Although we will use the terms somewhat synonymously, it is important to make a distinction between *groups* and *teams*. "A *work group* is a number of persons, usually reporting to a common superior and having some face-to-face interaction, who have some degree of interdependence in carrying out tasks for the purpose of achieving organizational goals."[1] A *team* is a form of group, but has some characteristics in greater degree than ordinary groups, including a higher commitment to common goals and higher degree of interdependency and interaction. Jon Katzenbach and Douglas Smith define *team* as follows: "A team is a small number of people with complementary skills who are committed to a common purpose, set of performance goals, and approach for which they hold themselves mutually accountable."[2] This distinction is particularly relevant in conceptualizing the kinds of teams desired in organization development efforts, in the creation of self-managed teams, and in the development of high-performance teams, including cross-functional teams.

Cross-Functional Teams

Even though a high proportion of OD team interventions involve working with what we call " intact work teams" (or "formal work groups," or "natural teams"), OD interventions are also applicable to other team configurations. In particular, cross-functional (or multi-functional) teams are widely used in organizations, and OD approaches have great utility in the formation and ongoing functioning of these teams.

Cross-functional teams typically comprised individuals who have a functional home base—e.g., manufacturing, design, engineering, or marketing, etc—but who meet regularly to solve ongoing challenges requiring inputs from a number of functional areas. Such cross-functional teams might be *permanent*, but *temporary* teams can be created to solve short-term problems. Temporary teams might tackle problems such as planning a product changeover or solving a key customer problem.[3]

Large companies such as Motorola, Ford, 3M, and General Electric, as well as many small and medium-sized organizations, have used cross-functional teams.[4] As a specific example, in the development of the Saturn automobile at General Motors, cross-functional teams were used from the outset. Rather than have one functional team (say, design) do its work and then "throw the plans over the wall" to the next functional team (say, production), cross-functional teams provide oversight throughout the entire project.[5] In his book, *Thriving on Chaos,* Tom Peters advocates increasing the use of cross-functional teams as a means for U.S. industry to compete successfully in today's fast-paced environment.[6]

Effective Teams

Early writers who directed attention to the importance or team functioning included Rensis Likert and Douglas McGregor, Likert, for example, suggested that organizations are best conceptualized by systems of interlocking groups connected by *linking pins*—individuals who occupy membership in two groups by being a boss in one group and a subordinate in another.[7] Through these interlocking groups the work of the organization gets done. The key reality seems to be that individuals in organizations function not so much as *individuals* alone but as *members* of groups or teams. For an individual to function effectively, frequently a prerequisite is that the team must function effectively.

CHARACTERISTICS OF AN EFFECTIVE TEAM

Clear purpose [defined and accepted vision, mission, goal or task, and an action plan]

Informality [informal, comfortable, and relaxed]

Participation [much discussion with everyone encouraged to participate]

Listening [use of effective listening techniques such as questioning, paraphrasing, and summarizing]

Civilized disagreement [team is comfortable with disagreement; does not avoid, smooth over, or suppress conflict]

Consensus decision making [substantial agreement through thorough discussion, avoidance of voting]

Open communications [feelings seen as legitimate, few hidden agendas]

Clear roles and work assignments [clear expectations and work evenly divided]

Shared leadership [in addition to a formal leader, everyone shares in effective leadership behaviors]

External relations [the team pays attention to developing outside relationships, resources, credibility]

Style diversity [team has broad spectrum of group process and task skills]

Self-assessment [periodic examination of how well the team is functioning][8]

High-Performance Teams

High-performance teams have the same characteristics but to a higher degree. Katzenbach and Smith say that strong personal commitment to each other—commitment to the others' growth and success—distinguishes high-performance teams from effective teams.

Team interventions in OD tend to be congruent with the characteristics identified in the preceding lists and are designed to bring about these conditions. Parenthetically, when groups are asked to describe what their groups would be like if they were operating at a highly effective level, they generate lists similar to the preceding lists.

Again, team and work groups are considered to be the fundamental units of organizations as well as key leverage points for improving the functioning of the organization. The following are among the interventions that have been developed to help teams become more effective while simultaneously addressing organizational problems and challenges.

BROAD TEAM-BUILDING INTERVENTIONS

Probably the most important single group of interventions in OD are team-building activities, the goals of which are the improvement and increased effectiveness of various teams within the organization. Some interventions focus on the intact work team composed of a boss and subordinates, which we call the *formal group*. Other interventions focus on special teams such as startup teams, newly constituted teams due to mergers, organization structure changes, or plant startups; task forces; cross functional project teams; and committees.

Team-building interventions are typically directed toward four main areas: diagnosis, task accomplishments, team relationships, and team and organization processes. These separate thrusts are diagrammed in Figure 8-1. In the following pages we describe the formal work group team-building, such as the formal work group diagnostic meeting, the formal work group team-building meeting, process consultation, and Gestalt OD, as well as a number of techniques and exercises used within team-building sessions to address specific issues.

Let us examine several of these interventions as they might be conducted with a formal group. The major actors are a consultant, who is not a member of the group (the *third party*), the group leader, and the group members.

THE FORMAL GROUP DIAGNOSTIC MEETING

The purpose of the formal group diagnostic meeting is to conduct a general critique of the performance of the group, that is, to take stock of: "where we are going" and "how we are doing," and to uncover and identify problems so that they may be worked on. Typically the leader and the consultant discuss the idea first, and if a genuine need for a diagnostic meeting exists, the idea is put to the group for their reactions. The leader may structure

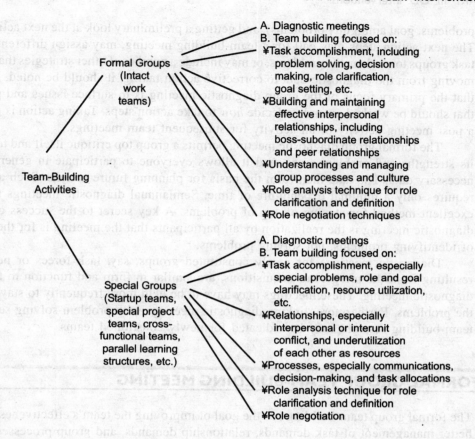

Formal Groups
(Intact
work
teams)

A. Diagnostic meetings
B. Team building focused on:
¥ Task accomplishment, including
   problem solving, decision
   making, role clarification,
   goal setting, etc.
¥ Building and maintaining
   effective interpersonal
   relationships, including
   boss-subordinate relationships
   and peer relationships
¥ Understanding and managing
   group processes and culture
¥ Role analysis technique for role
   clarification and definition
¥ Role negotiation techniques

Team-Building
Activities

Special Groups
(Startup teams,
special project
teams, cross-
functional teams,
parallel learning
structures, etc.)

A. Diagnostic meetings
B. Team building focused on:
¥ Task accomplishment, especially
   special problems, role and goal
   clarification, resource utilization,
   etc.
¥ Relationships, especially
   interpersonal or interunit
   conflict, and underutilization
   of each other as resources
¥ Processes, especially communications,
   decision-making, and task allocations
¥ Role analysis technique for role
   clarification and definition
¥ Role negotiation

FIGURE 8-1 Varieties of Team-Building Interventions

his or her testing for the group's reaction in the form of the following questions: What are our strengths? What problems do we have that we should work on? How are we doing in regard to our assigned tasks? How are our relationships with each other? What opportunities should we be taking advantage of?

If the group decides to conduct the formal group of diagnostic meeting after some thinking about their own performance, the group assembles for a half-day or a day meeting. Several ways are available for getting the diagnostic data out, that is, making the information public:

A total group discussion involves everyone making individual contributions to the total assemblage.

Sub grouping involves breaking down into smaller groups where a more intensive discussion takes place, then the subgroups report back to the total group. (This method is particularly effective because people have more "air time" and feel a higher degree of safety in the anonymity of a subgroup report.)

A pairing of two individuals interviews each other or simply discusses their ideas with each other; each other reports back to the total group.

After the data are shared throughout the group, the next steps consist of discussing the issues, grouping the issues in terms of themes (say, planning problems, interface problems, goal ambiguity problems), and getting a preliminary look at the next action steps. The next action steps may call for a team-building meeting, may assign different persons task groups to work on the problems, or may include a number of other strategies that involve moving from the diagnostic data to corrective action taking, it should be noted, however, that the primary focus of the group diagnostic meeting is to surface issues and problems that should be worked on and to decide *how* to take action steps. Taking action is generally a post meeting activity or an activity for subsequent team meetings.

The formal group diagnostic meeting permits a group top critique itself and to identify its strengths and problem areas, and it allows everyone to participate in generating the necessary data. The data then form the basis for planning future actions. Such a meeting requires only a minimal expenditure of time. Semiannual diagnostic meetings afford an excellent method for staying on top of problems. A key secret to the success of a short diagnostic meeting is the realization by all participants that the meeting is for the purpose of identifying problems, not solving problems.

Diagnostic meetings for newly constituted groups, say, task forces or new teams resulting from the mergers or acquisitions, are similar in form and function to the group diagnostic meeting. These meetings may have to be held more frequently to stay ahead of the problems. Furthermore, linking diagnostic meetings with problem-solving sessions or team-building sessions may be indicated for newly constituted teams.

THE FORMAL GROUP TEAM-BUILDING MEETING

The formal group team-building has the goal of improving the team's effectiveness through better management of task demands, relationship demands, and group processes. It is an inward look by the team at its own performance, beehive, and culture for the purposes of eliminating dysfunctional behaviors and strengthening functional ones. The group critiques its performance, analyzes its way of doing things, and attempts to develop strategies to improve its operation. Sometimes the purpose of the meeting is a special agenda item, such as developing the group's performance goals for the coming year. Often the purpose of the meeting is for the more general charge expressed in the question: How can we build ourselves into a better functioning team? And how can we do the job better?

The team-building session is usually initiated by the manager in consultation with the third party. The idea is then tested for reactions within the group. (Conversely, the group may initiate the idea and take it to the boss if they sense pressing problems that need examination and solution). A good length of time for the meeting is anywhere from one to three days. The session should be held away from the work place.

The usual practice for these sessions is to have the consultant interview each of the group members and the leader prior to the meeting, asking them what the strengths of the group are, what their problems are, how they think the group functions, and what obstacles are in the way of the group performing better. These interview data are categorized into themes by the consultant, who presents the themes to the group at the beginning of the meeting. The group examines and discusses the issues, ranks them in order to their importance, examines the underlying dynamics of the problems, begins to work on solutions to the problems, and establishes some action steps to bring about the changes deemed desirable. It is imperative to have follow-up meetings to determine whether the action steps that were outlined were taken and to determine whether those steps had the desired effects. This flow of events constitutes the team-building meeting. But let us look closer at the components.

The meeting may be called for a special purpose, such as a new member coming into the group, an organization structure change or planning for the next year; or it may primarily be devoted to maintaining and managing the group's culture and processes. If it is a special-purpose meeting, time should still be allocated to an examination and critique of the group's dynamics.

As mentioned previously, it is often desirable for the consultant to interview the entire group, using an open-ended approach, such as "What things do you see getting in the way of this group being a better one?" This procedure introduces the consultant to the group members and allows the consultant to assess commitment to the team-building session. The consultant decides in advance and informs the interviewees whether the information each gives will be considered public or confidential. Each approach has advantages and disadvantages. For example, if the information in the interviews is confidential, the interviewees may be more candid and open than if the information is to be public. On the other hand, treating the information as public data helps to set a climate of openness, trust, and constructive problem solving. If the information is considered confidential, the consultant is careful to report the findings in a general way that does not reveal the sources of information. Other ways the agenda items for the meetings are developed are through such devices as the formal group diagnostic meeting or through a society.

The consultant presents the interview results in terms of themes. When everyone understands these themes, these themes are ranked by the group in terms of their importance; the most important ones form the agenda for the meeting. In the course of the meeting, much interpersonal and group process information will be generated, which may also be examined. The group thus works on two sets of items: the agenda items and the items that emerge from the interactions of the participants.

As important problems are discussed, alternatives for action are developed. Generally, the team-building meeting involves deciding on action steps for remedying problems and setting target dates for "*who* will do *what when.*"

Significant variations of the team-building session entail devoting time to problem-solving methods, planning and goal-setting methods, conflict resolution techniques, and the like. These special activities are usually initiated in response to the needs demonstrated or stated by the group. The consultant offers makes conceptual inputs (mini-lectures) or structures the situation so that a particular problem or process becomes the focus. A wide variety of exercises may be interspersed into the three-day meeting, depending upon the problems identified and the group phenomena that emerge.

Purposes of Team Building

Figure 8-1 suggests that team-building sessions may be directed toward problem-solving for task accomplishment, examining and improving interpersonal relationships, or managing the group's culture and processes. In fact, one of these issues may be the principal reason for holding the team-building meeting. For example, suppose that the meeting is designed as a team problem-solving session to examine the impact on the team of a new function or task being added to the group's work requirements. Even in this case a portion of the session will probably be reserved for reflecting on *how* the team is solving its problems, that is, critiquing the group's processes. In this way the team becomes more effective at both the task level and the process level.

Richard Beckhard lists, in order of importance, the four major reasons or purposes involved in having teams meet other for the sharing of information: (1) to set goals and/or priorities... (2) to analyze or allocate the way work is performed ... (3) to examine the way a group is working, it processes (such as norms, decision making, communications)... and (4) to examine relationships among the people doing the work.[9] He notes that often all four items will be covered in a single team-building session, but it is imperative that the primary goal be clear and accepted by all. It is especially important to have a priority list of items that are inverse to those just given—from relationships among people as most important, to the way the group works together as next most important, to the work itself next, and to goals and priorities as least important. Lack of generation on the primary goal can lead to wasted energy and a generally unproductive and frustrating team-building session. We agree with Beckhard when he states that the consultant should help to implement the group leader's goals for the session, not the consultant's goals.

Bell and Rosenzweig relied heavily upon team-building workshops in an OD program in a municipal government organization and came to the following assessment:

> Our experience leads us to the tentative conclusion that some relatively simple notions underlie success, namely:
>
> 1. Get the *right people* together for
> 2. A *large block of uninterrupted time*
> 3. To work on *high-priority problems or opportunities* that
> 4. *They have identified* and that are worked on
> 5. In ways *that are structured* to enhance the likelihood of
> 6. *Realistic solutions* and action plans that are
> 7. *Implemented* enthusiastically and
> 8. *Followed up* to assess actual versus expected results.[10]

When a team engages in problem-solving activities directed toward task accomplishment, the team members build something together. It appears that the act of building something together also builds a sense of camaraderie, cohesion, and espirit de corps. The major ingredients involved in a team's building something together are probably the eight steps identified by Bell and Rosenzweig.

In our own consulting we have increasingly come to designate these sessions as "team-building" problem-solving workshops"—a clear signal to us and the client that both building a more effective team and solving priority problems constitute the business at hand. We consider team-building problem-solving interventions to be a cornerstone of OD technology.

AN EXAMPLE OF LARGE INDIAN ORGANIZATION

The National Thermal Power Corporation (NTPC), India's largest power utility company, was established in 1975. Today, it is the sixth largest power generating company globally.

It is a geographically diversified company or a mini India in itself with a strong workforce of about 24,000 employees working in 23 plants and corporate centers all across the country. While this size and diversity can be a hell to manage, it also gives the opportunity for brighter ideas and innovation to bring about the greatest change. The NTPC felt building a strong team-based environment is a must if it has to not only sustain but improve its productivity in order to realize its vision of becoming a global giant in the field of power sector. The NTPC implemented an OD intervention successfully in order to analyze and strengthen its team-based environment. A team-oriented approach to management is both dynamic and progressive yielding higher performance, improved quality, and utilization of creative power and higher level of job satisfaction.

At NTPC, a very comprehensive approach was adopted and the whole Team Building Intervention (TBI) was conducted in three stages with the following objectives:

1. To exploit the competitive advantage inherent in cross-functional teams.
2. To build successful cross-functional teams with an effective leader and effective plans.
3. To recognize and remove team obstacles and build bridges for success.

Stage-I: Diagnostic Phase
The diagnostic study was done at different levels from

a. The highest level *cross-functional executive team* of the plant at Talcher comprising its GM and HODs
b. The *functional teams* of the Head of the Departments from the critical areas and their executives.
c. *Cross-functional teams* comprising executives from the different areas.

The data was collected using the famous standardized tool—'Team Effectiveness Questionnaire' by Moxon, Gower and Aldershot.

The questionnaire provided the quantitative data on the following dimensions.

1. Team atmosphere
2. Result focus
3. Participation in decision making
4. Comfort with conflict
5. Real time agreements
6. Response to criticism
7. Open dialogue
8. Responsibility-Authority Match
9. Situation leadership
10. Empowered for team progress.

The quantitative data that emerged around these building blocks was crosschecked through following qualitative methods.

1. One to one in-depth interview with the GM and HODs.
2. Focused group discussions with cross-functional team of executives.

The total sample size used for the diagnostic phase was 30 percent of the total executives. The findings indicated that on the dimensions like empowerment, openness in dialogue, situational leadership and responsibility authority match, the two plants of NTPC (Talcher and Badarpur) were doing reasonably well but there was still scope for improvement. On analyzing and comparing the data gathered through questionnaire, it was evident that TTPS (Talcher) certainly had more issues, which needed attention. Even though the general team environment was given a high ranking, the results clearly bring to the surface the deeper issues of low result focus and participation in decision making and openness. Also the response to criticism was found low.

These concerns were crosschecked with the help of small focus groups, group discussion and personal interview.

The major strengths which were reflected in terms of teams and team work were

1. Enabling and informal atmosphere where seniors were easily approachable.
2. Shared vision and objective—well understood and accepted by members.
3. High level of commitment for the organization despite dissatisfaction on many fronts.
4. HODs team having good inter personal relationship response though it does not percolate downwards.

Major areas of improvement, which came to light, were also in line with the survey conducted. They can be summed up as follows-

1. Discussions though taking place often in groups tend to be dominated by few. Others feel left out & then develop disgruntled feeling.
2. Meetings tend to overstretch and go out of focus.
3. Hesitation in disagreement- fearing victimization / transfer.
4. Lack of open communication in interdepartmental communications at middle level executives.
5. Buck passing attitude or not owning up of responsibility.
6. Lack of transparency in critical issues like that of promotion and transfer thus creating lack of trust.
7. Lack of understanding about others roles.

It can be clearly inferred from the findings that there were two major root causes of all these symptoms—

a. Lack of trust amongst the seniors and their subordinates.
b. Lacking in interpersonal skills.

Dennis Kirlaw in his book *Developing Superior Work Teams*, has also emphasized that one of the greatest inhibitors to team effectiveness is the fear and distrust that people have while contacting. Hence, to stop these from becoming one of the biggest impediments for NTPC these needed to be addressed immediately, which thankfully the company got into doing.

Two other major concerns were voiced at the TTPS about the project not being effectively showcased at NTPC level and its turnaround not properly recognized. Also, although the PLF (Plant Load Factor) had risen significantly in last six years—the same pace has not been found in welfare measures. The two issues may have been responsible in contributing to apathy as reflected in survey findings, which were so alarmingly different from that of Badarpur plant.

Stage-II: Intervention—The Action Step

The second phase of Team Building Intervention was in the form of three-day intervention constituting of the following steps.

> **a.** *Presentation* of survey findings to the core executive team of GM and HODs.
> **b.** *Workshop* on team building with focus on techniques of effective dialogue, building of trust, receiving and learning from feedback. Workshop essentially made use of role-plays to develop proficiency and to master the skill.
> **c.** *Dialogue champions* were selected to observe and check the 'dialogue' process in meetings.
> **d.** *Preparation of action plans*. Groups met to identify key pernicious elements. Task forces were formed within each group to work on action plan and eliminate the problems.
> **e.** Attaching *time frame* to each action plan.

It can be seen that the phase resulted in

- Defining a clear purpose.
- Active participation of all key members
- Enforcement of self-discipline to keep the schedule.

Third Phase Review of Action Plan

This phase took place almost after 3-5 months after the expiry of phase II. This was done so that sufficient time was allowed to carry out the action plans and also to see, if any, problems surfaced.

For the review the agenda was fixed and circulated in advance and the Business Unit head—the general managers of the plant—chaired the sessions. The whole exercise took place in the presence of external consultant and an HR representative.

Each HOD first displayed his action plan and then explained in details how it was implemented. Both the process and the outcomes were discussed. The other teams and HODs gave feedbacks on their action plans. Further suggestions were provided and incorporated for the smooth functioning of teams.

Conclusion

The study successfully brought to the light the positive and negative approaches prevalent in various groups of these two plants of the NTPC. Further, it took the employees through the experiences of team effectiveness. The sense of ownership and participation was created. The NTPC did not become complacent and carried out an impact assessment of the intervention.

Impact assessment clearly showed marked improvements in

- The role played by the leader in providing support and being responsive to the needs of the team.

- More clarity about individual roles and responsibility.
- Productivity in team meetings.

Hence, to get the sustained improvement in team effectiveness and productivity, it is felt that team building should be taken as a journey and not as an end in itself.

PROCESS CONSULTATION INTERVENTIONS

The process consultation model is similar to team-building interventions except that process consultation places greater emphasis on diagnosing and understanding process events. Furthermore, the consultant's role is more nondirective and questioning as he or she gets the groups to solve their own problems.

Process consultation (PC) represents an approach or a method for intervening in an ongoing system. The crux of this approach is that a skilled third party (consultant) works with individuals and groups to help them learn about human and social processes and learn to solve problems that stem from process events. This approach has been around a long time; many practitioners operate from this stance. Edgar Schein pulled together the disparate practices and principles of process consultation in a comprehensive exposition.[11] Schein also describes the role of PC in organization development.

Some particularly important organizational processes are communications, the roles and functions of group members, group problem solving and decision-making, group norms and group growth, leadership and authority, and intergroup cooperation and competition.[12] The PC consultant works with the organization, typically in work teams, and helps them to develop the skills necessary to diagnose and solve the process problems that arise.

Schein describes the kinds of interventions he believes the process consultant should make:

1. Agenda-setting interventions, consisting of:
   — questions which direct attention to interpersonal issues.
   — process-analysis periods.
   — agenda review and testing procedures.
   — meetings devoted to interpersonal process.
   — conceptual inputs on interpersonal-process topics.
2. Feedback of observations or other data, consisting of:
   — feedback to groups during process analysis or regular work time.
   — feedback to individuals after meetings or after data-gathering.
3. Coaching or counseling of individualize [see discussion following].
4. Structural suggestions:
   — pertaining to group membership.
   — pertaining to communication or interaction patterns.
   — pertaining to allocation of work, assignment of responsibility, and lines of authority.[13]

In Schein's view, the process consultant would often make interventions in that same order: agenda setting, feedback of observations or other data, counseling and coaching, and, least likely, structural suggestions. Specific recommendations for the solution of substantive problems are not listed because to Schein such interventions violate the underlying values of the PC model in that the consultant so acting as an expert rather than as a resource.[14]

In *coaching and counseling interventions*, which may be considered either as a part of PC or as a set of interventions in their own right, the consultant is placed in the role of responding to such questions from groups or individuals as "What do you think I should do in this sentence to improve any performance?" "Now that I can see some areas for improvement, how do I go about changing my behavior?"

Schein sees the consultant's role in coaching and counseling situations to be the following: "The consultant's role then becomes one of adding alternatives to those already brought up by the client, and helping the client to analyze the costs and benefits of the various alternatives which have been mentioned."[15] Thus the consultant, when counseling either individuals or groups, continues to maintain the posture that real improvements and changes in behavior should be those decided upon by the client. The consultant serves to reflect or mirror accurate feedback, to listen to the alternatives and suggest new ones (often through questions designed to expand the client's horizons), and to assist the client in evaluating alternatives for feasibility, relevance, and appropriateness.

The basic congruence between theories of counseling and the theory of process consultation is pointed out by Schein: "In both cases it is essential to help the client improve his ability to observe and process data about himself, to help him accept and learn from feedback and to help him become an active participant with the counselor/consultant in identifying and solving his own problems."[16]

A GESTALT APPRAOCH TO TEAM BUILDING

A form of team building that focuses more on the individual than the group is the Gestalt approach to OD. The major advocate of this orientation is Stanley M. Herman, a management and OD consultant. The approach rests on a form of psychotherapy developed by Fredrick S. "Fritz" Perls called Gestalt therapy.[17] Gestalt therapy is based on the belief that persons function as whole, total organisms. And each person possesses positive and negative characteristics that must be "owned up to" and permitted expression. People get into trouble when they do not accept their total selves, and when they are trying to live up to the demands ("shoulds") of others rather than being themselves. Robert Harman lists the goals of Gestalt therapy as awareness, integration, maturation, authenticity, self-regulation, and behavior change.[18] Basically, one must come to terms with oneself, must accept responsibility for one's actions, must experience and live in the "here and now," and must stop blocking off awareness, authenticity, and the like by dysfunctional behaviors.

Stanley Herman applies a Gestalt orientation to organization development, especially in working with leader-subordinates relations and team building. The primary thrust is to make the individual stronger, more authentic, and more in touch with the individual's own feelings; building a better team may result, but it is not the primary desired outcome.

To do this people must be able to express their feelings fully, both positive and negative. They must "get in touch" with "where they are" on issues, relations with others, and relations with others and work them through to resolution rather than suppressing negative feelings or cutting off the transactions prematurely. They must learn to accept the polarities within themselves—weakness-strength, autocratic-democratic urges, and so forth.

The Gestalt OD practitioner fosters the expression of positive and negative feelings, encourages people to stay with transactions, structures, exercises that cause individuals to become more aware of what they want from others, and pushes toward greater authenticity for everyone. The Gestalt OD practitioner often works within a group setting, but the focus is usually on individuals.

Use of the Gestalt orientation to OD is not widespread. An interesting book by Herman and Korenich gives a theoretical framework, examples, and exercises for Gestalt OD, and this intervention may become more popular in organization development.[19]

We are somewhat ambivalent about the Gestalt orientation to OD. On the one hand, better individual functioning is a laudable goal and deserves support. On the other hand, it is an intervention of considerable "depth" and one that people might not choose to expose themselves to—they may believe they are being coerced into a therapeutic situation that they would prefer to avoid. One thing is certain: the Gestalt orientation to team building should not be used except by practitioners trained in this method.

TECHNIQUES AND EXERCISES USED IN TEAM BUILDING: SELECTED EXAMPLES

A number of techniques and exercises are used in team building to facilitate team performance and to address specific problematic issues. They are useful and powerful ways to structure the team's activities and energies in order to achieve understanding of the issues and to take corrective actions. Before using these techniques, a careful diagnosis should be made to ensure that the technique is appropriate. Team-building sessions often include many of these techniques and exercises.

Role Analysis Technique

The role analysis technique (RAT or RAP*) intervention is designed to clarify role expectations and obligations of team members to improve team effectiveness. In organizations individuals fill different specialized roles in which they manifest certain behaviors. This session of labor and function facilitates organization performance. Often, however, the role incumbent may not have a clear idea of the behaviors expected of him or her by others and, equally often, what others can do to help the incumbent fulfill the role is not understood. Ishwar Dayal and John M. Thomas developed a technique for clarifying the roles of the top management of a new organization in India.[20] This technique is particularly applicable for new teams, but it may also be helpful in established teams where role ambiguity or confusion exists. The intervention is predicated on the belief that consensual determination of role requirements for team members, consisting of a joint building of the requirements by all concerned, leads to more mutually satisfactory and productive behavior. Dayal and Thomas call the activity the *role analysis technique*.

---

*Our colleague Charles Hosford suggests the more euphonic label *role analysis process* for this procedure.

In a structured series of steps, role incumbents, in conjunction with team members, define and delineate role requirements. The role being defined is called the *focal role*. In a new organization, it may be desirable to conduct a role analysis for each of the major roles.

The first step consists of the focal role initiated by the focal role individual. The role, its place in the organization, the rationale for its existence, and its place in achieving overall organization goals are examined along with the specific duties of the office. The specific duties and behaviors are listed on a chalkboard and are discussed by the entire team. Behaviors are added and deleted until the group and the role incumbent are satisfied that they have defined the role completely.

The second step examines the focal role incumbent's expectations of others. The incumbent lists his or her expectations, of the other roles in the group that most affect the incumbent's own role are performance, and these expectations are discussed, modified, and agreed upon by the group and the focal role person.

The third step consists of explicating others' expectations and desired behaviors of the focal role, that is, the members of the group describe what they want from and expect from the incumbent in the focal role. These expectations of others are discussed, modified, and agreed upon by the group and the focal role person.

Upon conclusion of this step, the focal role person assumes responsibility for making a written summary of the role as it has been defined; this summary is called a role profile and is derived from the results of the discussions in steps 1 through 3. Dayal and Thomas describe the role profile as ... (a) a set of activities classified as to the prescribed and discretionary elements of the role, (b) the obligation of the role to each role in its set, and (c) the expectations of this role from others in its set. Viewed in toto, this provides a comprehensive understanding of each individual's "role space."[21]

The written role profile is briefly reviewed at the following meeting before another focal role is analyzed. The accepted role profile constitutes the role activities for the focal role person.

This intervention can be a nonthreatening activity with high payoff. Often the mutual demands, expectations, and obligations of interdependent team members have never been publicly examined. Each role incumbent wonders why "those other people" are "not doing what they are supposed to do," while in reality all the incumbents are performing as they think they are supposed to do," Collaborative role analysis and definition by the entire work group not only clarifies who is to do what but ensures commitment to the role once it has been clarified.

From our experience, this procedure can be shortened if there is already high visibility and understanding of the current activities of various role incumbents. For example, if one of the problems facing an organization is confusion over the duties of the board of directors and the president or the executive director, the following sequence can be highly productive.

1. With the board listening, the president and his/her staff members discuss this question: "If the board were operating in an optimally effective way, what would they be doing?"
2. During this discussion, responses are made visible on a chalkboard or on large newsprint, and disagreements are recorded.

3. After 45 minutes or so, the last is modified on the basis of general consensus of the total group.
4. The procedure is repeated, but this time the president listens while staff and board members discuss the question. "If the president were operating in an optimally effective way, what would he/she be doing?" Again, responses are made visible during the discussion. The discussion responds, and then the group attempts consensus.

As with the longer technique, this procedure helps to clarify role expectations and obligations and frequently leads to some significant shifts in the whole network of activities of the management group, including the board. For example, we have seen this procedure result in boards shifting their activities almost exclusively to policy determination, pulling away from previously dysfunctional tinkering with day-to-day operating problems and delegating operations to the president and the staff.

Interdependency Exercise

An interdependency exercise is a useful intervention if team members have expressed a desire to improve cooperation among themselves and among their units. This exercise is also useful for assisting people in getting better acquainted, in surfacing problems that may be latent and not previously examined, and in providing useful information about current challenges being faced in others' areas of responsibility.

The interdependency exercise can be structured as follows, although facilitators can invent other versions. It works well with up to approximately ten people, but can become too cumbersome and time consuming if more than that number are involved. Let's assume the top ten people of an organization or a division of the organization are present.

1. Two straight lines of five persons each are formed with the lines facing each other. Each person is seated facing one other person, but with pairs of people seated far enough apart to minimized distractions. Thus, persons 1,2,3,4, and 5 will be seated facing persons 6,7,8,9, and 10. Person 1 faces person 6; person 2 faces person 7, and so on.
2. Using the assignment sheets of taking notes as shown in Figure 9-2 persons facing each other are instructed to interview each other about the important interdependencies between their two jobs and/or units. Furthermore, they are instructed to interview each other about what seems to be going particularly well in the interdependencies and what present or potential snags are perceived. They are also instructed to make mutual action plans at the end of the interview or to meet further, if desired.
3. At the end of ten minutes, people in one row are asked to shift positions one chair within their row. That is, person 1 moves to where person 2 had been sitting, 2 moves to where 3 had been sitting, and so on, and 5 moves from the end of the row to where 1 had been sitting. (Persons 6 to 10 keep their same seats. Only the one row moves.)
4. Once the first round of five interviews is completed, the group takes a break. After the break, the person in *each row* pair up and interview each other. This requires a series of five more interview periods with one person sitting out each period.

Since there are ten persons involved, each person must interview nine others, for a total of 90 minutes of interviewing. Approximately two hours should be allocated for the total exercise. Participants report that this procedure is tiring, but in many ways exhilarating and extremely productive. Participants report considerable follow-up after the workshop.

(For taking notes: for your use only)

Person being interviewed _____

Unit _____

Please ask these questions:
What/where are the most important interdependencies between our two units (or our two jobs)?

What's going particularly well?

Present or potential snags?

Any action plans or agreement to meet further _____

Tailor the dialogue to fit your circumstances. For example, if there is very little interdependency, learn a few things about the other person's job, etc.

FIGURE 8-2 Interdependency Interviews

Obviously, this exercise requires the participants' cooperation and assumes no serious conflict situations. Serious intense conflict situations require a different structure and more time.

A shortened version of this same technique can be used in a large group of say, 60 people, if clusters of ten people interview each other, each having a different question. Each cluster has the same assignment and the same questions. For example, in each cluster of ten people, each person 1 through 10 is assigned a different question. Each interviews the five people seated in the opposite row through the procedure of asking people in one row to move over one chair at specified intervals of time. People who move take their question with them.

After the five paired interviews are completed, all of the "experts" about one question are now asked to meet together. Thus, ten new groups are formed by asking all six people who had the same question to meet and share what they found out. That is, person 1 from each of the six clusters meet together, and so on. These new groups share the data, extract the themes, and report the themes to the total group. This procedure is a rapid way to gather a great deal of data for diagnostic purposes.

---

*We are indebted to Herman (Hy) Resnick for introducing us to this "phalanx" technique of interviewing We are uncertain as to its origin.

A Role Negotiation Technique

When the causes of team effectiveness are based on people's behaviors that they are unwilling to change because it would mean a loss of power or influence to the individual, a technique developed by Roger Harrison called "role negotiation" can often be used to great advantage.[22]

> Role negotiation intervenes directly in the relationships of power, authority, and influence within the group. The change effort is directed at the work relationships among members. It avoids probing into the likes and dislikes of members for one another and their personal feelings about one another.[23]

The technique is basically an imposed structure for controlled negotiations between parties in which each party agrees in writing to change certain behaviors in return for changes in behavior of the other. The behaviors relate to the job. Specifically, I ask you to change some of your behaviors so that I can do my job more effectively; and you ask me to change some of my behaviors so that can do your job more effectively. Harrison states that the technique rests on one basic assumption: "*Most people prefer a fair negotiated settlement to a sense of unresolved conflict*, and they are willing to invest some time and make some concessions in order to achieve a solution."[24]

The role negotiation technique usually takes at least one day to conduct. A two-day session with a follow-up meeting a month later is best. We will outline the steps of the technique as given by Harrison.[25] The first step is *contract setting*. Here the consultant sets the climate and establishes the ground rules: we are looking at work behaviors, not feelings about people; be specific in stating what you want others to *do more* of or do better, to *do less* of or stop doing, or *maintain unchanged*; all expectations and demands must be *written*; no one is to agree to changing any behavior unless there is a quid pro quo in which the other must agree to a change also; the session will consist of individuals negotiating with each other to arrive at a *written contract* of what behaviors each will change.

The next step is *issue diagnosis*. Individuals think about how their *own effectiveness* can be improved if others change their work behaviors. Then each person fills out an issue Diagnosis Form for every other person in the group. On this form the individual states that he or she would like the other to do more of, do less of, or maintain unchanged. These messages are then exchanged among all members, and the messages received by each person are written on a chalkboard or newsprint for all to see.

The next step is the *influence trade* or negotiation period, in which two individuals discuss the *most important* behavior changes they want from the other and the changes they are willing to make themselves. A quid pro quo is required in this step: each person must give something in order to get something. Often this step is demonstrated by two individuals with the rest of the group watching. Then the group breaks into negotiating pairs. "The negotiating process consists of parties making contingent offers to one another such as 'If you do X, I will do Y.' The negotiation ends when all parties are satisfied that they will receive a reasonable return for whatever they are agreeing to give."[26] All agreements are written, with each party having a copy. The agreement may or may not be published for the group to see. The influence trade step is concluded when all the negotiated agreements have been made and written down. It is best to have a follow-up meeting to determine whether the contracts have been honored and to assess the effects of the contracts on effectiveness.

In our view Harrison's role negotiation technique is an effective way of bringing about positive improvement in a situation where power and influence issues are working to maintain an unsatisfactory status quo. We have used this technique successfully with several groups and have found that it is an intervention that leads to improved team functioning. It is based on the fact that frequently individuals must change their work behaviors for the team to become more effective.

The Appreciations and Concerns Exercise

The appreciations and concerns exercise may be appropriate if interview data suggest that one of the deficiencies in the interactions of members of a group is lack of expression of appreciation, and that another deficiency is the avoidance of confronting concerns and irritations. Various versions of the appreciations and concerns exercise can be used, but basically it is conducted as follows.

1. The facilitator asks each member of the group to jot down one to three appreciations for each member of the group.
2. Each member is also asked to jot down one or two minor irritations or concerns relative to each person that may be interfering with communications, getting the work done effectively, and so on.
3. Along with the assignment, the facilitator may make some suggestions, such as: "You be the judge of which concerns to raise—will it be helpful to the relationship? To the group? Can the person do anything about it? Would it be better to talk privately with the person? On the positive side, sometimes raising concerns in a team setting can provide an opportunity for others to validate what is being perceived or to provide another perspective, By the way, there will be plenty of time to work things through if there are any misunderstandings."
4. Someone is asked to volunteer to be the first person to listen to members of the group. Each group member mentions both the appreciations and concerns about the volunteer who hears from all of the group members before responding, with the exception that questions of clarification are encouraged after each person mentions his or her items.
5. Each group member listens, in turn, either through volunteering to be next or through the simple procedure of rotating clockwise or counterclockwise from the first person.

One variation of this exercise is to have each member of the group put his or her name on the top of a sheet of flip-chart paper, and make two column headings (1) appreciations, and (2) concerns (or what to do differently or consider, and so on). Sheets are taped to the walls, and with a marking pen each member writes appreciations and concerns on each sheet. Once the writing is finished a volunteer is asked to display his or her sheet and read the items aloud to the group. This version is usually productive, but the first version permits more face-to-face interaction.

In instances in which lack of appreciation is a much more serious deficiency than concerns, focusing solely on appreciations can be a powerful and positive intervention in the life of the group. When the concerns segment is used, a mini-lecture from the facilitator on the nature of constructive feedback is desirable. Whenever a substantial conflict exists within the group, a more structured exercise, such as the role negotiation technique, is likely to be more appropriate.

Responsibility Charting

In work teams decisions are made, tasks are assigned, and individuals and small groups accomplish the tasks. This process is easily described on paper, but in reality a decision to have someone do something in somewhat more complex way than it appears because multiple actors are in fact involved in even the simplest task assignment. The person who does the work, one or more people who may approve or veto the work, and persons who may "contribute" in some way to the work while not being responsible for it all play a part in a given task. The issue is, *who is to do what, with what kind of involvement by others*?

A technique called *responsibility charting* helps to clarify who is responsible for what on various decisions and actions.[27] It is a simple, relevant, and effective technique for improving team functioning. Richard Beckhard and Ruben Harris explain the technique as follows:

> The first step is to construct a grid; the types of decisions and classes of actions that need to be taken in the total area of work under discussion are listed along the left-hand side of the grid, and the actors who might play some part in decision making on those issues are identified across the top of the grid....

The process, then, is one if assigning a behavior to each of the actors opposite each of the issues. There are four classes of behavior:

1. *Responsibility (R)*—the responsibility to initiate action to ensure that the decision is carried out. For example, it would be a department head's responsibility (R) to initiate at the departmental budget.
2. *Approval required, or the right to veto (A -V)*—the particular item must be reviewed by the particular role occupant, and this person has the option of either vetoing or approving it.
3. *Support (S)*—providing logistical support and resources for the particular item.
4. *Inform (I)*—must be informed and, by inference, cannot influence.[28]

A fifth behavior (or nonbehavior) is noninvolvement of a person with the decision; this is indicated on the chart with a dash (—). One type of responsibility chart is in Figure 8-3.

Responsibility charting is usually done in a work team context. Each decision or action is discussed and responsibility is assigned. Next, approval-veto, support, and form functions are assigned. Beckhard and Harris offer some guidelines for making the technique more effective. First, assign responsibility to only one person. That person initiates and then is responsible and accountable for the action. Second, avoid having too many people with an approval-veto function on an item. That will slow down task accomplishment or will negate it altogether. Third, if one person has approval-veto involvement on most decisions, that person could become a bottleneck for getting things done.

Fourth, the support function is critical. A person with a support role has to expend resources or produce something that is then used by the person responsible for the action. This support role and its specific demands must be clarified and clearly assigned. And, finally, the assignment of functions (letters) to persons at times becomes difficult. For example, a person may want A–V on an item, but not really need it; a person may not want S responsibility on an item, but should have it; or two persons each want R on a particular item, but only one can have it.

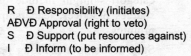

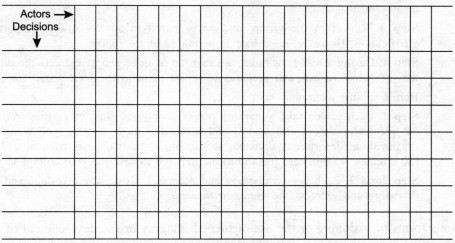

Source: Richard Beckhard and Reuben T. Harris, *Organizational Transitions: Managing* Complex Change (Figure 6.1), © 1977 by Addison-Wesley Publishing Company, Inc. Reprinted by permission of the publisher.

FIGURE 8-3 Responsibility Chart

A responsibility charting session can quickly identify who is to do what on new decisions as well as help to pinpoint reasons why old decisions are not being accomplished as desired. Responsibility charting is a good intervention to use to improve the task performance of a work team.

Visioning

Visioning is a term used for an intervention in which group members in one or more organizational groups develop and/or describe their vision of what they want the organization to be like in the future. The time frame may be anywhere from, say, six months to five years in the future.

The concept of visioning is credited to Ronald Lipitt. According to Weisbord, Lipitt began to tape-record planning meetings in 1949 and found that "people's voices grew softer, more stressed, depressed, as problems were listed and privatized. You could hear the energy drain away as the lists grew longer.[29] "In the 1950s, Lipitt, Ronald Fox, and Eva Schlinder-Rainman began referring to 'images of potential' rather than to problems as starting points for change, and by the 1970s were involving people in workshops visualizing "preferred futures."[30]

Various visioning techniques are used in team building. Here is an example:

Step 1. On notepaper, write down the characteristics you would like to see this organization have one and then two years from now. Use the following categories: (the categories might include products, customer and supplier relationships, human resources practices, leadership style, organizational structure, and so on). You have 90 minutes.

Step 2. Using a marking pen, make the characteristics visible on flipchart paper and display on the wall.

Step 3. Report to the group, and be prepared to answer questions pertaining to clarification. However, no debate is permitted at this point.

Step 4. During a half-hour break, a subgroup of three people extracts the themes from the individual reports and prepares to report them to the total group for discussion.

Here's another example:

Step 1. Each person take a marking pen (and/or yarn, glue, magazines from which to cut pictures, scissors and so on) and make a collage of what you would like this organization (department, division, and so on) to be two years from now: In an hour (30 minutes, 90 minutes, and so on) be prepared to describe your collage to the group.

Step 2and 3. Each person displays and describes his or where collage and the group discusses and extracts the common themes.[31]

Various forms of visioning or the use of mental imagery or the development of cognitive maps, are extensively used in strategic planning and in future search conferences. Strategic management activities and future search conferences are described in chapter 10.

Force-Field Analysis

Probably the oldest intervention in the OD practitioner's kit bag is the force-field analysis, a device for *understanding* a problematic situation and *planning corrective actions*. This technique rests on several assumptions; the present state of things (the current condition) is a quasi-stationary equilibrium representing a resultant in a field of opposing forces. A desired future state of affairs (the desired condition) could only be achieved by dislodging the current equilibrium, moving it to the desired state, and equilibrium at that point. To move the equilibrium level from the current to the desired condition the field of forces must be altered—by adding driving forces or by removing restraining forces.

This technique was first proposed by Kurt Lewin in 1947.[32] It is essentially a vector analysis—an analytical tool learned in first-year engineering classes. But the genius of Lewin was to apply the device to social problems, social equilibria, and social change. Lewin proposed that social phenomena—productivity of a factory, morale on a sports team, level of prejudice in a community, and so forth—could best be understood as processes being influenced by social forces and events. Furthermore, social phenomena tends to stabilize at equilibrium points because opposing forces come into balance over time.[33] The force-field analysis involves the following steps:

Step 1. Decide upon a problematic situation you are interested in improving, and carefully and completely describe the current condition. What is the status quo? What is the current condition? Why do you want it changed?

Step 2. Carefully and completely describe the desired condition, Where do you want to be? What is the desired state of things?

Step 3. Identify the forces and factors operating in the current force filed. Identify the driving forces pushing in the direction of the desired condition; identify the restraining forces pushing away from the desired condition. Identification and specification of the force field should be thorough and exhaustive so that a picture of why things are as they are becomes clear.

Step 4. Examine the forces. Which ones are strong, which are weak? Which forces are susceptible to influence, which are not? Which forces are under your control, what are not? (Important individual forces could themselves be subjected to a force-field analysis in order to understand them better).

Step 5. Strategies for moving the equilibrium from the current conditions to the desired condition are the following: add more driving forces; remove restraining forces; or do both. Lewin advises against simply adding new driving forces because they may increase both. Lewin advises against simply adding new driving forces because they may increase resistance and tension in the situation. Therefore, in this step select several important, adaptable restraining forces and develop action planes to remove them from the field of forces. As restraining forces are removed, the equilibrium shifts toward the desired condition. New driving forces may also be proposed and action plans developed to implement them.

Step 6. Implement that action plans that should cause the desired condition to be realized.

Step 7. Describe what actions must be taken to stabilize the equilibrium at the desired condition and implement those actions.

An example of the force-field analysis is shown in Figure 8-4. Assume that the management team of Plant X is concerned about excessive turnover and wants to correct that situation. They generate the force-field analysis shown in the figure.

Mapping the field of forces in this way permits the management team of plant X to understand the multiple facets of the problem. They would next decide which restraining forces should be removed and develop action plans to initiate those changes.

This technique is excellent for diagnosing change situations. We label it a team intervention (although it is also a tool for individuals) because it can be powerful and exciting when used by groups. Group analysis typically yields a comprehensive understanding of what is happening to cause the problem and what must be done to correct it.

Constructive Interventions

The team interventions described in this chapter can be highly rewarding for participants, but the dynamics must be addressed with empathy and skill. For example, the basic team-building process can generate both positive and negative feedback. The appreciation and concerns and the appreciative inquiry have major personal feedback components. Negative feedback can create considerable defensiveness, including denial, arguing or verbal retaliation. Even positive feedback can be awkward for some recipients, as well as for the persons offering the feedback. Team members need to behave in a way that creates a situation in which it is okay for someone to become teary or embarrassed when expressing or receiving positive sentiments. On the negative side, it needs to be clear that any name-calling or punitive or threatening behavior is off limits.

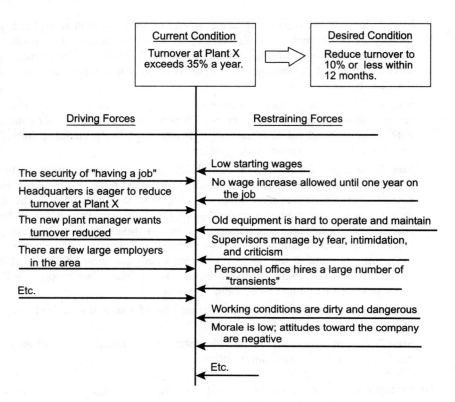

FIGURE 8-4 Force-Field Analysis of a Turnover Problem at Plant X.

To maximize the odds of such exercises being constructive for the entire team

- participants, particularly the formal leader, need to be informed of the nature of the intervention and largely "buy in" to the process beforehand
- the team needs some training in effective group skills
- team members need some coaching and practice in giving constructive feedback, in dealing with a range of feelings including defensive ones, and in processing conflict.
- the facilitator needs counseling and listening skills of a high order
- the formal leader needs some coaching to assure no punitive or retaliatory behavior will be a consequence of the exercise.

Ideally, some of this training occurs prior to the team-building sessions. However, training can be conducted in the context of team-building workshops. Team-building sessions can be ongoing laboratories for enhancing interpersonal, group, and leadership skills.

CONCLUDING COMMENTS

Team building produces such powerful positive results because it is an intervention in harmony with the nature of organizations as social systems. Further, under a system of division of labor, parts of the total organizational task are assigned to teams; and then that team assignment is subdivided and assigned to individuals. In most cases individual members of the team are *interdependently* related to each other and must coordinate and integrate individual efforts in order to achieve successful task accomplishment. Conceptualizing the team as the relevant system rather than individuals was the profound insight developed by early OD pioneers such as Blake, Shepard, Mouton, and McGregor; the team is the relevant unit for making individuals more effective. The efficacy of team building confirms the validity of that view.

In addition to discussing the nature of effective teams, in this chapter we have examined the major sets of activities that constitute team-building interventions and their rationales. They are at the center of OD activities. However, without the interventions directed to improving intergroup relations or interventions directed to improving the total organization, OD would not exist as a discipline today; instead it would only be an expanded "small-group" discipline. We want to underscore that while the small group or team is an entry point in most OD strategies, and while ongoing attention to team effectiveness is a sine qua non for successful OD efforts, achieving total organizational improvement.

NOTES

1. Wendell L. French, *Human Resources Management*, 4th ed. (Boston: Houghton Mifflin, 1998), p. 111.
2. Jon R. Katzenbach and Douglas K. Smith, "The Discipline of Teams," *Harvard Business Review*, 71 (March–April 1993), p. 112.
3. Richard S. Wellins, William C. Byham, and George R. Dixon, *Inside Teams* (San Francisco: Jossey-Bass, 1994), pp. 9–10. See also Susan Albers Mohrman, Susan G. Cohen, and Allan Mohrman, Jr., *Designing Team-Based Organizations* (San Francisco: Jossey-Bass, 1995).
4. Jon R. Katzenbach and Douglas K. Smith, *The Wisdom of Teams: Creating the High-Performance Organization* (Boston: Harvard Business School Press, 1993), p. 15.
5. Described in the symposium "The Role of OD in General Motor's Saturn Project" at the 1987 Academy of Management Annual Meeting in New Orleans, October 11, 1987.
6. Tom Peters, *Thriving on Chaos* (New York: Alfred A. Knopf, 1988). For more on cross-functional teams, see Rebecca A. Proehl, "Enhancing the Effectiveness of Cross-Functional Teams," *Leadership & Organization Development Journal* 17, no. 5 (1996), pp. 3–10.
7. Rensis Likert, *New Patterns of Management* (New York: McGraw-Hill, 1961).
8. Glenn M. Parker, *Team Players and Teamwork: The New Competitive Business Strategy* (San Francisco: Jossey-Bass, 1990), p. 33.
9. From Richard Beckhard, "Optimizing Team-Building Efforts," *Journal of Contemporary Business*, 1, no. 3 (Summer 1972), pp. 23–32.
10. Cecil Bell, Jr. and James Rosenzweig, "Highlights of an Organization Improvement Program in a City Government," in W. L. French, C. H. Bell, Jr., and R. A. Zawacki, eds., *Organization Development Theory, Practice, and Research* (Dallas: Business Publications, 1978).
11. Edgar H. Schein, *Process Consultation: Its Role in Organization Development* (Reading, MA: Addison-Wesley Publishing Company, 1969; 2d ed., 1988).
12. Schein, 1st ed., p. 13.
13. Ibid., pp. 102–103.
14. Ibid., p. 103.

15. Ibid., p. 116.

16. Ibid., p. 116. For more on process consultation, see Jane Moosbruker, "The Consultant as Process Leader," *OD Practitioner*, 21 (March 1989), pp. 10–12.

17. F. Perls, R. Hefferline, and P. Goodman, *Gestalt Therapy* (New York: Julian Press, 1951). See also F. Perls, *Gestalt Therapy Verbatim* (Lafayette, CA: Real People Press, 1969).

18. Robert L. Harman, "Goals of Gestalt Therapy," *Professional Psychology*, (May 1974), pp. 178–184.

19. Stanley M. Herman and Michael Korenich, *Authentic Management: A Gestalt Orientation to Organizations and Their Development* (Reading, MA: Addison-Wesley, 1977).

20. I. Dayal and J. M. Thomas, "Operation KPE: Developing a New Organization," *Journal of Applied Behavioral Science*, 4, no. 4 (1968), pp. 473–506. The present discussion is based on this article.

21. Ibid., p. 488.

22. Roger Harrison, "When Power Conflicts Trigger Team Spirit," *European Business* (Spring 1972), pp. 27–65.

23. Ibid., p. 58.

24. Ibid., p. 58. [Harrison's emphasis.]

25. These steps are paraphrased from ibid., pp. 59–63.

26. Ibid., p. 63.

27. See Richard Beckhard and Reuben T. Harris, *Organizational Transitions: Managing Complex Change* (Reading, MA: Addison-Wesley, 1977), pp. 76–82.

28. Ibid., p. 76. See also Richard Beckhard and Wendy Pritchard, *Changing the Essence: The Art of Creating and Leading Fundamental Change in Organizations* (San Francisco: Jossey-Bass Publishers, 1992), pp. 83–84.

29. Marvin R. Weisbord, "Toward Third-Wave Managing and Consulting," *Organizational Dynamics*, 15 (Winter 1987), pp. 20–21.

30. Marvin R. Weisbord, *Productive Workplaces* (San Francisco: Jossey-Bass Publishers, 1987), p. 283.

31. For more on the use of collages, see Fordyce and Weil, *Managing WITH People*, pp. 152–155.

32. Kurt Lewin, "Frontiers in Group Dynamics: Concept, Method, and Reality in Social Science; Social Equilibria and Social Change," *Human Relations*, 1, no. 1 (June 1947), pp. 5–41.

33. See the following articles in *The Planning of Change*, W. G. Bennis, K. D. Benne, and R. Chin, eds., (New York: Holt, Rinehart and Winston, 1964): "The Utility of System Models and Developmental Models for Practitioners" by Robert Chin, pp. 201–214; "Force Field Analysis Applied to a School Situation" by David H. Jenkins, pp. 238–244.

CHAPTER 9

Intergroup and Third-Party Peacemaking Interventions

W hen tension, conflict, or competition exist among groups, some predictable things happen: each group sees the other as an "enemy" rather than as a neutral object; each group describes the other in terms of negative stereotypes; interaction and communication between the two groups decrease, cutting off feedback and data input between them; what intergroup communication and interaction does take place is typically distorted and inaccurate; each group begins to prize itself and its products more positively and to denigrate the other group and its products; each group believes and acts as though it can do no wrong and the other group can do no right; under certain circumstances the groups may commit acts of sabotage (of various kinds) against the other group.[1] Most people are aware of the existence of considerable intergroup conflict in organizations, and most people are aware of the patterns of behavior of groups in conflict. But few people knew ways to alleviate the conflict to avoid the consequences of the conflict.

Several strategies for reducing intergroup conflict have been identified in the literature. They include a "common enemy" (an outside object or group that both groups dislike, which brings the groups closer together); increasing the interaction and communication among the groups (increased interaction under favorable conditions tends to be associated with increased positive feelings and sentiments); finding a supraordinate goal (a goal that both groups desire to achieve but that neither can achieve without the help of the other); rotating the members of the groups; and instituting some forms of training.[2] Even knowing these strategies for reducing intergroup conflict may not be especially helpful—the questions still remain. How can we *implement* conflict-reducing mechanisms? and How do we *begin*?

The dynamics of conflict and its resolution between *two persons* in organizations are similar to between-group conflict and, therefore, in this chapter we will examine the technology to reduce interpersonal conflict as well as intergroup conflict. These interventions are important because of the serious impact intergroup and interpersonal conflict has on team and organizational functioning and on human satisfaction. In addition, the development of techniques to improve systems larger than single teams has marked a significant step toward being able to improve total systems.

INTERGROUP TEAM-BUILDING INTERVENTIONS

The focus of this team-building group of OD interventions is on improving intergroup relations. The goals of these activities are to increase communications and interactions between work-related groups, to reduce the amount of dysfunctional competition, and to replace a parochial independent point of view with an awareness of the necessity for interdependence of action calling on the best efforts of both groups. A significant amount of dysfunctional energy spent in competition, misunderstanding, miscommunication, and misperception is not uncommon between groups. Organizational reward structures often encourage such behavior through emphasis on unit goal attainment as contrasted with total-organization goal attainment. Organization development methods provide ways of increasing intergroup cooperation and communication, as we will see in the following series of interventions.

One set of activities developed by Blake, Shepard, and Mouton is widely applicable to situations where relations between groups are strained or overtly hostile.[3] The steps are these:[4]

Step 1. The leaders of the two groups (or the total membership) meet with the consultant and are asked if they think the relations between the two groups can be better and are asked if they are willing to search for mechanisms or procedures that may improve intergroup relations. Their concurrence that they are willing to search for ameliorative mechanisms is all that they are asked to commit themselves to at that time. If they agree, with some prior planning as to time and place, the following activities take place.

Step 2. The intergroup intervention per se begins now. The two groups meet in separate rooms and build two lists. In one list they give their thoughts, attitudes, feelings, and perceptions of the other group—what the other group is like, what it does that gets in their way, and so on. In the second list the group tries to predict what the other group is saying about them in its list—that is, they try to anticipate what the other group dislikes about them, how the other group sees them and so on. Both groups build these two lists.

Step 3. The two groups come together to share with each other the information on the lists. Group A reads its list of how it sees Group B and what it dislikes about Group B. Group B reads it list of how it sees Group A and what it dislikes about it. The consultant imposes a rule of no distinction of the items on the lists and limits questions to clarifying the meaning of the lists only. Next, Group A reads its list of what is expected Group B would say about it, and Group B reads its list of what it thought Group A would say about it.

Step 4. The two groups return to their separate meeting places and are given two tasks. First, they react to and discuss what they have learned about themselves and the other group. It typically happens that many areas of disagreement and friction are discovered to rest on misperceptions and miscommunication; these issues are readily resolved through the information sharing of the lists. The differences between the two groups are seen not to be as great as was imagined, and the problems between them are seen to be fewer than imagined. After this discussion, the group is given a second task: to make a list of the priority issues that still need to be resolved between the two groups. The list is generally much smaller than the original list. Each group builds such a list.

Step 5. The two groups come back together and share lists with each other. After comparing their list, they then make one list containing the issues and problems that should be resolved. They set priorities on the items in terms of importance and immediacy. Together they generate action steps for resolving the issues and assign responsibilities for the actions. "Who will do what when" is agreed upon for the most important items. That concludes the intervention.

Step 6. As a follow-up to the intergroup team–building activity, a meeting of the two groups or their leaders is desirable to determine whether the action steps have in fact occurred and to assess how the groups are doing on their action plans. This step ensures that the momentum of the intergroup intervention is not lost.

This procedure can also be used with large groups drawn from two large populations. For example, after an expression of interest by parole officers and police officers in improving mutual understanding and relationships, we spent an evening with the two groups in an exercise called Project Understanding. By coincidence, members of the two groups happened to be attending workshops the same week at the same conference center. We simply divided the two large populations into small groups and paired off these small groups and conducted an exercise almost identical to the sequence given. Tentative action recommendations were posted in the large general session room for informal perusal during a social activity that followed.

A slightly modified version of this procedure is presented by Fordyce and Weil based on their experience at TRW Systems.[5] In this version, two groups that have decided to work on improving their intergroup relations come together for the intergroup team-building meeting and are separated into two meeting rooms. Each group is assigned the task of building three lists as follows:

1. A "positive feedback" list containing the things the groups values and likes about the other group;
2. A "bug" list containing the things the group does not like about the other group;
3. An "empathy" list containing a prediction of what the other group is saying in its list.

The two groups come together, and spokespeople for the groups read their lists. Questions are limited to issues of clarification only; discussion of the items is disallowed.

At this point, instead of breaking into separate groups again, the total group together builds an agenda or a master list of the major problems and unresolved issues between the two groups. The issues are ranked in terms of importance.

Subgroups are formed containing members from each group and are given the task of discussing and working on each item. The subgroups all report back to the total group.

On the basis of the information from the subgroups, the work on the issues that has been going on, and the total information shared by the two persons, the participants now build a list of action steps for improving intergroup relations and commit themselves to carrying out the actions. For each of the action steps, people are assigned specific responsibilities and an overall schedule of completion for the action steps is recorded.

THIRD- PARTY PEACEMAKING INTERVENTIONS

Conflict management can be a major component in the professional life of the OD practitioner. As Fisher, Ury, and Patton say in their book *Getting to Yes*, "More and more occasions require negotiation; conflict is a growth industry."[6] In this section we will discuss OD interventions that can be used when two persons are in conflict and some of the theory underlying these interventions.

Walton's Approach to Third-Party Peacemaking

Third-party interventions into conflict situations have the potential to control (contain) the conflict or resolve it. R. E. Walton has presented a statement of theory and practice for third-party peacemaking interventions that is both important in its own right and important for its role in organization development.[7] His book is directed toward interpersonal conflict-understanding and intervening in ways to control or resolve the conflict. This intervention technique is somewhat related to intergroup relations described previously, but many aspects are unique to conflict situations involving only two people. In this section, rather than describe specific interventions, we explicate some of the features of the theory presented by Walton.

A basic feature of third-party intervention is confrontation: the two principals must be willing to confront the fact that conflict exists and that it has consequences for the effectiveness of the two parties involved. The third party must know how, when, and where to utilize confrontation tactics that expose the conflict for examination.

The third party must be able to diagnose conflict situations, and Walton presents a diagnostic model of interpersonal conflict based on four basic elements: the conflict issues, the precipitating circumstances, the conflict-relevant acts of the principals, and the consequences of the conflict.[8] In addition, conflict is a cyclical process, and the cycles may be benevolent, malevolent, or self-maintaining. For accurate diagnosis it is particularly important to know the source of the conflict. Walton speaks to this issue:

> A major distinction is drawn between substantive and emotional conflict. Substantive issues involve disagreements over policies and practices, competitive bids for the same resources, and differing conceptions of roles and role relationships. Emotional issues involve negative feelings between the parties (e.g., anger, distrust, scorn, resentment, fear, and rejection).[9]

This distinction is important for the third-party consultant in that substantive issues require problem-solving and bargaining between the principals, while emotional issues require restructuring perceptions and working through negative feelings.

Intervention tactics for the third party consist of structuring confrontation and dialogue between the principals. Many choice points exist for the consultant. Walton lists the ingredients of productive confrontation. (Our interpretation is shown in brackets).

1. Mutual positive motivation [both parties are disposed to attempt to resolve the conflict].
2. Balance in the situational power of the two principals [power parity is most conducive to success].

3. Synchronization of their confrontation efforts [initiatives and readiness to confront should occur in concert between the two parties].
4. Appropriate pacing of the differentiation and integration phases of a dialogue [time must be allowed for working through of negative feelings and clarification of ambivalent or positive feelings].
5. Conditions favoring openness in dialogue [norms supporting openness should be structured for the parties].
6. Reliable communicative signs [making certain each can understand the other].
7. Optimum tension in the situation [there should be moderate stress on the parties].[10]

Most of these ingredients are self-explanatory, but some elaboration may be helpful on the differentiation and integration phases. In the differentiation phase of conflict, the principals clarify the differences that divide them and sort out the negative feelings they have; in the integration phase, the principals seek to clarify their commonalities, the positive feelings or ambivalence that may exist, and the commonality of their goals.

The third party will intervene directly and indirectly in facilitating dialogue between the principals. Examples of direct interventions would be interviewing the principals before a confrontation meeting, helping to set the agenda, attending to the pace of the dialogue, and refereeing the interaction; examples of more subtle interventions of the third party would be setting the meeting on neutral turf, setting time boundaries on the interaction, and the like.

ORGANIZATION MIRROR INTERVENTIONS

The *organization mirror* is a set of activities in which a particular organizational group, the host group, gets feedback from representatives from several other organizational groups about how it is perceived and regarded. This intervention is designed to improve the relationships between groups and increase the intergroup work effectiveness. It is different from the intergroup team-building intervention in that three or more groups are involved, representatives of other work-related groups typically participate rather than the full membership, and the focus is to assist the host unit that requested the meeting.[11]

The flow of events is as follows: an organizational unit that is experiencing difficulties with units to which its work is related may ask key people from those other units to come to a meeting to provide feedback on how they see the host unit. The consultant often interviews the people attending the meeting before the meeting takes place in order to get a sense of the problems and their magnitude, to prepare the participants, and to answer any questions that the participants may have.

After opening remarks by the manager of the host group, in which he or she sets the climate by stating that the host group genuinely wants to hear how the unit is perceived, the consultant feeds back to the total group information from the interviews. The outsiders "fishbowl" to discuss and explore the data presented by the consultant. (The fishbowl is a group seating and talking configuration in which there is an inner circle of chairs for people who talk and an outside circle of observers and noninteractors.)

The fishbowl allows the invited participants to talk about the host unit in a natural, uninterrupted way while the host group members listen and learn. Following this, the host group members fishbowl and talk about what they have heard, ask for any clarification, and generally seek to understand the information they have heard. At this point, a general discussion can ensure that everyone understands what is being said, but at this time these participants do not start to work on the problems that have been recovered.

For actually working on the problems, subgroups composed of both host group members and invited participants are formed. The subgroups are asked to identify the most important changes that need to be made to improve the host unit's effectiveness. After the small groups have identified the key problems, the total group convenes to make a master list to work out specific action plans for bringing about the changes deemed most important. The total group hears a summary report from each subgroup. Action plans are firmed up, people are assigned to tasks, and target dates for completion are agreed upon. This last group of activities concludes the organization mirror intervention, but a follow-up meeting to assess progress and to review action steps is strongly recommended.

In a short period of time an organizational unit can get the feedback it needs to improve its relations with significant work-related groups. The organization mirror intervention provides this feedback effectively. It is imperative that following the meeting the host group in fact implements the action plans that were developed in the meeting.

PARTNERING

In situations in which two or more organizations are likely to incur unnecessary conflict and cost overruns such as in the owner-contractor relationship in a large construction project, an intervention called *partnering* can be productive for both parties. Partnering is a variation of team building, intergroup team-building, and strategic planning having the objective of forming 'an effective problem-finding/problem-solving management team composed of personnel from both parties, thus creating a single culture with one set of goals and objectives for the project."[12] Partnering has been used in the private sector—for example, Fluor Daniel and Du Pont—and in military and government construction.[13]

The people from both parties who should be involved are identified by Donald Mosely and colleagues: "Ideally, partnering involves all the functions in the construction project, including engineering and design, site management, and home office support.[14] In a typical partnering project involving the U.S. Army Corps of Engineers and a contractor, interventions included these steps or events:

1. The Corps of Engineers selected the consultants.
2. A retreat at a neutral site lasting form two and one-half to four and one-half days was scheduled prior to the beginning of construction. Participants included key managers from home offices, site managers from both the Corps and the contractor, and the consultants.
3. The workshop focused on "team-building, action research, and planning including advanced conflict resolution methods, developing a shared vision, and strategic planning with "break the ice" and to demonstrate the utility of group decision making. Lists were developed and shared showing both "strengths" and "problems" of the Corps and the contractor. Mixed groups, comprised members from both parties, selected one or more of the problems to diagnose further, identified and evaluated possible courses of action, and made recommendations to the total group.

4. At the workshop, mutual commitment to team work, equitable problem solving and open communications was made.
5. A follow-up workshop—this one two days in length—was held three months after construction began.
6. At six months, "on-site data-gathering visits were conducted with follow-up two-day workshops involving all key players."

While partnering did not solve all of the problems that surfaced during the life of the various projects, high success rates have been reported, and participants tended to report "better results than on previous non-partnered projects." As a result, partnering has been used on several other large government projects involving the Air Force, Navy, and NASA, and their contractors.[15]

CONCLUDING COMMENTS

Intergroup team building, third-party peacemaking, the organization mirror, and partnering are four major interventions that have been developed to improve intergoup and interpersonal relations. They all work; that is, they actually reduce intergroup and interpersonal conflict and improve relationships.

Why these interventions work is not totally understood. But the underlying dynamics that cause these techniques to be efficacious are probably the following:

1. The interactions between the groups are *controlled* and a *structure is imposed to maintain control.*
2. The interventions are based on data, and the *data are complete and public.*
   When group A puts down all the things about group B that it dislikes, that gives group B a grasp of the scope of the problem issues and permits a comprehensive understanding of the differences and problems. Knowing the scope of the issues and having a comprehensive understanding of them is probably a necessary ingredient in making a group (or an individual) move from a defensive posture to a problem-solving stance.
3. The early stages of these interventions—making lists and sharing them and using the fish-bowl technique—lead the participants to *experience feelings of success in dealing with the other group.* Feelings of anxiety, apprehension, and hostility start to give way to feelings of competence and success as the early stages of the interventions produce better communication and understanding than the participants had expected. Nothing succeeds like success, and when the early stages are perceived as a success experience by both groups they feel optimistic that "We *can* work together with those people." Participants are watching for subtle cues of defensiveness, resistance to the data, stubbornness, and the like, and the controlled nature of the process make most of these unnecessary.
4. The *constructive, problem-solving* tone of the meetings, set by the leaders or the consultant, *carries a force of its own.* If people want to be negative, destructive, and defensive, they have to go against the tenor of the meeting. This attempt to sabotage is increasingly difficult to do if a clear problem-solving climate has been established.

Of all the dynamics of the intergroup and interpersonal interventions, those just listed indicate some of the reasons why such interventions usually work. The intergroup and interpersonal interventions are an important part of the OD practitioner's repertoire. They require some skill in their execution, but the process itself carries the brunt of the work in making them effective interventions.

NOTES

1. Research evidence for these statements comes from the following sources: M. Sherif and Carolyn Sherif, *Groups in Harmony and Tension* (New York: Harper & Row, 1953); and R. R. Blake and Jane S. Mouton, "Conformity, Resistance, and Conversion," in I. A. Berg and B. M. Bass, eds., *Conformity and Deviation* (New York: Harper & Row, 1961). For a succinct summary of this issue, see E. H. Schein, *Organizational Psychology*, 2d ed. (Englewood Cliffs, NJ: Prentice-Hall, 1970), chapter 5.
2. Schein, *Organizational Psychology*, chapter 5.
3. R. R. Blake, H. A. Shepard, and J. S. Mouton, *Managing Intergroup Conflict in Industry* (Houston: Gulf, 1965).
4. This discussion is based on R. Beckhard, *Organization Development: Strategies and Models* (Reading, MA: Addison-Wesley, 1969), pp. 33–35.
5. This discussion is taken from J. K. Fordyce and R. Weil, *Managing WITH People* (Reading, MA: Addison-Wesley, 1971), pp. 124–30.
6. Roger Fisher and William Ury, with Bruce Patton, *Getting to Yes*, 2d ed. (New York: Penguin Books, 1991), p. xvii.
7. R. E. Walton, *Interpersonal Peacemaking: Confrontations and Third Party Consultation* (Reading, MA: Addison-Wesley, 1969).
8. Ibid., p. 71.
9. Ibid., p. 73.
10. Ibid. This list is from p. 94; Walton's discussion of the list is on pp. 94–115. For a newer edition of this work, see Richard E. Walton, *Managing Conflict: Interpersonal Dialogue and Third-Party Roles*, 2d ed. (Reading, MA: Addison-Wesley Publishing Company, 1987). For a classic statement on interpersonal conflict, see Carl R. Rogers, "Dealing With Psychological Tensions," *Journal of Applied Behavioral Science*, 1 (First Quarter 1965), p. 13.
11. Fordyce and Weil, in *Managing WITH People*, discuss this intervention in detail, pp. 101–105.
12. Carl Moore, Donald Mosley, and Michelle Slagle, "Partnering: Guidelines for Win-Win Project Management," *Project Management Journal*, 23 (March 1992), p. 18.
13. In addition to the other sources cited, this description of partnering is based on Donald Mosley, Carl Moore, Michelle Slagle, and Daniel Burns, "Partnering in the Construction Industry: Win-Win Strategic Management in Action," *National Productivity Review*, 10 (Summer 1991), pp. 319–325.
14. Ibid., p. 320.
15. Ibid., pp. 320–325. See also Donald C. Mosley, Jeanne Maes, Michelle L. Slagle, and Carl Moore, "An Analysis & Evaluation of a Successful Partnering Project: The Bonneville Navigation Lock," *Organization Development Journal*, 11 (Spring 1993), pp. 57–65.

CHAPTER 10
Comprehensive OD Interventions

In this chapter we examine OD interventions that are comprehensive in terms of the extent to which the total organization is involved and/or the depth of cultural change addressed. Included are discussions of "getting the whole system in the room," "search and future search conferences." Beckhard's confrontation meeting, strategic management activities, real time strategic change, stream analysis, survey feedback (linked to system 4T), appreciative inquiry, Grid OD, and Schein's cultural analysis. We will also discuss large-scale change and high-performance systems, and transorganizational development (TD), a variation of OD that involves several organizations.

"GETTING THE WHOLE SYSTEM IN THE ROOM"

Phrases like "getting the whole system in the room" are appearing with increasing frequency in OD practice.[1] What OD professionals are talking about is the usefulness of getting all of the key actors of a complex organization or system together in a team-building, future-planning kind of session. Future search conferences comprise one version of "getting whole systems in the room," and Beckhard's confrontation meeting is another version. In a sense, partnering, as described in Chapter 10, operates from the same mode.

The rationale for inviting all of the key actors of a complex system to meet together is congruent with systems theory and an extension of the assumptions underlying team building. If you get all of the people with crucial interdependencies together to work on matters of mutual concern, good things can happen. In this case, the system is conceptualized as a total organization or as several organizations in interaction.

"Getting the whole system in one room" has a long and venerable history, including the art and science of *conference planning* and running large meetings. For example, Burke and Beckhard's book, *Conference Planning*, has essays that go back to the 1940s and that are relevant to today's OD practice.[2] Examples of the "whole system" might be as follows:

- Managers of all of the functional areas in a business.
- Representatives of top management, a cross section of employees from all levels, and supplier and customer representatives.
- All of the librarians in a state or region plus the direct and staff of the state library system.
- Directors of all of the social service agencies in a community.

The latter is an example of the overlap between OD and community development, an overlap that has been apparent since scholar/practitioners like Eva Schindler–Rainman were working with community agencies in the 1950s and 1960s (see chapter 2).

SEARCH CONFERENCES AND FUTURE SEARCH CONFERENCES

"Search conferences" and "future search conferences" are similar, but have slightly different geographical and theoretical foundations. "Search" conferences largely emerged with consulting practices in Great Britain, Europe, and Australia, while "future search" conferencing has been largely an American phenomenon, although both have had extensive applications in the United States. In comparing these two large group interventions in their book *The Search Conference*, Merrelyn Emery and Ronald Purser, who have been associated with British/Australian practice, see U.S. "future search" literature as taking "a more psycho-therapeutic view of humanity" in contrast to the Births and Australian orientation.[3] However, both consulting modalities stem from the interaction extensively influenced by the works of Kurt Lewin.

The basic design of the search conference has the three following phases as quoted from Emery and Purser's *The Search Conference*:

Phase One: Environmental Appreciation
Changes in the world around us
Desirable and probable future

Phase Two: System Analysis
History of the system
Analysis of the present system
Desirable future for the system

Phase Three: Integration of System and Environment
Dealing with constraints
Strategies and action plans[4]

One version of Weisbord's future search conference model consists of the following steps.[5]

1. The consultants (or conference managers) meet with a voluntary committee of four to six potential participants. Many aspects are planned, including the overall focus, who should attend, dates, and times, locations and meals, group tasks, and so on. The conferences are usually planned to start on Wednesday evening (with dinner followed by the first working session) and to end up on Friday afternoon.

2. Up to 50 or 60 people are invited. Depending on the nature of the focus, the whole system is represented in the conference. Such representation might mean people from all of the functional areas and levels of the organization; persons from all racial, ethnic, sex, and age backgrounds; and might include customers, suppliers, and union leaders. People are asked to bring newspaper and magazine clippings that describe events they believe are influencing and shaping the organization's future.

3. Participants sit at tables of six to eight, with an easel, marking pens, and tape. Depending on the focus and assigned tasks, groupings may vary during the conference, with group membership assigned or based on self-selection. All group output is recorded on easel paper, all ideas are valid, and agreement is not required. The conference is not to solve problems, but to generate awareness, understanding, and mutual support. (Conference members, however, make action recommendations at the end of the workshop.)

4. The conference has four or five segments, each listing up to a half day. As Weisbord describes it, "Each one requires that people (a) build a database, (b) look at it together, (c) interpret what they find, and (d) draw conclusions for action.[6]

5. *The first major activity focuses on the past.* Although sitting at a table with others, each person individually is asked to make notes on significant events, milestones, and so on, that they can recall relative to each of the past three decades and from three perspectives; self, company (or town or industry), and society. These individual notes are transferred to sheets on the wall that is organized by topic and by decade.

   The group at each table is asked to analyze one theme—self, company, or society—across the three past decades and to extract patterns and meanings. Each table then reports to the total group, and a consultant notes trends. The total conference then interprets "good and bad trends and the direction of movement of each."

6. *The second major activity focuses on present factors*—both external and internal—that are shaping the future of the organization. Relative to the external environment, participants are asked to share their newspaper and magazine clippings, with their table group and indicate why they think the article is important. Each group selects priorities from lists that are developed. Next, internal events and trends are surfaced by asking people to generate a list of "prouds" and "sorries" relative to what is currently going on within the organization. People vote for the "proudest prouds" and the "sorriest sorries," and the results are displayed and discussed. The conference managers probe, note key statements, and summarize on flip charts.

7. *The third major activity focuses on the future.* New groups are formed and are given one to two hours to develop a draft of a preferred future scenario. "They are asked to imagine the most desirable, attainable future five years out.[7] Varieties of media are used like colored paper, crayon, scissors, tape, and so on. The groups then report to the total conference.

BECKHARD'S CONFRONTATION MEETING

The *confrontation meeting*, developed by Richard Beckhard, is a one-day meeting of the entire management of an organization in which they take a reading of their own organizational health.[8] In a series of activities, the management group generates information about its major problems, analyzes the underlying causes, develops action plans to correct the problems, and sets a schedule for completed remedial work. This intervention is an important one in organization development; it is a quick, simple, and reliable way in which to generate data about an organization and to set action plans for organizational improvement. Beckhard says of the confrontation meeting:

Experience shows that it is appropriate where

- there is a need for the total management group to examine its own workings.
- very limited time is available for the activity.

- top management wishes to improve the conditions quickly.
- there is enough cohesion in the top team to ensure follow-up.
- there is enough real commitment to resolving the issue on the part of top management.
- The organization is experiencing, or has recently experienced, some major change.[9]

The steps involved in the confrontation meeting are as follows:[10]

Step 1. Climate Setting (45 to 60 minutes). The top manager introduces the session by stating his or her goals for the meeting, citing the necessity for free and open discussion of issues and problems, and making it clear that individuals will not be punished for what they say. This introduction is generally followed by a statement from the consultant regarding the importance of communication within organizations, the practicability of organization problem solving, and the desirability of addressing and solving organizational problems.

Step 2. Information Collecting (1 hour). Small groups of seven or eight members are formed on the basis of heterogeneity of composition; that is, a maximum mixture of people from different functional areas and working situations compose each team. The only rule is that bosses and subordinates cannot be put together on the same team. The top management group meets as a separate group during this time. The charge to all the groups is as follows:

Think of yourself as an individual with needs and goals. Also think as a person concerned about the total organization. What are the obstacles, "demotivators," poor procedures or policies, unclear goals, or poor attitudes that exist today? What different conditions, if any, would make the organization more effective and make life in the organization better?[11]

The groups work on this task for an hour and recorder/ reporters list the results of the discussion.

Step 3. Information Sharing (1 hour). Reporters from each small group report the group's complete findings to the total group, which are placed on newsprint on the walls. The total list of items is categorized, usually by the meeting leader, into a few major categories that may be based on type of problems (e.g., communications problems), type of relationship (e.g., troubles with top management), or type of area (e.g., problems with the accounting department).

Step 4. Priority Setting and Group Action Planning (1 hour and 15 minutes). This step typically follows a break during which time the items from the lists are duplicated for distribution to everyone. In a 15-minute general session, the meeting leader goes through the list of items and puts a category assignment so that everyone has his or her own copy of the categorized items. Next the participants form into functional, natural work teams reflecting the way they are organized in the organization. Each group is headed by the top manager in the group. The groups are asked to respond to a three-part charge, that is, to do three tasks. First, they are to identify the problems they think should be the priority issues for top management. Third, they are to determine how they will communicate the results of the confrontation meeting to their subordinates. This activity completes the confrontation meeting for all the managers except for the top management group.

Step 5. Immediate Follow-Up by Top-Team (1 to 3 hours). The top management team meets after the rest of the participants have left to plan the first follow-up action steps and to determine what actions should be taken on the basis of what they have learned during the day. These follow-up action plans are communicated to the rest of the management group within several days.

Step 6. Progress Review (2 hours). A follow-up meeting with the total management group is held four to six weeks later to report progress and to review the actions resulting from the confrontation meeting.

These steps represent the flow of activities for the confrontation meeting. It is an excellent way to get fast results leading toward organization improvement. Beckhard believes that the confrontation meeting provides a quick and accurate means for diagnosing organizational health, promotes constructive problem identification and problem solving, enhances upward communication within the organization, and increases involvement and commitment to action on the part of the entire managerial group.[12] We agree with his assessment.

STRATEGIC MANAGEMENT ACTIVITIES

Many OD programs and interventions are directed toward the internal workings of the organization. Interventions such as team building, managing intergroup relations, survey feedback, and conflict resolution are intended to fine tune the organization to make it function better. This internal focus must be complemented with an external focus if OD is truly to serve the best interests of the organization. In other words, OD must develop outward-looking interventions directed toward environmental analysis and strategic planning to ensure that the organization is in synchrony with its environment.

The field of business policy developed the concept of strategic management, which is defined as the development and implementation of the organization's grand design or overall strategy for relating to its current and future environmental demands. The concept is described by Schendel and Hofers as follows: "There are six major tasks that comprise the strategic management process: (1) goal formulation; (2) environmental analysis; (3) strategy evaluation; (4) strategy evaluation; (5) strategy implantation; and (6) strategic control.[13]

Developing organizational goals is the first step, which means defining the mission and purpose of the organization. Next an assessment is made of the constraints and opportunities afforded by the environment. The present environment can be monitored directly; constraints and opportunities of the future environment must be predicted. Strategic plans, derived from goals and environmental analysis, are then developed, implemented, and monitored for results. Generally, some dominant coalition of key decision-makers in the organization is responsible for the strategic management process.

Additional OD strategic planning techniques will be described here. One technique, used by our colleague Charles E. Summer who conducts strategic planning activities with organizations, is based on four questions:

1. What is your present strategy?
2. What are the opportunities and threats to that strategy?
3. What are your strengths and weaknesses to meet those threats and opportunities?
4. What kind of future policies must you adopt to avoid the threats and maximize your strengths?[14]

A top management team will work for six months to a year answering these four questions. Meetings are held every one to two months; extensive data collection and analysis take place between meetings. It can be seen that the first question requires an in-depth analysis of what the organization is currently doing or what it thinks it is doing. The second question directs attention to the external environment and to forces that may affect the organization's ability to compete and remain viable. The third question starts to mesh organizational capabilities with environmental demands. The fourth question addressees the actions and changes needed to allow the organization to operate as desired in the future.

Open systems planning (OSP) is a technique developed by Charles Krone, G. K. Jayaram, and others to assess the environment in a systematic way.[15] Here the top team develops a number of scenarios. The Present scenario is a description of the expectations and demands of environmental domains and internal groups and subgroups, along with a description of the current response to those demands. The Realistic Future scenario projects what the future demand picture is likely to be and what the future response pattern is likely to be *if the organization makes no adaptive changes*. This extrapolation is likely to highlight impending undesirable events if the organization simply maintains the status quo. Next, an Idealistic Future scenario is developed that describes what an ideal or desired demand system would be like and identifies what actions would have to be taken by the organization to cause the desired state to exist. These needed changes are then analyzed for feasibility and costs. Open systems planning thus helps decision-makers to move back and forth from present to future and from "what is" to "what should be." These word pictures make salient the need for organizational adaptation and change and lead to action planning and implementation.

Organization development practitioners need to become experts in strategic management processes and need to have a thorough knowledge of strategic management content. Excellent sources for learning about strategic management content are the following: Michael Porter's books, *Competitive Advantage*, and *Competition in Global Industries*, summarize and synthesize the field.[16] Tregoe and Zimmerman's *Top Management Strategy* presents the practical side of strategic planning.[17] These two authors worked with hundreds of top management teams helping them to develop strategic plans for their organizations. Kenichi Ohmae's book, *The Mind of the Strategist*, is highly recommended.[18] *Strategy Pure and Simple* by Michel Robert is clear and practical.[19] *The Art of the Long View* by Peter Schwartz describes scenario planning, a strategic planning method developed by Royal Dutch Shell Company,[20] *Strategic Planning: Models and Analytical Techniques* by Robert Dyson gives a thorough coverage of different strategic planning techniques.[21]

A number of OD practitioners have realized the necessity for OD to become more actively involved in strategic management issues in organizations. Zand observed that there is considerable mistrust and conflict often separating strategic management people and D people in organizations.[22] As a result, both strategic planning and implementation suffer. Zand calls for closer cooperation between these two fields that can offer so much to each other. Greiner and Schein challenge OD practitioners to become more involved in the strategic management process—both to improve these activities in organizations and to build a power base for the practitioner.[23] Paul Buller recommends blending practices with strategic management to enhance the effectiveness of both disciplines.[24] Buller suggests six areas where OD can assist strategic management as follows: "The six primary activities that promote a better strategic management OD blend are: to assess and develop the organization's state of readiness for strategic change, facilitate the strategic planning process, implement strategy, create the conditions for successful mergers and acquisitions, manage organizational decline, and develop leadership skills."[25] He explains how specific OD interventions can facilitate these processes. We agree with Buller in these six strategic areas OD can and should make valuable contributions to organization leaders.

REAL TIME STRATEGIC CHANGE

A process congruent with search conferences and strategic management activities is Robert Jacob's "real time strategic change" intervention. Some aspects of this intervention are derived from the work of Ronald Lippitt.[26] "Real time " as used in the Jacob's book refers to "the simultaneous planning and implementation of individual, group, or organizationwide changes."[27]

As part of this unfolding intervention, a critical mass of organizational members— sometimes hundreds—come together for a three-day meeting to discuss organization-wide issues. The assumptions underlying this event are:

- A leadership team has decided that its organization needs a new strategic direction based on drivers for change either from inside or outside their own organization;
- A draft strategy has been developed by a leadership team prior to the event;
- The leadership group is open to feedback on the strategy by participants, and to revising it based on this feedback; and
- The participants in this event comprise the entire organization, or a critical mass of people from a larger organization.[28]

A strategy for the change effort is crucial. Jacobs describes six key steps for developing strategy:

1. Identifying and clarifying the basic, important issues facing the organization as a whole.
2. Agreeing on an overall purpose for the change effort.
3. Deciding which people need to be involved in the change effort and how.
4. Determining how much influence these people need to have over the development of this strategy.
5. Clarifying the information people will need to do quality work and make wise decisions regarding their collective future.
6. Exploring the methods, processes, and approaches that will boost support people in making real time strategic changes.[29]

Although the three-day event is much more complex than can be shown in an agenda, the planned flow of events is shown in Figure 10–1. The setting includes flipcharts, break tables set with refreshments and snacks, and a podium and microphone. While most of the participation is in small groups with maximum diversity of function and level (called "max–mix groups), on the third day participants self-select themselves into action planning groups focusing on a subpart of the overall strategy that is of the most interest to them. Later in that day, participants also work in their "back home" work groups for planning next action steps. Throughout the process, participants are asked to react to material that has been generated by voting on items as "glads", "sads", and "mads," or posting gold stars ("great idea") or red dots ("you gotta be kidding!").[30]

This process requires a great deal of planning and a great deal of facilitator assistance. As Jacobs states it, "Large group events are tightly orchestrated and flexibly implemented to provide the most freedom and to maximize the group's chances for success.[31] A "logistics

---

Real Time Strategic Change Event

PURPOSE: To work together as leaders of this organization to:
- Build a common picture of where we are right now,
- Explore and agree on where we must be in the future if we are to be successful, and
- Make commitments to each other on what we need to do differently, individually, and collectively, to get there.

AGENDA

Day 1

8:00 AM	Coffee, etc.
8:30	Welcome and Purpose
	Agenda and Logistics
	Telling Our Stories
	View from the Leadership Perspective
	Organization Diagnosis
	Lunch
	Content Expert Input
	View from the Customer's Perspective
5:00 PM	Evaluation/Close/Debrief

Day 2

8:00 AM	Coffee, etc.
8:30	Feedback on Evaluations/Agenda for the Day
	Change Possibilities Panel
	Valentines
	Organizational Norms
	Organization Strategy: Revisit
	Feedback on Strategy by Participants
5:00 PM	Evaluation/Close/Debrief
	Leadership Turnaround on Strategy

Day 3

8:00 AM	Coffee, etc.
8:30	Feedback on Evaluations/Agenda for the Day
	Response from the Leadership Group: Finalized Strategy
	Preferred Futuring
	System-Wide Action Planning
	Back Home Teamwork
	Back Home Planning
5:00 PM	Wrap-Up/Evaluation/Close

Figure 10-1 Schedule for a Real Time Strategic Change Intervention

czar" is appointed to coordinate details, and teams of consultants are usually involved. Teams of two sometimes work with smaller groups, but teams of three, four, or five are frequently used. Jacobs reports that a team of thirteen consultants supported a 2,200-person event at Ford's Dearborn, Michigan, assembly plant.[32]

Extensive follow-up back on the job, or course, is essential. Implementation plans need to be made, and leaders continuously need to keep the broader system in mind so that plans and implementation will occur both within and across units.[33] According to Jacobs, some of the organizations that have used this process include Boeing, Marriott Hotels, METRO (Seattle), Health and Hospitals Corporation (New York City), United Kingdom's Employment Service, Kaiser Electronics, and Corning–Asahi Video Products Company.[34]

STREAM ANALYSIS

As developed by Jerry Porras, stream analysis, although complicated and somewhat difficult to use, is a valuable model for thinking about change and for managing change.[35] Stream analysis is a system for graphically displaying the problems of an organization, examining the interconnections between the problems, identifying core problems (those with many interconnections), and graphically tracking the corrective actions taken to solve the problems.

Porras categorized the important features of the organizational work setting (the environment in which people work) into four classes of variables labeled "organizing arrangements," include such things as goals, strategies, structure, administrative policies and procedures, administrative systems, reward systems, and ownership. "Social factors" include culture, management style, interaction processes, informal patterns and networks and individual attributes. "Technology" includes tools, equipment, and machinery, information technology, job design, workflow design, and technical systems. "Physical setting" includes space configuration, physical ambince, interior design, and architectural design.[36] These four classes of variables constitute the four "streams" of stream analysis.

Next, a thorough diagnosis of the organization's problems and barriers to effectiveness is performed, via brainstorming sessions, interviews, questionnaires, and other methods. A task force of representatives from all parts of the organization reviews the problems and barriers, discusses them until reaching agreement on what they mean, and categorizes each problem into one of the "streams." Four columns are drawn on paper; the column headings are labeled "organizing arrangements," "social factors," "technology," and "physical setting." Porras writes:

> As the problems are categorized, they are placed on Stream Charts in their appropriate columns. After all identified problems have been classified, an analysis of the entire set usually reveals much overlap among the various problem statements. What is usually required then is a grouping of problems and a condensation of the larger set of problems into a much smaller collection of relatively unique issues.[37]

Next, the interconnections between the problems are noted; problems that have many interconnections are identified as core problems. Action plans are developed to correct the core problems. The action plans and their results are tracked on stream charts.

The action plans are OD interventions directed solving the core problems. The OD program systematically addresses and resolves the issues identified, and by so doing correct dysfunctional aspects of the four classes of variables that make up the organizational work setting. OD programs modify organizing arrangements, social factors, technology, and physical settings, which in turn precipitate changes in individuals' on-the-job behaviors Thus, in stream analysis, OD programs change the work setting, which leads to organizational improvement. Porras and Robertson say: "Since the work setting is the environment in which people work, and since the environment plays a key role in determining the behavior of people, these factors define the characteristics that, if changed, will induce change in on-the-job behaviors of individual employees.[38] We believe stream analysis is a valuable model for understanding planned change processes.

SURVEY FEEDBACK

An important and widely used intervention for organization development rests on the process of systematically collecting data about the system and feeding back the data for individuals

	Traditional Approach	Survey Feedback or OD Approach
Data collected from:	Rank and file, and maybe supervisors	Everyone in the system
Data reported to:	Top management, department heads, and perhaps to employees through newspapper	Everyone who participated
Implications of data are worked on by:	Top management (maybe)	Everyone in work teams, with workshops starting at the top (all superiors with their subordinates)
Third-party intervention strategy:	Design and administration of questionnaire, development of a report	Obtaining concurrence on total strategy, design and administration of questionnaire, design of workshops, appropriate interventions in workshops
Action planning done by:	Top management only	Teams at all levels
Probable extent of changes and improvement:	Low	High

Figure 10-2 Two Approaches to the Use and Attitude or Climate Surveys

and groups at all levels of the organization to analyze, interpret meanings, and design corrective action steps. These activities—which have two major components, the use of a climate or attitude survey and the use of feedback workshops—are called *survey feedback*. This approach is based on the Systems 1-4 "management system" to be described later.

An attitude survey, if properly used, can be a powerful tool in organization improvement. Most surveys are not used in an optimal way—at maximum, most give top management some data for changing practices or provide an index against which to compare trends. At minimum, they are filed away with little of consequence resulting. (See Figure 10-2 for a comparison of two approaches to the use of attitude surveys—the traditional approach and the survey feedback approach.)

Research at the Institute for Social Research at the University of Michigan indicates that if the survey is to be optimally useful, the following steps must occur.[39]

Step 1. Organization members at the top of the hierarchy are involved in the preliminary planning.
Step 2. Data are collected form all organizations.
Step 3. Data are fed back to the top executive team and then down through the hierarchy is functional teams. Mann refers to this as "interlocking chain of conferences."[40]
Step 4. Each superior presides at a meeting with his or her subordinates in which the data are discussed and in which (a) subordinates are asked to help interpret the data, (b) plans are made for making constructive changes, and (c) plans are made for the introduction of the data at the next lower level.
Step 5. Most feedback meetings include a consultant who has helped prepare the superior for the meeting and who serves as a resource person.

The conclusions regarding the usefulness of survey feedback grew out of a four-year program with a large organization. In the first phase, data were gathered from some 8,000 employees throughout the company (1948). Comparable data were gathered two years later (1950) from the eight accounting departments, involving 800 employees and 78 supervisors. In this phase, four of the eight departments carried on feedback activities as described earlier; two departments served as control groups with nothing further done after one all-department meeting; and two departments were eliminated from the design because of changes in key personnel. Two years later (1952), another survey was made and the researchers found that "more significant positive changes occurred in employee attitudes and perceptions in the four experimental departments than in the two control departments.[41] In particular, important changes occurred relative to how employees felt about "(1) the kind of work they do (job interest, importance, and level of responsibility); (2) their supervisor (ability to handle people, give recognition, direct their work, and represent them in building complaints); (3) their progress in the company; and (4) their group's ability to get the job done."[42]

From our experience, feedback workshops take on many of the characteristics of team-building sessions but are less likely to deal with interpersonal matters. However, they frequently focus on leadership style or on matters pertaining to cooperation and teamwork. For example, the following two items were included in a questionnaire used by one of the authors:

Management side-steps or evades things that bother people on the job	Strongly Agree	Agree	Undecided	Disagree	Strongly disagree

There is good cooperation and teamwork in my work group	Strongly Agree	Agree	Undecided	Disagree	Strongly disagree

In this questionnaire, items were included pertaining to "Organizational Climate," "Pay and Benefits," "Relations with Other Units," "Communications," "Supervisor/Employee Relations," "Performance Counseling," "My Job," "Pressure of Work," "Management by Objectives," "Opportunities for Personal Growth and Advancement," and "Training."

This kind of attitude or climate survey, coupled with a series of workshops involving work teams at successively lower levels of the organization, can be used to create action plans and change across a wide range of variables in the social, structural, goal, and task subsystems of an organization. We think this approach has exciting possibilities because, in the words of Baumgartel (also quoted 3), *"it deals with the system if human relationships as a whole ... and it deals with each manager, supervisor, and employee in the context of his own job, his own problems, and his work relationships."*[43] Feedback permeates most OD activities and is one of the dimensions that differentiates OD from traditional interventions in organizations.

A closer look at some of the underlying dynamics of survey feedback reveals why it works. The survey feedback technique is essentially a procedure for giving objective data about the system's functioning to the system members so that they can change or improve selected aspects of the system. The objective data are obtained by a survey; working with the data to improve the organization is done in feedback sessions.

Frank Neff states that for organization improvement (change) to take place, three things must happen. First, the work group must accept the data as valid. Often people are defensive and resistant to data about their own organization. This resistance must be overcome. Second, the work group must accept responsibility for the part it plays in the problems identified.

The leader plays an important role in this regard—he or she should "model" behaviors indicating that the problem is "owned" by the leader and the group. Third, the work group must commit himself to solving problems; that is, its members must commit themselves to doing something about the problems. In summary, the work group must accept the data from the survey as valid, must accept responsibility for the problems identified, and must start solving the problems.[44]

Bowers and Franklin state that the rationale for survey feedback, or what they also call "survey-guided development," is based on a model that views people as rational, cognitive, information processing individuals. Furthermore, differences in a person's perceptions act as sources of motivation. New information leads to new perceptions that may be in conflict with old perceptions. In this way, new information becomes a force for changing perceptions and actions. Another basic assumption of survey-guided development is that human behavior is goal-oriented. Bowers and Franklin describe how the goal-seeking process works:

At least four elements are involved: (1) a model, (2) a goal, (3) an activity, and (4) feedback. The model is a mental picture of the surrounding world, including not only structural properties, but cause-and-effect relations. It is built by the person(s) from past accumulations of information, stored in memory. From the workings of the model and from the modeling process which he employs alternative possible future states are generated, of which one is selected as a goal. At this point, what is called the "goal selection system" ends and what is known as the "control system" ends and what is known as the "control system" per se begins. Activities are initiated to attain the goal, and feedback, which comes by some route from the person's environment, is used to compare, confirm, adjust, and correct responses by signaling departures from what was expected.[45]

A well-designed survey helps organization members to develop valid models of how organizations work and also provides information (feedback) about progress toward the goal.

Survey feedback has been shown to be an effective change technique in OD. In a longitudinal study evaluating the effects of different change techniques in 23 different organizations, survey feedback was found to be the most effective change strategy when compared with interpersonal process consultation, task process consultation, and laboratory training.[46] These results may be somewhat misleading, however, in that the survey feedback programs may have been more comprehensive than the other programs and the positive results may reflect the superiority of more comprehensive programs compared with less comprehensive ones. On the other hand, survey feedback is a cost-effective means of implementing a comprehensive program, thus making it a highly desirable change technique.

Appreciative Inquiry

An intervention broader than the appreciation and concerns exercise is appreciative inquiry. (Ai), developed by Frank Barrett and David Cooperrider and refined by Gervase Bushe. As discussed in chapter 7, this major intervention is based on the assertion that the organization "is a miracle to be embraced" rather than "a problem to be solved."[47] While interventions have evolved as consultant/researchers have experimented with the approach, basically the central interventions are interviews and then discussions in small groups or organizational meetings centering on such core questions as:

1. What have been the peak moments in the life of this organization—"when people felt most alive, most energized, most committed, and most fulfilled in their involvements?"
2. What do staff members value most "about themselves, their tasks, and the organization as a whole?"
3. Where excellence has been demonstrated, "what have been the organizational factors (structures, leadership approaches, systems, values, and so on) that most fostered realization of excellence?"
4. What are the "most significant embryonic possibilities, perhaps latent with the system," that indicate "realistic possibilities for an ever better organization?"[48]

A fairly detailed case study of the use of appreciative inquiry merging with a survey–guided intervention was reported in the OD practitioner.[49] The organization, an $11 billion commercial banking organization, conducted operations in several states. A hostile takeover attempt, large losses from a foreign loan portfolio, and a major drop in profits led to a layoff of more than 850 employees of its 8,000-member workforce. Outplacement assistance for laid-off employees and a comprehensive communications program assisted in managing the crisis, but top management recognized that more was needed to stabilize the organization, to retain a high-quality staff, and to move the organization forward. Led by the vice president who had been the project manager for the cost cutting, the corporate human resources staff, and external consultants, the following sequence of interventions emerged:

1. A vision statement and statement of values was developed by the top management and reviewed with bank managers, followed by a decision to proceed with a more aggressive intervention involving all employees.
2. An appreciative inquiry process was launched as a pilot project.
   a. An affirmative topic—the identification of the best of "what is"—was chosen.
   b. Two hundred and fifty employees representing a cross section of staff at all levels were selected at random to take part in one-on-one three interviews.
   c. Interviews with these employees were conducted by 20 of the bank's senior human resources staff members over a three-week period.
   d. Themes that "bridged the best of 'what is' with the understanding of 'what might be'" were extracted. The values were reported in the present tense because of a sense that people were reporting their present ideal experiences when the organization was at its best.
   e. A summary was reported to the CEO and to the president. These executives found the information so compelling that they decided the entire management team should be involved in reviewing it.
   f. The findings were presented to the management team at a two-day site conference, and plans were made to move the process forward.
3. The process then shifted to a survey-guided mode involving all employees, which included the administration of a questionnaire to all 8,000 employees over a period of a month.
   a. The survey reflected the themes that had emerged in the interviews and allowed employees to "have a voice in identifying what is important to the company and to learn as individuals," "evaluate how well they practice those ideals today;" and "indicate how much they have experienced their values in their career." They were also asked to think about the times they were really excited about their organization and what they were doing at that time to make their jobs exciting.[50]
   b. Approximately 6,500 employees participated in the survey, of which 4,000 provided extensive answers to the survey's open-ended comments.
4. A "preferred future" was then constructed involving employees throughout the organization.
   a. Team leaders were trained to conduct and facilitate brainstorming sessions with groups of employees.
   b. The purpose of these sessions was to build on the identified strengths and to take action of employees.
   c. The brainstorming sessions provided an opportunity for ongoing dialogue and action.
5. The overall results of the AI and the survey guided development were highly positive. According to the author,

The AI process powerfully affected the nature of conversations in the organization, causing a fundamental shift in the daily, dialogue. Employees began to view problems as opportunities and the optimism inherent in the conversations led to feelings of empowerment; employees were ready to take action in the face of possibility rather than staying frozen in the face of problems and circumstances. [52]

Researchers, while generally enthusiastic about the contribution that appreciative inquiry can make in "conditions of intergroup and interpersonal defensiveness," expresses the caution that this intervention could become "an unwilling accomplice in the dynamic of group flight."[53] Obviously, one of the important aspects that the approach seems to generate is more attention by the consultant to the strengths of the organization and its members.[54] Another important aspect, as evident in the case, is that AI can be productively combined with other OD approaches, in this application survey feedback.

GRID ORGANIZATIONAL DEVELOPMENT

A thoroughgoing and systematic organization development program, designed by Robert R. Blake and Jane S. Mouton, is *Grid Organization Development*.[55] In a six-phase program lasting about three to five years, an organization can move systematically from the stage of examining managerial behavior and style to the development and implementation of an "ideal strategic corporate model." The program utilizes a considerable number of instruments, enabling individuals and groups to assess their own strengths and weaknesses; it focuses on skills, knowledge, and processes necessary for effectiveness at the individual, group, intergroup, and total organization levels. The organizational program is conducted by internal members who have been pretrained in Grid concepts.

Basic to the Grid OD program are the concepts and methods of the Managerial Grid, also developed by Blake and Mouton, a two-dimensional schematic for examining and improving the managerial practices of individual managers. One dimension underlying this diagnostic questionnaire is "concern for people;" the other dimension is "concern for production." The most effective managers are those who score high on both of these dimensions—a 9,9 management style is described as follows: "Work accomplishment is from committed people; interdependence through a 'commonstake' in organization purpose leads to relationships of trust and respect."[56]

The relations between the Managerial Grid diagnostic questionnaire and Grid OD is explained by Blake and Mouton: "The single most significant premise on which Grid Organization Development rests is that the 9,9 way of doing business is acknowledged universally by managers as the soundest way to manage to achieve excellence."[57] As used in the Grid OD process, the Managerial Grid questionnaire becomes one vehicle for individuals and groups to examine and explore their styles and modify prevailing practices.

Behavioral science concepts and rigorous business logic are combined in the Grid OD program's six phases. These phases are as follows:[58]

Prephase 1: Before an organization (usually a business corporation) begins a grid organization development program, selected key managers who will later be instructors in the organization attend a Grid Seminar. In this week-long experience-based laboratory, managers learn about Grid concepts, asses their own styles using the Managerial Grid questionnaire and the two-dimensional schematic, develop team action skills, learn problem-solving and critiquing skills, work at improved communication skills, and learn to analyze the culture of a team and of an organization. Learning takes place through the use of instruments, and team performance, and conceptual inputs.

After several managers have gone to a Grid Seminar, some might go on to advanced Grid courses or for further exposure to the Grid OD approach. At a Grid OD Seminar, participants are taught the materials involved in phases 2 to 6. They learn both what the Grid OD program is all about and how to conduct it in their own company.

Another advanced course is the Instructor Development Seminar, in which participants actually learn to conduct an in-company phase 1 Grid Seminar. Training these managers in the various seminar accomplishes two things: the managers learn how to conduct a Grid approach to determine whether they think it is a good idea for their organization to embark on such a course of action.

If, at this point, the company decides to implement a Grid organization development program, it might conduct a pilot phase 1 program for volunteer managers. If the result of this *pilot* is a "go," then phase 1 begins.

Phase 1: The Managerial Grid   In this phase, Grid Seminar, conducted by in-company managers, is given to all the managers of the organization. The focus of the training is similar to that just described: attention is given to assessing an individual's managerial styles; problem-solving, critiquing, and communications skills are practiced; the skills of synergistic teamwork are learned and practiced. In this phase, managers learn to become 9,9 managers.

Phase 2: Teamwork Development   The focus of this phase is work teams in the organization. The goal is *perfecting* teamwork in the organization through analysis of team culture, traditions, and the like are also developing skills in planning, setting objectives, and problem solving. Additional aspects of this phase include feedback given to each manager about his or her individual and team behavior; this critique allows the manager to understand how others see his or her strengths and weaknesses in the team's working.

Working on teamwork is done in the context of actual work problems. The problems and issues dealt with are the real ones of the team. In this process of phase 2, individuals learn how to study and manage the culture of their work teams.

Phase 3: Intergroup Development   The focus of this phase is intergroup relations, and the goal of this phase is to move groups from their ineffective, often win-lose *actual* ways of so relating between groups toward an *ideal* model of intergroup relations. The dynamics of intergroup cooperation and competition are explored. Each group separately analyzes what an ideal relationship would be like; these analyses are shared between groups. Action steps to move toward the ideal are developed and assigned to individuals. The phase thus includes building operational plans for moving the two groups from their actual state of intergroup relations.

The phase consists of teams convening in twos, to work on the previously stated issues. Not all teams would pair with all others; only teams that have particularly important interface relationships do so. Often only selected members of the teams—people who have close working relations with the other team—take part in the exercises and activities.

Phase 4: Developing an Ideal Strategic Corporate Model   In this phase the focus shifts to corporate strategic planning, with the goal being to learn the concepts and the skills of corporate logic necessary to achieve corporate excellence. The top management group engages in the strategy planning activities of this phase, although their plan and ideas are tested, evaluated, and critiqued in conjunction with other corporate members. The charge to the top management group is to design an ideal strategic corporate model that would define what the corporation would be like if it were truly excellent. Fact-finding, technical inputs, and so on maybe contributed from all persons in the organization.

Using the comparisons of ideal corporate logic versus real corporate logic, the top management team is better able to recognize what aspects of the culture must be changed to achieve excellence.

In a process that may take up to a year, the top executives build the ideal strategic corporate model *for their particular organization.* This model is then used in the next phase.

Phase 5: Implementing the Ideal Strategic Model In several different steps, the organization seeks to implement the model of corporate excellence developed in phase 4. To execute the conversion of the ideal strategic model, the organization must be reorganized. Logical components of the corporation are designated (profit centers, geographical locations, product lines, etc.). Each component appoints a planning team whose job is to examine every phase of the component's operation to see how the business may be moved more in line with the ideal model. Every concept of the ideal strategic corporate model is studied by the planning team for its implications for the component. In addition, a phase 5 coordinator is appointed to act as a resource to the planning teams.

The planning teams thus conduct "conversion studies" to see how the components must change to fit the ideal, strategic corporate model. An additional planning team is formed and is given the charge of designing a headquarter that would operate effectively and yet keep overhead to a minimum. After the planning and assessment steps are completed, conversion of the organization to the ideal condition is implemented.

Phase 6: Systematic Critique In this phase the results of the Grid OD program, from prephase 1 to phase 5, are measured. Systematic critiquing, measuring, and evaluating lead to knowledge of what progress has been made, what barriers still exist and must be overcome, and what new opportunities have developed that may be exploited. This phase is begun after phase 5 is going well and is beginning to convert the organization to the ideal model. Taking stock of where the corporation has been, how far it has come, and where it currently is thus represents a "new beginning" from which to continue striving toward corporate excellence.

Grid organization development is an approach to organization improvement that is complete, systematic, and difficult. Does it work? Blake, Mouton, Barnes, and Greiner evaluated the results of a Grid OD program conducted in a large plant that was part of a large multiplant company. The 800 managers and staff personnel of the 4,000-person workforce at the plant were all given training in the Managerial Grid and Grid OD concepts. Significant organizational improvements showed up on such "bottom-line" measures as greater profits, lower costs, and less waste.[59] Managers themselves, when asked about their own effectiveness and that of their corporation, likewise declared that changes for the better had resulted from the program.

SCHEIN'S CULTURAL ANALYSIS

A particularly deep and difficult intervention is Edgar Schein's cultural analysis. This intervention is complex, probes deeply into the organization, and is not for every OD consultant nor for every client organization. Indeed, as Schien says:

If someone says "We want to do a cultural analysis, 'I spend quite a bit of time probing why, what for, and where we are going with it... Sometimes it will in fact lead to a workshop dealing with culture, but that same set of questions may lead to some other form of consultation or counseling'".[60]

Basically, when Schein and clients agree that the intervention is appropriate, the flow is as follows. We will use Schein's words to describe the process.

Once the purpose is established I would suggest to the immediate clients that they consider bringing together groupings of managers and/or employees to discuss the culture concept and to begin to identify some of their own assumptions. When such a group is assembled, I give a short lecture on the distinction between artifacts, espoused values, and underlying assumptions, followed by an invitation to the group to start brainstorming on what they see as the artifacts of their organization. If there are newcomers in the organization they are often a good group to begin with.

As various artifacts such as the architecture, the office layout, the mode of dress, the prerequisites and status symbols, etc., are identified, I write them down on flip charts and fill the walls with them. Within an hour or less, the group participants will begin to see some of the values that lie behind the artifacts and these are now written down for common observation. As this process proceeds, the outsider should begin to push for some of the underlying assumptions by noting areas of consistency and areas of inconsistency. Sometimes the best way to get at an underlying assumption is to note where espoused values are out of line with observed artifacts. The outsider can also offer hypotheses at this point to further stimulate the group's efforts to identify assumptions and begin to help the group classify them if they fall into clusters or form a pattern.

The next step in the intervention is typically to see the participants off in smaller groups with the task of further identifying assumptions and then classifying them into two categories: (1) those cultural assumptions that will aid us in getting to our goals; and 2) those cultural assumptions that will hinder us in getting to our goals. This self-diagnosis is then reported back to the total group and analyzed with the help of the outside consultant to determine what steps might be appropriate.

In this discussion it is crucial that the consultant help the group to focus on the helpful parts of the culture, and help the group to recognize what the consequences are of saying that they want to change those parts of the culture that they may view as non-helpful. But all of this only makes sense in the context of some strategic or tactical goals that the group is pursuing. Doing a cultural analysis for its own sake is at best boring and at worst dangerous.[61]

Schein goes on to note that the client system "is fully involved in owning both diagnosis and interventions." He further emphasizes that the role of the OD consultant is to provide the conceptual framework for the analysis and to "manage the process."[62]

LARGE-SCALE CHANGE AND HIGH-PERFORMANCE SYSTEMS

When a number of OD and other interventions are combined to create major changes in the total culture and operations of an organization, the term *large-scale change* is frequently used. Similarly, the creation of *high-performance systems*, *high-performance organizations*, *high-involvement organizations*, or *self-designing organizations*—terms that are used somewhat synonymously[63]—usually involve a broad array of interventions, and typically feature extensive member participation and involvement. Changes in such areas as job design and workflow, staffing procedures, training, and compensation are usually combined with such interventions. These matters will be discussed in greater detail in the next chapter. (See, in particular, the multiple interventions at British Airways described toward the end of chapter 12.)

TRANSORGANIZATIONAL DEVELOPMENT

When consultants get "the whole system in the room" and that system is conceptualized as involving several organizations (for example, in connection with some future search conferences, Weisbord talks about getting customers, suppliers, and union leaders together with organizational members), we can begin to sense some of the complexities of *transorganizational development*. Thomas Cummings has provided one of the best descriptions of this form of OD, which he says is "not simply an extension of OD, but constitutes a distinct level of practice commensurate with the dynamics emerging at this higher level of social system."[64]

Transorganizational development (TD) is seen by Cummings to be an important form of organizational change process for transorganizational systems (TSs), TSs comprise business alliances, consortia, or "network alliances" formed for such purposes as coordinating services to the public, conducting joint research and development, exchanging technology, or gaining access to worldwide markets. Linkages among members are "loosely coupled" or indirect. Power and leadership are dispersed rather than hierarchical, with wide fluctuations in commitment to the collaboration over time.[65]

Cummings sees three phases in typical TD practice:

Phase 1: Potential Member Organizations Are identified. TD practitioners assist early members in forming a steering committee, establishing criteria for membership, and perhaps serving as brokers to introduce potential partners to each other.

Phase 2: Member Organizations Are Convened. Representatives from member organizations are brought together, sometimes in a search conference, to assess the desirability and feasibility of creating a TS. These conferences permit members to share perceptions and ideas, to negotiate equitable benefits, and to develop action plans.

Phase 3: The TS Is Organized. Once common purposes and sufficient motivation have been generated, TD practitioners help members create the roles, structures, and mechanisms needed to coordinate the collaborative efforts of TS members.[66]

Practitioners need to play more of an activist role than is traditionally seen in OD. Furthermore, practitioners need to maintain a neutral role and not be seen as being aligned with particular member organizations or people.[67]

CONCLUDING COMMENTS

Comprehensive OD interventions are very much alive and visible in contemporary OD practice. Some, like Beckhard's confrontation meeting and strategic management activities, involve all of top management or, in the case of smaller organizations, the entire management group. (The confrontation meeting is also applicable to all employees of very small organizations.) Others, like future search conferences, tend to involve a wide spectrum of organizational members and can involve others beyond the immediate organization. Some, like survey feedback, based on Systems 1–4 T theory, are designed to involve all members of an organization. One intervention, Schein's cultural analysis, is a fairly deep intervention in the organization's basic culture. Appreciative inquiry focuses on the strengths of the organization and what is most valued by its members, and has an important future component when deliberations move to "what might be."

Some comprehensive interventions involve "getting the whole system in the room," a feature that a number of interventions have in common, including search conferences, transorganizational development, partnering, and the confrontation meeting. Search conferences and future search conferences have been visible in the United States and abroad during the last two decades, and have been utilized by many different types of organizations.

Transorganizational development (TD) aimed at assisting organizations in forming and developing alliances, has many similarities to the planning and conducting of future search conferences. However, TD requires practitioners to take on a more activist, brokerage role and to give considerable assistance and leadership in developing appropriate structures for communications and decision making.

Like all OD interventions, these comprehensive interventions must involve a collaborative effort between the client organization(s) and the consultant(s) in both diagnosis and intervention. To be successful, they must fit the realities being experienced by the client system and must engage the cooperation and goodwill of client system members.

Notes

1. See, for example, Marvin Weisbord, "Toward Third-Wave Managing and Consulting," *Organizational Dynamics*, 15 (Winter 1987), p. 9.
2. W. Warner Burke and Richard Beckhard, *Conference Planning*, 2d ed. (San Diego: University Associates, 1970).
3. Merrelyn Emery and Ronald E. Purser, *The Search Conference* (San Francisco: Jossey-Bass, 1996), pp. 215–217.
4. Ibid., p. 40.
5. Ibid., p. 10.
6. Ibid., p. 11.
7. Marvin R. Weisbord, *Productive Workplaces* (San Francisco: Jossey-Bass Publishers, 1987), p. 283.
8. Richard Beckhard, "The Confrontation Meeting," *Harvard Business Review*, 45 (March–April 1967), pp. 149–155.
9. Ibid., p. 150.
10. This discussion represents paraphrasing, ibid., p. 154.
11. Ibid., p. 154.
12. Ibid., p. 153.
13. Dan E. Schendel and Charles W. Hofer, eds., *Strategic Management* (Boston: Little, Brown, 1979), p. 14.

14. Charles E. Summer, *Strategic Behavior in Business and Government* (Boston: Little, Brown, 1980), chapter 10.

15. See Charles Krone, "Open Systems Redesign," in John Adams, ed., *Theory and Management in Organization Development: An Evolutionary Process* (Roslyn, VA: NTL Institute, 1974); and G. K. Jayaram, "Open Systems Planning," in W. G. Bennis, K. D. Benne, R. Chin, and K. Cory, eds., The Planning of Change, 3d ed. (New York: Holt, Rinehart and Winston, 1976), pp. 275–283. This discussion is based primarily on Jayaram's article.

16. Michael Porter, *Competitive Strategy* (New York: The Free Press, 1980), *Competitive Advantage* (New York: The Free Press, 1985), and *Competition in Global Industries* (Boston: Harvard Business School Press, 1986).

17. B. B. Tregoe and J. W. Zimmerman, *Top Management Strategy* (New York: Simon and Schuster, 1980).

18. Kenichi Ohmae, *The Mind of the Strategist* (New York: Penguin Books, 1982).

19. Michel Robert, *Strategy Pure and Simple* (New York: McGraw-Hill, Inc., 1993).

20. Peter Schwartz, *The Art of the Long View* (New York: Doubleday Publishing Co., 1991).

21. Robert G. Dyson, *Strategic Planning: Models and Analytic Techniques* (Chichester, West Sussex, England: John Wiley and Sons, Ltd., 1990).

22. Dale E. Zand, "Organization Development and Strategic Management," *OD Newsletter* (Winter 1984), pp. 1, 6–7.

23. Larry E. Greiner and Virginia E. Schein, "A Revisionist Look at Power and OD," *The Industrial-Organizational Psychologist*, 25, no. 2 (1988), pp. 59–61.

24. Paul F. Buller, "For Successful Strategic Change: Blend OD Practices with Strategic Management," *Organizational Dynamics*, 16 (1988), pp. 42–55.

25. Ibid., p. 43.

26. Robert W. Jacobs, *Real Time Strategic Change* (San Francisco: Berrett-Koehler Publishers, 1994).

27. Ibid., p. 21.

28. Ibid., pp. 54–55.

29. Ibid., p. 154.

30. Ibid., pp. 67–118.

31. Ibid., p. 44.

32. Ibid., p. 247.

33. Ibid., pp. 274–275.

34. Ibid., pp. 173–189.

35. Jerry I. Porras, *Stream Analysis: A Powerful Way to Diagnose and Manage Organizational Change* (Reading, MA: Addison-Wesley Publishing Company, 1987).

36. This discussion comes from Jerry I. Porras and Peter J. Robertson, "Organizational Development: Theory, Practice, and Research," in Marvin D. Dunnette and Leaetta M. Hough, eds., *Handbook of Industrial and Organizational Psychology*, 2d ed., vol. 3 (Palo Alto, CA: Consulting Psychologists Press, 1992), pp. 719–822. The work-setting elements are listed on p. 729.

37. Porras, *Stream Analysis*, p. 23.

38. Porras and Robertson, "Organizational Development," p. 728.

39. Floyd C. Mann, "Studying and Creating Change," in W. G. Bennis, K. D. Benne, and R. Chin, eds., *The Planning of Change* (New York: Holt, Rinehart and Winston, 1961), pp. 605–613.

40. Ibid., p. 609.

41. Ibid., p. 611.

42. Ibid., p. 611.

43. Howard Baumgartel, "Using Employee Questionnaire Results for Improving Organizations: The Survey 'Feedback' Experiment," *Kansas Business Review*, 12 (December 1959), p. 6. [Baumgartel's emphasis.]

44. Frank W. Neff, "Survey Research: A Tool for Problem Diagnosis and Improvement in Organizations," in A. W. Gouldner and S. M. Miller, eds., *Applied Sociology* (New York: Free Press, 1966), pp. 23–38.

45. David G. Bowers and Jerome L. Franklin, "Survey-Guided Development: Using Human Resources Measurement in Organizational Change," *Journal of Contemporary Business*, 1, no. 3 (Summer 1972), pp. 43–55. This passage is taken from p. 48.

46. David G. Bowers, "OD Techniques and Their Results in 23 Organizations: The Michigan ICL Study," *Journal of Applied Behavioral Science*, 9, no. 1 (1973), pp. 21–43.

47. Frank J. Barrett and David L. Cooperrider, "Generative Metaphor Intervention: A New Approach for Working with Systems Divided by Conflict and Caught in Defensive Perception," *The Journal of Applied Behavioral Science*, 26, no. 2 (1990), pp. 219–239.

48. Based on or inferred from Barrett and Cooperrider, p. 229; and a draft of an unpublished paper by Gervase R. Bushe, "Advances in Appreciative Inquiry as an Organization Development Technique," (September 1992), pp. 1–7. (Gervase Bushe, Simon Fraser University, Burnaby, British Columbia.)

49. Rita F. Williams, "Survey Guided Appreciative Inquiry: A Case Study," *OD Practitioner*, 28, nos. 1 & 2 (1996), pp. 43–51.

50. Ibid., pp. 47–48.

51. Ibid., p. 49.

52. Ibid., pp. 49–50.

53. Barrett and Cooperrider, p. 237.

54. Bushe, "Advances in Appreciative Inquiry as an Organization Development Technique," p. 6.

55. Robert R. Blake, Jane S. Mouton, and Anne A. McCanse, *Change by Design* (Reading, MA: Addison-Wesley, 1989), pp. 116–216; R. R. Blake and J. S. Mouton, *The Managerial Grid* (Houston: Gulf Publishing, 1964); and *The New Managerial Grid* (Houston: Gulf Publishing, 1978).

56. R. R. Blake and J. S. Mouton, *Building a Dynamic Corporation Through Grid Organization Development* (Reading, MA: Addison-Wesley, 1969), p. 61.

57. Ibid., p. 63.

58. This discussion is based on ibid., pp. 76–109.

59. R. R. Blake, J. S. Mouton, L. B. Barnes, and L. E. Greiner, "Breakthrough in Organization Development," *Harvard Business Review*, 42 (November–December 1964), pp. 133–155.

60. Fred Luthans, "Conversation with Edgar H. Schein," *Organizational Dynamics*, 17 (Spring 1989), p. 73.

61. Edgar H. Schein, "Organization Development and the Study of Organizational Culture," *Academy of Management OD Newsletter* (Summer 1990), pp. 4–5. Used by permission.

62. Ibid., p. 5. For a more detailed description of the process, see Edgar H. Schein, *Organizational Culture and Leadership*, 2d ed. (Jossey-Bass Publishers, 1992). For more on organizational culture, see Ralph H. Kilmann, Mary J. Saxton, Roy Serpa and Associates, *Gaining Control of the Corporate Culture* (San Francisco: Jossey-Bass Publishers, 1985); and J. Steven Ott, *The Organizational Culture Perspective* (Pacific Grove, CA: Brooks/Cole Publishing Company, 1989).

63. Gerald E. Ledford, Jr. and Susan Albers Mohrman, "Self-Design for High Involvement: A Large-Scale Organizational Change," *Human Relations*, 46 (February 1993), p. 145.

64. Thomas G. Cummings, "Transorganizational Development," *Academy of Management OD Newsletter* (Summer 1989), p. 9.

65. Ibid., pp. 8–9.

66. Ibid., pp. 9–10.

67. Ibid., p. 10. See also Thomas G. Cummings and Christopher G. Worley, *Organization Development and Change*, 5th ed. (Minneapolis/St. Paul: West Publishing Company, 1993); and Jerry I. Porras and Peter J. Robertson, "Organization Development: Theory, Practice, and Research," in Marvin D. Dunnette and Leaetta M. Hough, *Handbook of Industrial and Organizational Psychology*, 2d ed., vol. 3 (Palo Alto, CA: Consulting Psychologists Press, 1992), pp. 719–822.

CHAPTER 11

Structural Interventions and the Applicability of OD

In this chapter we will examine what we call *structural interventions*, sometimes called *technostructural interventions*, a shorthand term for a broad class of interventions or change efforts aimed at improving organizational effectiveness through changes in the task, structural, technological, and goal processes in the organization. This class of interventions includes changes in how the overall work of the organization is divided into units, who reports to whom, methods of control, the spatial arrangements of equipment and people, work flow arrangements, and changes in communications and authority.

In particular, we want to examine the structural interventions that are frequently labeled OD or linked to OD: sociotechnical systems (STS), self-managed teams, work redesign, management by objectives (MBO), quality circles, quality of work life projects (QWL), parallel learning structures (or collateral organizations), physical settings, and total quality management (TQM). (We will also examine reengineering, an intervention modality that is usually not considered OD, but nevertheless, needs to be understood by OD practitioners and clients.) We will also look at the concepts of "self-designing," "high-involvement," "high-commitment,"and high-performance" organizations. These concepts overlap and are somewhat synonymous, but are frequently used in the literature.

Most of the structural interventions we will discuss seek a joint optimization of the social and technological systems of organizations. Applications are properly called OD to the extent that the latter is true; they use the participant action research model, and other characteristics are congruent with how OD has been described in earlier chapters. We would hope the OD label would not be applied whenever structural interventions are carried out without attention to the social system or to humanistic values.

Finally, we want to look briefly at the concept of large-scale systems change. In this discussion, we also want to examine organization transformation, or second-order change, which usually involves a variety of OD interventions over a relatively long time frame.

SOCIOTECHNICAL SYSTEMS

The term *sociotechnical systems* (or STS) is largely associated with experiments that emerged under the auspices of the Tavistock Institute in Great Britain or have stemmed from the Tavistock approach. In recent years, additional institutions, such as the University of

Southern California, have been associated with STS innovations. These efforts have generally attempted to create a better "fit" among the technology, structure, and social interaction of a particular production unit in a mine, factory, or office.

As described by Cummings and Worley, STS theory has two basic premises. One is that "effectiveness work systems must jointly optimize the relationship between their social and technical parts." The second premise is that "such systems must effectively manage the boundary separating and relating them to the environment" in such a way that effective exchanges occur with the environment along with protection from external disruptions. Furthermore, the implementation of STS is seen as "highly participative" involving all of the relevant stakeholders, including employees, engineers, staff experts, and managers.[1]

As indicated in chapter 5, STS projects tend to feature the formation of autonomous workgroups (the terms *self-managing* or *self-managed* are now more frequently used), the grouping of core tasks so that a team has a major unit of the total work to be accomplished, the training of group members in multiple skills, delegation to the work group of many aspects of how the work gets done, and the availability of a great deal of information and feedback to work groups for the self-regulation of productivity and quality. The theory suggests that effectiveness, efficiency, and morale will be enhanced, which has been generally confirmed by numerous studies carried out over the years.

One of the earliest studies was in British coal mining where the consultant-researchers found that by reintroducing a team approach to mining coal, broadening job scope, and providing team pay incentives, a number of benefits resulted, including improved productivity, safety, and morale.[2] An experiment in India in a textile-weaving mill also utilized increased job scope and autonomous work groups with beneficial consequences.[3] Other experiments and research have appeared with increasing frequency around the world, particularly in Norway and Sweden[4] and the United States.

Part of the heritage of these experiments was the emergence of *work restructuring* projects such as at the Volvo plants in Sweden, and the General Foods pet-food plant in Topeka, Kansas. Common characteristics have been the use of autonomous work teams, participative decision making, considerable team autonomy in planning and controlling production and in screening new team members, and pay geared to the number of tasks mastered by each team member ("skill-based pay").[5] These experiments have sometimes overlapped with programs called quality of work life (QWL) projects.

Other organizations where self-managed teams have been used extensively include Digital, Frito-Lay, General Electric, Hewlett-Packard, Honeywell, Pepsi-Cola, the Oregon Department of Transportation, the San Diego Zoo, and many smaller organizations.[6] Lawler has followed up on a number of plants using self-managed teams, including the General Foods plant, and concluded "virtually every plant has thrived and continues to be managed in a very participative way."[7]

Unfortunately, in some instances STS and self-managed teams have languished or disappeared because of changes in management, internal company politics, divestitures, or mergers. For example, in his book *The Age of Heretics*, Art Kleiner chronicles the successes of the STS efforts at the former General Foods plant at Topeka. This remarkably successful program continued through several corporate owners only to fall into disuse when the plant was purchased by Heinz in 1995.[8]

SELF-MANAGED TEAMS: PROBLEMS IN IMPLEMENTATION

Several problems are typically encountered in moving toward the use of self-managed teams. The first problem is what to do with the first-line supervisors who are no longer needed as supervisors. Some can assume new responsibilities as coordinators or coaches; some can rejoin the work group, but many will no longer be needed. Another problem is that the managers (or coordinators) that are now one level above the teams will likely oversee the activities of several teams, and their roles will change to emphasize planning, expediting, and coordinating. These managers will need considerable training to acquire skills in group leadership and the ability to delegate to the teams. Furthermore, team members will need to develop new skills in running and participating in team meetings, as well as in planning, quality control, budgeting, and so forth. Frequently, all team members learn all of the technical tasks performed by the team.[9]

OD interventions such as team-building activities are relevant to sociotechnical systems design and the development of self-managed teams. Furthermore, these activities need to be ongoing because, as Lawler puts it, well-run plants using self-managed teams "run the risk of becoming stagnant and complacent." He suggests the development of "on going organizational assessment capability that constantly surfaces issues of organizational effectiveness and renewal."[10]

WORK REDESIGN

Richard Hackman and Greg Oldham have provided an OD approach to work redesign based on a theoretical model of what job characteristics lead to the psychological states that produce what they call "high internal work motivation." Their approach has OD characteristics in its use of diagnosis, participation, and feedback, and particularly in applications to the redesign of group work where extensive use of the facilitator role in team development is recommended. Their model is shown in Figure 11-1.

Hackman and Oldham recommend that organizations analyze jobs using the five core job characteristics shown in Figure 11-1 and then redesign jobs to maximize worker motivation. The five core job characteristics are skill variety, task identity, task significance, autonomy, and feedback from the job. The first three are related to "experienced meaningfulness of the work." Job autonomy is related to the psychological state of "knowledge of the results of the work activities." The expected outcomes, in turn, are high work motivation, high satisfaction with the job and with one's growth on the job, and high work effectiveness.[11]

As noted at the bottom of Figure 11-1, some factors can minimize or moderate these outcomes. One factor is knowledge and skill. Deficiencies in either can lead to less than desirable performance and a sense of failure. Another moderating factor is the strength of a person's need to learn and develop. If this need is low, the presence of the core job characteristics is less likely to high motivation and job satisfaction with the context of the job. Dissatisfaction with such matters as pay, job security, coworkers, or supervision is likely to minimize the otherwise favorable consequences of designing more complex and challenging jobs.[12]

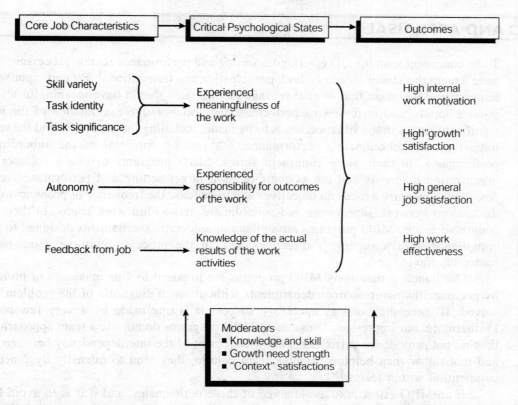

Source: J. Richard Hackman and Greg R. Oldham, *Work Redesign* (Figure 4.6), p. 90 © 1980 Addison-Wesley Publishing Company, Inc. Reprinted with permission of the publisher.

Figure 11-1 The Complete Job Characteristics Model

The same authors extend their concepts to the redesign of the work of teams, self-managed teams, in particular. In this context they describe an approach in which, an outstanding agent such as a consultant or manager helps group members develop and monitor their own performance norms:

> When a work group's is being formed, the person responsible for designing the group might meet with group members to discuss explicitly how they want to develop their performance strategies. Merely talking through this issue may foster a climate in which strategic questions can be openly discussed—both when initial norms about strategy are developed and in the future when circumstances change. In effect, the manager or consultant would be helping members develop a general norm that encourages open and self-conscious discussion of specific norms about how group members work together on the task.[13]

Hackman and Oldham offer both an endorsement and a caution about self-managed teams:

> Self-managing work teams are a powerful social invention. In a moderately supportive organizational context they can prompt significant alterations in how work gets done and how the organization itself is managed. But if the people or the managerial climate and style of the organization are clearly unsympathetic to a group design for work, the potential benefits of such groups are unlikely to be realized.[14]

MBO AND APPRAISAL

To be congruent with the OD effort, goal-setting and performance review processes should have a team thrust and should be both participative and transactional. By participative and transactional we mean that in goal setting, subordinates should have meaningful ways to provide inputs; and in reviewing performance, a collaborative examination of the major significant forces in the situation needs to be made, including the superior's and the team's impact of the subordinate's performance, not just an appraisal of the subordinate's performance. In their more congruent forms, MBO programs evolve a collaborative organization diagnosis and are systems of joint target setting and performance review designed to increase a focus on objectives and to increase the frequency of problem-solving discussions between supervisors and subordinates and within work teams. In their least congruent forms, MBO programs are unilateral, autocratic mechanisms designed to force compliance with a superior's directives and, in the process, reinforce a one-on-one leadership mode.

Our hunch is that many MBO programs are imposed by line managers or promoted by personnel/human resources departments without much diagnosis of the problem to be solved. If some diagnosis is made, we suspect it is one made by a very few people. Furthermore, our impression is that most MBO programs do not use a team approach, that they do not provide for sufficient acknowledgement of the interdependency between jobs, and that rather than helping examine team culture, they tend to intensify dysfunctional competition within teams.[15]

If an MBO effort is to avoid some of these deficiencies, and if it is to avoid being punitive or overly constraining, we think it should include such ingredients as the following. We call this "Collaborative Management by Objectives" or CMBO:[16]

1. A collaborative diagnosis of organizational problems, from which it is concluded that a collaborative MBO effort would be functional.
2. Increased skills in interpersonal communications and group processes. (This point will be crucial to the team aspects if this approach.)
3. Real subordinate participation, in team configurations, in setting goals.
4. A team approach to reviewing individual and group targets and their achievement.
5. Ongoing individual and team problem-solving discussions with superiors.
6. A continuous helping relationship within teams and in superior-subordinate relationships. (This characteristic will not occur quickly; a win-win climate that says "Let's try to help each other succeed" needs to emerge.)
7. Attention to personal and career goals in a real effort to make them complementary to organizational goals.

Some research evidence supports arguments for some of these ingredients. Research at General Electric, for example, found that criticism by the superior tended to produce defensiveness and impaired performance, that goal setting and mutual goal setting between superior and subordinate were associated with improved performance and that coaching needed to be a day-to-day activity.[17] A follow-up study at General Electric found that appraisals went better in a climate promoting trust, openness, support, and development.[18] Research in a public utility also found the organizational climate dimension of support to be a criteria factor in the perceived success of MBO efforts.[19]

Likert and Fisher describe a participative, team approach to MBO in use in a retail division of a consumer products organization and in an automobile plant. They report impressive increases in contribution to corporate profits in the retail sales division and substantially increased productivity and reduced scrap and rejects in the automobile plant. They call the approach Management by Group Objectives (MBGO).[20]

QUALITY CIRCLES

The quality circle concept is a form of group problem solving and goal setting with a primary focus on maintaining and enhancing product quality. Quality circles have been extensively used in Japan since the introduction of quality control techniques there in the 1950s and 1960s by W. Edwards Deming, Joseph Juran, and A. W. Feigenbaum.[21] It is reported that Kaoru Ishikawa of Tokyo University integrated these techniques with the theories of American behavioral scientists such as Maslow, McGregor, and Herzberg, and thus, the quality circle was born.[22]

The Lockheed Missile and Space Company appears to be the first American firm to study the emerging Japanese approach and to implement an extensive program.[23] By 1995 it was estimated that over 90 percent of the Fortune 500 companies were utilizing quality circles, including such firms as Honeywell, Digital Equipment, TRW, and Westinghouse.[24]

Quality circles consist of a group of seven to ten employees from a unit (or across units) who have volunteered to meet together regularly to analyze and make proposals about product quality and other problems. Recommendations are forwarded to a coordinating or steering committee; meetings are typically held once a week for an hour or chaired by an employee elected from the group. Leaders are encouraged to create a high degree of participation within the group.

Prior to the formation of quality circles, those supervisors who have volunteered to participate are trained by quality control experts and facilitators in such matters as quality control concepts, including the necessary statistical tools, in leading participative group discussions, and in group dynamics and communications skills. In turn, the supervisors, with the help of facilitators, train those subordinates who volunteer to participate. The facilitators also help each circle in its linking with other groups and with the overall coordinating committee. Groups are encouraged to use experts from within the organization when their specialties are relevant and are frequently authorized by management to make changes without higher authority whenever feasible. Once or twice a year, a member of higher management meets with each group.[25]

Favorable results have generally been reported in the popular and technical media. In the first three years of Lockheed's experimentation with the process, the company was reported to have saved six dollars for every one it spent on the process, and defects in manufacturing declined by two–thirds. Morale and satisfaction among participants were reported to have increased.[26] At Nippon Kokan K. K., where thousands of employees are involved in quality control circles, savings were reported of some $86 million in one year, stemming from suggestions emerging from the groups.[27]

A 1990 study of 313 organizations found 52 percent evaluated their quality circle programs as successful, 36 percent were undecided, and 12 percent reported that they were unsuccessful.[28]

Favorable results have also been reported through the use of cross-functional (or multifunctional) quality circle teams at such organizations as Ford and IBM. The latter has an extensive program using "Process Improvement Teams" whose members are drawn from multiple functions.[29]

The use of quality circles has been one of the central aspects in the evolution of total quality management, a much broader intervention strategy. TQM will be discussed later in this chapter.

QUALITY OF WORK LIFE PROJECTS

The term quality of work life (QWL) has been applied to a wide variety of organizational improvement efforts. The common elements seem to be as, Goodman indicates, an "attempt to restructure multiple dimensions of the organization" and to "institute a mechanism which introduces and sustains changes over time."[30] Aspects of the change mechanism are usually an increase in participation by employees in shop floor decisions and an increase in problem solving between the union and management.

At some General Motor plants, QWL projects have included some of the following features:

- Voluntary involvement on the part of employees.
- Union agreement with the process and participation in it.
- Assurance of no loss or jobs as a result of the programs.
- Training of employees in team problem solving.
- The use of quality circles where employees discuss problems affecting the performance of the plant and the work environment.
- Work team participation in forecasting, work planning, and team leader and team member selection.
- Regular plant and team meetings to discuss such matters as quality, safety, customer orders, and schedules.
- Encouragement of skill development and job rotation within work teams.
- Skill training
- Responsiveness to employee concerns.[31]

While the specifics vary from one QWL project to another, both within a given organization and between organizations, several features tend to be common. These factors include union involvement; a focus on work teams; problem-solving sessions by work teams in which the agenda may include productivity, quality, and safety problems; autonomy in planning work; the availability of skill training; and increased responsiveness to employees by supervision.

Although many of these QWL projects have at least modest success, frequently difficulties arise in sustaining or expanding the process beyond a few years. Some of the reasons, according to Goodman, include changes in union leadership, expectations that were too high, efforts aimed at production and clerical levels, and too little attention to long-term financial rewards for the participants.[32] Major resistance from supervisors has frequently occurred when top management has paid insufficient attention to issues of job security and role definition for people at this level.[33]

PARALLEL LEARNING STRUCTURES

As discussed in chapter 4, in their most basic forms, parallel learning structures generally consist of a steering committee and a number of working groups that study what changes are needed in the organization, make recommendations for improvement, and then monitor the resulting change efforts. Use is made of the facilitator role, data gathering, data feedback, and process consultation. As described by Gervase Bushe and A. B. Shani, these parallel organizations, or collateral organizations as described by Dale Zand, are essentially microcosms of the total organization and are set up in tandem with the ongoing activities of the organization.

As viewed by Zand, the collateral organization is created to deal with "ill-structured" (i.e., complex, nonroutine, future-oriented) problems that have high priority and that are system wide, involving more than one unit. A deliberate effort is made to develop a set of norms different from those in the formal system. In particular, "careful questioning and analysis of goals, assumption, methods, alternatives, and criteria for evaluation" are encouraged.[34] Bushe and Shani also emphasize the importance of the creation of different norms and culture within the parallel or collateral organization. In particular, they say "What's important is that people act in a way that promotes learning and adaptation."[35]

Also as indicated in chapter 4, the parallel learning structure has been extensively used across a wide array of change programs. These have included quality of work life) QWL programs, sociotechnical systems (STS) work redesign efforts, open systems planning programs, and the coordination of employee involvement teams.

PHYSICAL SETTINGS AND OD

Some consultants have been active in working with clients and in conceptualizing about how to make physical settings congruent with OD assumptions and the OD process. A notable example of this thrust is Steele's work. To Steele, physical settings are an important part of organization culture that work groups should learn to diagnose and manage, and about which top management needs input in designing plants and buildings.

Steel cities many instances in which physical settings were found to interfere with effective group and organizational functioning. For example,

- A personnel director promoted to senior vice-president, a position inheriting the incredible, mandatory practice of having a secretary share the same office (which was supposed to signal high status), with the resulting lack of privacy and typewriter noise, adversely affecting the executive's ability to hold spontaneous meetings with employees.
- An executive group wanting to rearrange an office setting to increase interaction and rapport, but locked into status considerations relative to the larger and corner offices.
- A factory management encouraging group decision making, yet providing no space for more than six people to meet at one time.
- Classroom and lecture hall arrangements in universities reinforcing teacher-dominated and low-peer-interaction climate.[36]

Many OD consultants have long given considerable attention to the physical arrangements for team-building sessions, and Steele reinforces this approach by urging facilitators to include the dimension of physical arrangements in their "process consultation" interventions.[37] Steele describes a rating process he uses to examine things such as desks, lights, or machines, patterns of elements such as the arrangement of chairs, and sociological factors such as norms about the use of physical settings.[38]

Even though architecture and interior arrangements and design are not OD per se, both the approach used by Steele, which includes a strong emphasis on participative diagnosis, and the outcomes, which tend to meet client needs (e.g., enhancing team efforts when needed and privacy when needed) are highly congruent with OD. Steele's work is a notable example of some of the creative integrations that have occurred between OD and other consultancy modes.

TOTAL QUALITY MANAGEMENT

Total quality management (TQM), sometimes called continuous quality improvement, is a combination of a number of organization improvement techniques and approaches including the use of quality circles, statistical quality control, statistical process control, self-managed teams and task forces, and extensive use of employee participation. Much of the impetus for TQM has come from a growing awareness by American executives of the critical need for American corporations to compete on a global scale. In particular, it has become obvious that it is necessary to compete with the Japanese who have had great success in managing quality.

The following features tend to characterize TQM. This list is largely based on total quality conferences held in the United States and abroad by the Conference Board and on a special issue of Business Week entitled *The Quality Imperative*.[39]

Primary emphasis on customers. The development of an organizational culture in which employees at all levels, including the CEO, give paramount treatment to customer needs and expectations. Daily operational use of the concept of internal customers. Emphasis on the concept that work flow and internal interdependencies require that organizational members treat each other as valued customers across functional lines as well as within units.

An emphasis on measurement using both statistical quality control and statistical process control techniques. Statistical quality control is a method of measuring and analyzing deviations in manufactured products; statistical process control is a method of analyzing deviations in manufacturing processes.

Competitive benchmarking. Continuous rating of the company's products and practices against the world's best firms, including other organizations in other industries.

Continuous search for sources of defects with a goal of eliminating them entirely. The Japanese call it Kaizen.

Participative management. It includes extensive delegation and involvement and a coaching, supportive leadership style.

An emphasis on teams and teamwork. The typical vehicle for such a focus is self, managed teams. Cross-functional and multilevel task forces are also used extensively.

A major emphasis on continuous training. Learning new and better ways of doing things and adding new skills are essential. In many organizations training is reinforced by changes in the reward system, for example, the introduction of skill-based or knowledge-based pay.

Top management support on an ongoing basis. A long-term perspective and a long-term commitment is required on the part of top management.

Because of the emphasis on creating an organizational culture that features extensive participation, an emphasis on teams and teamwork, cooperation between teams and units, the generation of valid data,[40] and continuous learning, TQM appears to be highly congruent with OD approaches and values. Indeed, Dan Ciampa states that a major aspect of TQM is derived from OD:

> The people side of Total Quality is a direct descendant of Organization Development. To truly understand TQ and to be able to make it a reality, one must be an expert in creating change on the people side of the organizational excellence equation. The values on which OD is based, its dedication to human learning, its elements of adult education and management training are all necessary parts of a true, successful TQ effort.[41]

Although this historical connection can be made, many TQM practitioners would probably not consider themselves to be involved in organization development, the improvement strategy based on behavioral science described in this book. At this point the two fields are relatively independent of each other. The great potential for synergy between TQM and OD is evident, however, as indicated by the Lawler et al research just mentioned and the book on total quality by Dan Ciampa.

THE SELF-DESIGN STRATEGY

What the literature has dubbed a "self-design strategy" has components in common with a number of the comprehensive and structural interventions described in this and the previous chapter. Basically, according to Cummings and Worley, it is a "learning model" to help organizations develop "the built-in capacity to transform themselves to achieve high performance in today's competitive and changing environment.[42] The action research model is evident throughout the process as it unfolds. The basic components are:

- An educational component consisting of "readings, presentations, visits to other companies, and attendance at conferences."
- "Clarifications of the values that will guide the design process," which might include the use of values of visioning process.
- "Diagnosis of the current state of the organization using the values as a template"— these diagnostic activities might include "interviews, focus groups, survey data, and benchmark performance data."
- "Changes are then designed and implemented in an interactive manner."[43]

This process acts as a roadmap for large-scale organizational change.[44] This large-scale change would be conceptualized as the development of a high-involvement and/or a high-performance work system, concepts to which he will turn next.

HIGH-INVOLVEMENT AND HIGH-PERFORMANCE WORK SYSTEMS

The terms "high-involvement organizations," "high-commitment, organizations," and "high-performance organizations" are seen by Ledford, Lawler, and Mohrman as largely synonymous, but they see "high-involvement" as more descriptive and less loaded than the other terms. High performance and high commitment are possible outcomes in organizations that are designed for high involvement, but may not occur if environmental conditions are unfavorable "or if the high-involvement design is poorly implemented.[45] Thus, they prefer the term that connotes the basic strategy or process that is used—high involvement—rather than one that connotes a desired outcome.

Typically, as described by various authors, "high-involvement organizations" feature decision making moved downward as far as possible, extensive use of self–managed teams, compensation systems that link rewards to individual and team performance, widely shared information, participative and shared leadership, and extensive training.[46] Many of the OD interventions we have described in this book, if not all, contribute to the development of high-involvement (and high-performance) organizations, particularly when linked to modifications in leadership style, staffing, appraisal, reward, communications, and in structures that are congruent with high involvement.

LARGE-SCALE SYSTEMS CHANGE AND ORGANIZATIONAL TRANSFORMATION

Any of the interventions described in earlier chapters and in this chapter could be part of a large-scale systems change effort. Typically, when OD approaches are used in large-scale change efforts, multiple types of OD interventions are utilized.

By *large-scale systems change* we mean organizational change that is massive in terms of the number of organizational units involved, the number of people affected, the number of organizational subsystems altered, and/or the depth of the cultural change involved. For example, a major restructuring with objectives including a reduction in hierarchical levels from eight to four and shifting to a more participative leadership style might involve every unit of the organization, affect the responsibilities of every employee at every level, and would require changes in such aspects as work flow, reporting relationships, job descriptions and titles, compensation, and training programs.

Figure 11-2 portrays some of the differences between evolutionary, incremental or mid-range, and large-scale systems change.[47] Included in the latter is what Levy and Merry call "second-order change," that is, "…a multidimensional, multi-level, qualitative, discontinuous, radical organizational change involving a paradigmatic shift." Their use of the term second-order change is essentially synonymous with "organization transformation."[48]

Organizational transformation, or second-order change, usually requires a multiplicity of interventions and takes place over a fairly long period of time. For example, the five-year organizational transformation process at British Airways, as reported by Goodstein and Burke, included the following:

	Evolutionary Change	Incremental or Mid-Range Change	Large-Scale Systems Change
Problem Solving	Business as usual. Some employee and supervisory training of a technical nature that enhances job performance.	OD helps with participative problem solving. Several units, beginning with top management, hold periodic retreats to take a reading on strengths and problem areas—largely the technological and task aspects of their units—and to make action plans. Task forces are utilized.	Technological/structural approaches. Organization engages in massive reengineering program to speed up product development and customer service. Or Organization, in an efficiency move, merges several divisions, sells two, eliminates two layers of management, lays off ten percent of the workforce.
Problem Solving Plus Cultural Change	Business as usual plus modest shift in culture. Some managers and employees, in addition to technical training, attend various seminars courses. Individual managers begin to shift toward a more participative, open, supportive leadership style.	OD begins to have a significant impact on organizational culture. Units holding retreats include a collaborative look at functional and dysfunctional consequences of technological/task aspects plus leadership, group process, teamwork, and conflict management aspects. Process matters begin to be a legitimate part of any meeting agenda.	Organizational transformation including OD. Organization reconceptualizes the nature of its business, reduces management levels, uses multiple OD interventions, including the collateral organization, team building, survey feedback, task forces, and intensive leadership training; revises staffing and compensation systems. Or Organization reconceptualizes the nature of its business and engages in a comprehensive TQM effort, including extensive use of survey feedback, team building, and organization mirror techniques.

Figure 11-2   Examples of Different Types and Degrees of Organizational Change

- Replacement of the top management team
- Redefining the nature of the business from transportation to service.
- Diagonal task forces to plan changes.
- A reduction in hierarchical levels.
- Substantial downsizing of the workforce, including middle management, without layoffs
- Team building (off site), including role clarification and negotiation.
- Process consultation.
- Modifying the budget process
- Top management commitment and involvement

- Personnel staff trained to be internal consultants
- Peer support groups
- Performance-based compensation and profit sharing
- Experiential training programs for senior and middle managers including feedback on managerial behavior.
- Open communications.
- Continuous data-based feedback on work group and organizational climate and management practices.
- A new appraisal system emphasizing both behavior and performance
- Continuous use of task forces[49]

The reader will note that a wide variety of interventions were utilized in this large-scale systems change program.

SUMMARY OF THE CHARACTERISTICS OF SELECTED STRUCTURAL INTERVENTIONS

The following summarizes some of the differences and similarities as well as the overlap between sociotechnical systems (STS), self-managed teams, work redesign, MBO, quality circles, quality of work life, (QWL) programs, parallel or collateral structures, physical settings, total quality management (TQM), and large-scale systems change:

1. *Sociotechnical systems (STS) theory* is based on joint optimization of the social and technological systems of organizations. Furthermore,

   a. the boundary between the organization and its environment should be managed in such a way as to allow effective exchanges, but protection from external disruptions,

   b. the implementation of STS should be highly participative, and

   c. the creation and development of self-managed teams is an important implementation (Cummings and Worley; Trist, Higgin, Murray, and Pullock; and others).

2. The creation of *self-managed teams* involves

   a. providing teams with a grouping of tasks that comprises a major unit of the total work to be performed.

   b. training group members in multiple skills, including team-effectiveness skills

   c. delegating to the team many aspects of how the work gets done;

   d. providing a great deal of information and feedback for self-regulation of quality and productivity;

   e. solving the problem of dislocation of first-line supervisors; and coordinating (Walton, Lawler, and others).

3. *Work redesign theory* suggests that

   a. motivation and performance can be enhanced through redesigning jobs to heighten skill variety, task identity, task significance, autonomy, and feedback from the job;

      b. the concept can be extended to the creation of self-managed teams; and

      c. third-party assistance in the development and monitoring of group norms can be useful (Hackman and Oldham).

4. *Traditional MBO targets* assumes the need for systematic goal setting linking the goals of superiors to subordinates and that

      a. objectives or targets should be stated in quantitative terms whenever possible,

      b. goal setting and appraisal should be one-on-one dialogue between superiors to subordinate. However, additional conceptualization and experience indicate that

      c. MBO can vary on a autocratic-participative continuum

      d. MBO can feature a participative team approach (French and Hollmannn, Likert and Fisher).

5. *Quality circles*, at least the participative, problem-solving versions, are based on the assumptions that many; if not most, employees are willing to work collaboratively in group settings—both natural work teams and cross-functional teams—on problems of product quality and system effectiveness, and that they can learn to effectively utilize both technical and process consultants, providing they are

      a. trained in quality control concepts and the relevant measuring techniques, and

      b. trained in group dynamics, team leadership, and interpersonal communication skills.

6. *Quality of work life (QWL) programs* vary in content but frequently include restructuring of several dimensions of the organization, including

      a. increased problem solving between management and the union;

      b. increased participation by teams of employees in shop floor decisions pertaining to production flow, quality control, and safety;

      c. skill development through technical skill training, job rotation, and training in team problem solving (Fuller, Carrigan, Bluestone, Goodman, Lawler, Ledford, Walton, and others).

7. *Parallel learning structures (or collateral organizations)* are organizations established within ongoing organizations and have the following features:

      a. a mandate to deal with complex, nonroutine, future-oriented problems and/or to coordinate large-scale systems change;

      b. the creation of different norms and culture to enhance creative problem solving and to create a model organization from which the organization can learn (Zand, Bushe, and Shani).

8. *Physical settings or arrangements* can be the focus of interventions that can utilize and be highly congruent with OD techniques and assumptions (Steele).

9. *Total quality management (TQM) programs* are combinations of a number of approaches, including

      a. a high emphasis on customers, including internal customers;

      b. the use of statistical quality control and statistical process control techniques;

      c. competitive benchmarking;

      d. participative management;

      e. an emphasis on teams and teamwork; and

      f. an emphasis on continuous training (Peters and Peters, Ciampa, Sashkin, and others).

10. *Large-scale systems change (including organizational transformation) with an extensive OD thrust* typically requires a multiplicity of interventions over an extended time frame, including

      a. a reconceptualization of the nature of the business;

      b. the use of a parallel learning structure;

      c. a reduction in hierarchical levels;

      d. team building and development, including the use of cross-functional teams;

      e. survey feedback;

      f. extensive use of task forces; and

      g. intensive leadership training (Nadler, Ackerman, Porras and Silvers, Cummings and Worley, Weisbord, and others).

NOTES

1. Thomas G. Cummings and Christopher G. Worley, *Organization Development and Change*, 5th ed. (St. Paul, MN: West Publishing Company, 1993), pp. 353–354.

2. E. L. Trist, G. W. Higgin, H. Murray, and A. B. Pollock, *Organizational Choice* (London: Tavistock, 1965).

3. A. K. Rice, "Productivity and Social Organization in an Indian Weaving Shed: An Examination of Some Aspects of the Socio-Technical System of an Experimental Automatic Loom Shed," *Human Relations*, 6 (1953), pp. 297–329.

4. See, for example, E. Thorsrud, "Socio-Technical Approach to Job Design and Organizational Development," *Management International Review*, 8 (1968), pp. 120–131. See also Calvin Pava, "Designing Managerial and Professional Work for High Performance: A Sociotechnical Approach," *National Productivity Review*, 2 (Spring 1983), pp. 126–135; and Calvin Pava, "Redesigning Sociotechnical Systems Design: Concepts and Methods for the 1990s," *The Journal of Applied Behavioral Science*, 22, no. 3 (1986), pp. 201–221.

5. Richard E. Walton, "From Hawthorne to Topeka and Kalmar," in E. L. Cass and Frederick G. Zimmer, eds., *Man and Work in Society* (New York: Van Nostrand Reinhold, 1975), pp. 116–129. See also William A. Pasmore, "Overcoming the Roadblocks in Work-Restructuring Efforts," *Organizational Dynamics*, 10 (Spring 1982), pp. 54–67; and Berth Jonsson and Alden Lake, "Volvo: A Report," *Human Resource Management*, 24 (Winter 1985), pp. 455–465.

6. David Barry, "Managing the Bossless Team: Lessons in Distributed Leadership," *Organizational Dynamics*, 20 (Summer 1991), p. 31; Oregon Department of Transportation, Region 4, and Gossard-Pyron Associates, *Self-Directed Maintenance Crews: Results of a Two-Year Pilot Program* (January 1993); *Fortune* (October 17, 1992), p. 113; and Jana Schilder, "Work Teams Boost Productivity," *Personnel Journal*, 71 (February 1992), pp. 67–71.

7. Edward E. Lawler III, "The New Plant Revolution Revisited," *Organizational Dynamics*, 19 (Autumn 1990), p. 10.

8. Art Kleiner, *The Age of Heretics* (New York: Doubleday, 1996), pp. 61–101.

9. For more on problems in the use of self-managed teams, see Tom Peters, Thriving on Chaos (New York: Alfred A. Knopf, 1988), pp. 299–300; and Tony Kulisch and David K. Banner, "Self-Managed Work Teams: An Update," *Leadership & Organization Development Journal*, 14, no. 2 (1993), pp. 25–29.

10. Lawler, "The New Plant Revolution," p. 11. For more on sociotechnical systems design and self-managed teams, see Abraham B. Shani and Ord Elliott, "Sociotechnical System Design in Transition," in Walter Sikes, Allan B. Drexler, and Jack Gant, eds. *The Emerging Practice of Organization Development* (Alexandria, VA: NTL Institute, and San Diego: University Associates, 1989), pp. 187–198; and Louis E. Davis, "Guides to the Design and Redesign of Organizations," in Robert Tannenbaum, Newton Margulies, and Fred Massarik and Associates, *Human Systems Development* (San Francisco: Jossey-Bass Publishers, 1985), pp. 143–166.

11. J. Richard Hackman and Greg R. Oldham, *Work Redesign* (Reading, MA: Addison-Wesley Publishing Company, 1980), pp. 77–83.

12. Ibid., pp. 82–88.

13. Ibid., p. 181.

14. Ibid., p. 184.

15. For a description of a federal government MBO program "laid on from the top" and the consequent resistance and token use, see Edward J. Ryan, Jr., "Federal Government MBO: Another Managerial Fad?" *MSU Business Topics*, 21 (Autumn 1976), pp. 35–43. For more on some of the basic faults in many MBO efforts, see Harry Levinson, "Management by Whose Objectives?" Harvard Business Review, 48 (July–August 1970), pp. 125–134.

16. See Wendell French and Robert Hollmann, "Management by Objectives: The Team Approach," *California Management Review*, 17 (Spring 1975), pp. 13–22. A workshop participant has suggested we call this "COMBO." See also Wendell L. French and John A. Drexler, Jr., "A Team Approach to MBO," Leadership & Organization Development Journal, 5, no. 5 (1984), pp. 22–26.

17. H. H. Meyer, E. Kay, and J. R. P. French, Jr., "Split Roles in Performance Appraisal," *Harvard Business Review*, 43 (January–February 1965), pp. 124–139.

18. Edward E. Lawler III, Alan M. Mohrman, Jr., and Susan M. Resnick, "Performance Appraisal Revisited," *Organizational Dynamics*, 13 (Summer 1984), pp. 20–35.

19. Robert W. Hollmann, "Supportive Organization Climate and Managerial Assessment of MBO Effectiveness," *Academy of Management Journal*, 19 (December 1976), pp. 560–576.

20. Rensis Likert and M. Scott Fisher, "MBGO: Putting Some Team Spirit into MBO," *Personnel*, 54 (January–February 1977), pp. 40–47. Actually, Likert had done some research on such an approach in the mid-1960s but had not called it a form of MBO. See Rensis Likert's discussion of "a group method of sales supervision" in his *The Human Organization: Its Management and Value* (New York: McGraw-Hill, 1967), pp. 55–71.

21. Peter F. Drucker, "Learning from Foreign Management," *The Wall Street Journal*, June 4, 1980, p. 20.

22. Donald L. Dewar, *Quality Circle Member Manual* (Red Bluff, CA: Quality Circle Institute, 1980), p. iii.

23. Robert E. Cole, "Made in Japan—Quality-Control Circles," *Across the Board*, 16 (November 1979), pp. 72–78.

24. Edward E. Lawler III and Susan A. Mohrman, "Quality Circles After the Fad," *Harvard Business Review*, 63 (January–February 1985), pp. 65–71.

25. Based on interviews and observations at Lockheed Shipbuilding; Robert E. Cole and Dennis S. Tachiki, "Forging Institutional Links: Making Quality Circles Work in the U.S." *National Productivity Review*, 3 (Autumn 1984), pp. 417–429; and Mary Zippo, "Productivity and Morale Sagging? Try the Quality Circle Approach," *Personnel*, 57 (May–June 1980), pp. 43–45.

26. Cole, "Made in Japan," p. 76.

27. "Quality Control Circles Pay Off Big," *Industry Week* (October 29, 1979), p. 17.

28. Edward E. Lawler III, Susan A. Mohrman, and Gerald E. Ledford, Jr., *Employee Involvement and Total Quality Management* (San Francisco: Jossey-Bass Publishers, 1992), p. 57.

29. Tom Peters, *Thriving on Chaos* (New York: Alfred A. Knopf, 1988), p. 85. For some of the potential problems with quality circles, see Gregory P. Shea, "Quality Circles: The Danger of Bottled Change," *Sloan Management Review*, 27 (Spring 1986), pp. 33–46; Donald D. White and David A. Bednar, "Locating Problems with Quality Circles," *National Productivity Review*, 4 (Winter 1984–85), pp. 45–52; and Edward E. Lawler III and Susan A. Mohrman, "Quality Circles: After the Honeymoon," *Organizational Dynamics*, 14 (Spring 1987), pp. 42–55.

30. Paul S. Goodman, "Quality of Work Life Projects in the 1980s," *Labor Law Journal*, 31 (August 1980), p. 487. See also Louis E. Davis, "Guides to the Design and Redesign of Organizations," in Robert Tannenbaum, Newton Margulies, Fred Massarik and Associates, *Human Systems Development* (San Francisco: Jossey-Bass Publishers, 1985), pp. 143–166.

31. Stephen H. Fuller, "How Quality-of-Worklife Projects Work for General Motors," *Monthly Labor Review*, 103 (July 1980), pp. 37–39; Irving Bluestone, "How Quality-of-Worklife Projects Work for the United Auto Workers" *Monthly Labor Review*, 103 (July 1980), pp. 39–41; and Patricia M. Carrigan, "Up from the Ashes," *OD Practitioner*, 18 (March 1986), pp. 1–6. See also Edward M. Glaser and Paul A. Nelson, "A Quality of Worklife Improvement Effort at Five Mental Health Facilities," *OD Practitioner*, 19 (March 1987), pp. 1–6.

32. Goodman, "Quality of Work Life Projects in the 1980s," pp. 387–494. See also Edward E. Lawler III and Gerald E. Ledford, Jr., "Productivity and the Quality of Work Life," *National Productivity Review*, 1 (Winter 1981–82), pp. 23–36. For further discussion of QWL projects see Louis E. Davis and Albert B. Cherns, eds., *The Quality of Working Life*, vol. II (New York: The Free Press, 1975); Richard E. Walton, "Work Innovations at Topeka: After Six Years," *Journal of Applied Behavioral Science*, 13, no. 3 (1977), pp. 422–433; and Richard E. Walton, "Work Innovations in the United States," *Harvard Business Review*, 57 (July–August 1979), pp. 88–98.

33. See Janice A. Klein, "Why Supervisors Resist Employee Involvement," *Harvard Business Review*, 62 (September–October 1984), pp. 87–95. See also Robert T. Golembiewski and Ben-Chu Sun, "Positive-Findings Bias in QWL Studies: Rigor and Outcomes in a Large Sample," *Journal of the Academy of Management*, 16, no. 3 (1990), pp. 665–674.

34. This discussion is based on Dale Zand, "Collateral Organization: A New Change Strategy," *Journal of Applied Behavioral Science*, 10, no. 1 (1974), pp. 63–89. See also Dale E. Zand, *Information, Organization, and Power* (New York: McGraw-Hill, 1981), chapter 4; and Barry A. Stein and Rosabeth Moss Kanter, "Building the Parallel Organization: Creating Mechanisms for Permanent Quality of Work Life," *The Journal of Applied Behavioral Science*, 16 (July–September 1980), pp. 371–386. See also Abraham B. Shani and Bruce J. Eberhardt, "Parallel Organization in a Health Care Institution," *Group & Organization Studies*, 12 (June 1987), pp. 147–173.

35. Gervase R. Bushe and A. B. (Rami) Shani, *Parallel Learning Structures* (Reading, MA: Addison-Wesley Publishing Company, 1991), p. 10.

36. Fred I. Steele, *Physical Settings and Organizational Development* (Reading, MA: Addison-Wesley, 1973), pp. 101–107.

37. Ibid., p. 131.

38. Ibid., pp. 97–98. See also Jerry I. Porras and Peter J. Robertson, "Organization Development: Theory, Practice, and Research," in Marvin D. Dunnette and L. M. Hough, *Handbook of Industrial & Organization Psychology*, 2d ed. (Palto Alto, CA: Consulting Psychologists Press, 1992), pp. 773–779.

39. Barbara H. Peters and Jim L. Peters, *Total Quality Management*, The Conference Board Report No. 963 (1991); and *Business Week* special issue "The Quality Imperative" (October 25, 1991).

40. Marshall Sashkin emphasizes the dimension of valid data in his paper distributed at a Bowling Green State University Master of Organization Development program in April 1992: "TQM Implications for OD," pp. 4–5.

41. Dan Ciampa, *Total Quality*, p. 33. For more on the cultural dimensions of TQM, see Marshall Sashkin and Kenneth J. Kiser, Total Quality Management (Seabrook, MD: Ducochon Press, 1991), chapters 4 and 5.

42. Thomas G. Cummings and Christopher G. Worley, *Organization Development and Change*, 5th ed. St. Paul, MN: West Publishing Company, 1993), p. 543.

43. Gerald E. Ledford, Jr. and Susan Albers Mohrman, "Self-Design for High Involvement: A Large-Scale Organizational Change, *Human Relations*, 46 (February 1993), p. 146.

44. Ibid. See also Susan Albers Mohrman and Thomas G. Cummings, Self-Designing Organizations: Learning How to Create High Performance (Reading, MA: Addison-Wesley, 1989).

45. Ledford and Mohrman, p. 145.

46. Ibid., pp. 144–145.

47. This conceptualizing of different types of change has been influenced by a number of authors and sources, including David A. Nadler, "Organizational Frame Bending: Principles for Managing reorientation," *Academy of Management* EXECUTIVE, 3 (August 1989), pp. 194–204; Linda Ackerman, "Development, Transition or Transformation: The Question of Change in Organizations," *OD Practitioner*, 18 (December 1986), pp. 1–8; Marvin R. Weisbord, "Toward Third-Wave Managing and Consulting," *Organizational Dynamics*, 15 (Winter 1987), pp. 5–25; Jerry I. Porras and Robert C. Silvers, "Organization Development and Transformation," *Annual Review of Psychology*, 42 (1991), pp. 51–78; and Thomas G. Cummings and Christopher G. Worley, *Organization Development and Change*, 5th ed. (St. Paul, MN: West Publishing Company, 1993), pp. 520–523.

48. Amir Levy and Uri Merry, *Organizational Transformation* (New York: Praeger Publishers, 1986), p. 5.

49. Leonard D. Goodstein and W. Warner Burke, "Creating Successful Organizational Change," *Organizational Dynamics*, 19 (Spring 1991), pp. 5–17.

CHAPTER 12

Training Experiences

A number of training or educational experiences aimed at individual have utility in the successful evolution of an OD effort. These OD interventions can be complementary and reinforcing adjuncts to the OD process. Many different kinds of seminars and workshops, of course, including those of a technical nature such as budgeting, statistical process control, and long-range planning, can be of assistance to individuals, depending upon their experiences to date and the problems faced by the organization. But we want to highlight several that focus on the human and social processes of organizations, especially those that are of relevance to leadership, interpersonal and group skills, and to career development.

In particular, we want to focus on T-groups, behavior modeling, and life and career planning, including the use of career anchors, and the use of collage and letters. There will also be a discussion of mentoring and coaching, and the use of instrumented training.

T-GROUPS

Early in the OD movement, T-groups ("T" for training)[1] were sometimes used with intact work teams, but such use has largely given way to team building. The latter has a much more diagnostic, issue-oriented, problem-solving, and organizational focus. Nevertheless, as an educational experience for the individual, the T-group has high relevance for developing skills of importance in the unfolding of an OD effort and for personal growth and development.

A T-group is an essentially unstructured, agendaless group session for about 10 to 12 members and a professional "trainer" who acts as catalyst and facilitator for the group. The data for discussion are the data provided by the interaction of the group members as they strive to create a viable society for themselves. Actions, reactions, interactions, and the concomitant feelings accompanying them are the data for the group. The group typically meets for three days up-to two weeks. Conceptual material relating to communication skills, interpersonal relations, individual personality theory, and group dynamics is a part of the program. But the main learning vehicle is the group experience.

Learnings derived from the T-group vary for different individuals, but they are usually described as learnings to be more competent in interpersonal relationships, learning more about oneself as a person, learning how others react to one's behavior, and learning about the dynamics of group formation, and group norms, and group growth. In an early work, Benne, Bradford, and Ronald Lippitt list the goals of the laboratory method as follows:

1. One hoped for outcome for the participant is increased awareness of and sensitivity to emotional reactions and expression in himself and in others.
2. Another desired objective is greater ability to perceive and to learn from the consequences of his actions through attention to feelings, his own and others. Emphasis is placed on the development of sensitivity to cues furnished by the behavior of others and ability to utilize "feedback" in understanding his own behaviors.
3. The staff also attempts to stimulate the clarification and development of personal values and goals consonant with a democratic and scientific approach to problems and personal decision and action ...
4. Another objective is the development of concepts and theoretical insights, which will serve as tools in linking personal values, goals, and intentions to actions consistent with these inner factors and with the requirements of the situation.... One important source of valid concepts is the findings and methodologies of the behavioral sciences....
5. All laboratory programs foster the achievement of behavioral effectiveness in transactions with one's environment.... The learning of concepts, the setting of goals, the clarification of values, and even the achievement of valid insight into self, are sometimes far ahead of the development of the performance skills necessary to expression in actual social transactions. For this reason laboratory programs normally focus on the development of behavioral skills to support better integration of intentions and actions.[2]

The T-group is a powerful learning laboratory where individuals gain insights into the meaning and consequences of their own behavior, the meaning and consequences of others' behaviors, and the dynamics and processes of group behavior. These insights are coupled with growth of skills in diagnosing and taking more effective interpersonal and group action. Thus, the T-group can give individuals the basic skills necessary for more component action taking in the organization.

Uses of T-groups relative to OD are varied, but they are particularly appropriate to introduce key members of the organization to group and interpersonal process issues and for enhancing basic skills relevant to group and interpersonal dynamics. The most frequently used T-group format is the "stranger" lab composed of people from a variety of organizations. To illustrate, a one-week T-group experience might involve three trainers and 30 to 36 participants, all strangers to each other at the beginning of the lab. Another format involves several clusters of two or three persons from the same organizations, with people who know each other assigned to different T-groups. (The Oregon Leadership Institute, for example, encourages this arrangement.)

Our impression from discussion with Warner Burke of Teachers College, Columbia University, Craig Lundberg of Cornell, and others is that a significant number of long-time, senior OD consultant-scholars see the need for more encouragement of managers and OD-practitioners to attend T-group experiences. A quote from Marvin Weisbord, in the context of commenting on research on the positive and negative uses of power and authority in self-managing groups, tends to support this. He states, "This confirms for me that the T-group, which put these issues in stark relief, is an important *learning* structure."[3] Peter Vaill says, "I think that sensitivity training is the most original and powerful contribution that the applied behavioral sciences have made to civilized culture.[4] "We agree and believe that T-group learnings provide numerous insights and skills of importance to successful OD efforts and to effective organizational functioning.

SENSITIVITY TRAINING IN INDIA

Rolf Lynton conducted the first T-group in India in 1957 for youth leaders under the aegis of the Aloka Foundation (Sinha, 1985). Sinha provides a detailed documentation of the historical development of sensitivity training (ST) in India till 1980s. Table 12.1 presents a list of some of the training institutions in India.

Table 12-1: Sensitivity Training Institutions in India

Year	Individual/Institution	Focus Area
1971	Indian Society for Applied Behavioral Science (ISABS)	NTL approach, Intra-personal, Interpersonal, and Group Processes-based Sensitivity Training
1979	Indian Society for Individual and Social Development (ISISD)	Departure: Role and Identity-based Sensitivity training—Broader perspective including mythology, existential, eastern phenomenological, and relativist philosophies
1996	Aastha	Role and Identity-based Sensitivity Training—Focus on Educational Sector
1996	Sumedhas: The Academy of Human Context	Role and identity-based Sensitivity Training—Invitation Rather Than Confrontation and Unfolding of Self in its Wholeness

Indian Innovations in Sensitivity Training

Sensitivity training in India has evolved from the initial influences of Western developments and has, in fact, built on them. Some of the significant new forms of lab are as follows:

- Facilitative leadership lab and explorations in personal and role effectiveness using 360 degrees feedback by Indian Society for Applied Behavioral Science (ISABS, 2001).
- Explorations in the dynamics of vitalizing life spaces and explorations in fostering growth by Indian Society for Individual and Social Development (ISISD, 2001).
- Bindu and Learning Theatre (LT) by Sumedhas, 2001).

COMPARATIVE ANALYSIS BETWEEN WESTERN PERSPECTIVE AND INDIAN PERSPECTIVE

Table 12-2 shows a comparative analysis between Western perspective and Indian perspective (Role and Identity Approach).

Table 12-2: Comparative analysis between Western Perspective and Indian Perspective

Western Perspective	Indian Perspective (Role and Identity Approach)
• Conceptual Understanding and Experiential Learning	• Experiential Learning, Self-reflectivity, and Awareness
• Emphasis on Gaining skills and Competencies	• Emphasis on Unfolding of Inherent Potential
• Focus on Individual Growth and Development Team Working and Role Taking Leadership Work Climate/Culture Resistance to Change and Mindset Change	• Focus on Individual Growth and Development Role Creation and Enactment Collective Leadership Co-creation of organizational Reality Self and Professional Renewal-Individuals, Teams, and Organization.
Balancing Individual and Organizational Goals	Aligning Simultaneous and Multiple Individual and Organization Goals
	• Intervention to change the working Paradigm/perspective
• Interventions to solve Problems • To Achieve Organizational Objectives	• To Co-create Organizational Reality and Future

Source: Golembiewski and Blumberg (1970); Sinha (1083); Garg and Parikh (1989);Sumedhas (2000); and Sumedhas (2001c).

NEW TRENDS OF SENSITIVITY TRAINING APPLIED IN ORGANIZATIONS (PARIKH AND JAYAVELU, 2002)

Unstructured Sensitivity Training Labs

Unstructured labs provide a space to voice the unvoiced, articulate the unarticulated, express the unexpressed, own up the disowned, and enact the withheld (Parikh, 1989). They are called by many names—Personal growth Lab, Exploration in Roles and Identity, Interpersonal Relations Lab, and so on—and provide the foundation for individual, group, and organizational transformation.

Semi-Structured Labs

Semi-Structures Labs have specific objectives and are designed to address the critical issues faced by the organizational members. Some examples are Interface Labs, Leadership Labs, Self-renewal labs, and Visioning and Co-creating labs.

Structured Workshops

Structured Workshops are experiential based conceptual training programmes. These aim at conceptual understanding along with experience of exploration of new beginnings and enhanced competencies. Examples of workshops are Managerial and Leadership Roles, Team Building/Building a Team across Functions, Divisions, and Organizations etc.

BEHAVIORAL MODELING

Behavior modeling is a training technique designed to improve interpersonal competence. It is not an OD intervention per se, but we believe it should be added to the OD practitioner's repertoire because it is such an effective tool, and because problems with interpersonal relations are common in organizations. For improving interpersonal skills, behavior modeling is an important training option.

Based on Albert Bandura's Social Learning Theory and utilizing procedures developed by Goldstein and Sorcher, behavior modeling has been shown to be an excellent way to make first-line supervisors more effective (Latham and Saari) and to improve organizational performance (Porras et al.)[5] The basic premise of Social Learning Theory is that for persons to engage successfully in a behavior, they (1) must perceive a link between the behavior and certain outcomes, (2) must desire those outcomes (called Positive valence), and (3) must believe they can do it (called self-efficacy).[6] For example, many first-line supervisors find it difficult to discipline employees. To learn this behavior they must see a link between successful disciplining from superiors or less hassle from subordinates) and must come to believe they can do it. This latter belief can be instilled through the methodology of behavior modeling: by viewing a model similar to them being successful, by discovering the specific behavioral skills that led to success, and by practicing the skills until they too are proficient.

A simple problem-solving model underlies most behavior modeling training, Porras and Singh describe it as follows:

> The problem-solving approach, a rather straightforward one consisting of three phases—problem identification, problem solving, and implementation, consisting of five behavioral skills:
>
> 1. *Behavior description.* The ability to describe behavior of self or others in specific concrete terms and to avoid generalizations or inferences drawn from observed behaviors.
> 2. *Justification.* The ability to clearly explain the impact of an observed behavior on the individual, the observer, or the organization.
> 3. *Active listening.* The ability to accurately reflect both content and feelings of another's communication.
> 4. *Participative problem solving.* The ability to involve another, meaningfully and appropriately, in the process of solving a work-related problem.
> 5. *Positive reinforcement.* The ability to compliment another in a sincere and authentic manner.[7]

The steps involved in behavior modeling are simple. First determine the most pressing problems facing a target group, say, first-line supervisors. These usually consist of such issues as counseling the poor performer, correcting absenteeism, encouraging the average performer, correcting unsafe work behavior, and so forth. Training modules for each of about ten problems are developed, the core of which are videotapes showing a person (model) correctly handling the situation. The specific behaviors exhibited by the model that cause success are highlighted as "learning points"—typically these are the behavioral skills mentioned by Porras and Singh. Weekly training sessions of four hours are scheduled for each module for groups of approximately ten participants.

At the training sessions the problem situation is announced and briefly discussed. Participants then observe a videotape in which the model (who looks similar to them) successfully solves the problem by enacting specific behavioral skills. The trainees discuss the behavioral skills and then *role-play the situation* receiving *feedback from the group and the trainer* in their performance. Role-playing continues until each participant successfully masters all the specific skills. Participants then commit to practicing the new skills on the job in the coming week. At the beginning of the next session, participants report on how their new skills worked on the job. If necessary, additional practice is held to ensure mastery of the skills. Then a new problem is addressed, the model is observed on videotape, and role-playing and feedback occur until all participants learn how to solve the new problem.

Behavior modeling works; it teaches the skills and behaviors needed to deal with interpersonal problems. It should be in the practitioner's kit bag.

LIFE AND CAREER PLANNING

A number of approaches exist to help the individual think through and analyze his or her life and career trajectory. This information is often used in workshop or other educational settings in the context of small-group discussions and some theory input. We will focus primarily on some contributions of Edgar Schein, Herbert Shepard, and Jack Fordyce and Raymond Weil.

Career Anchors

Edgar Schein has provided the concept of career anchors, which are useful individually and in voluntary group discussions in career development workshops. Based on a longitudinal study of MIT Sloan School alumni, Schein hypothesized five basic career anchors. He defines the career anchor as "the pattern of self-perceived talents, motives, and values" that serves "to guide, constrain, stabilize, and integrate the person's career" and that tends to" remain stable throughout the person's career.[8]

The five career anchors are as follows:

Technical/functional competence: The entire career is organized around a particular set of technical or functional skills which the person is good at and values, leading to a self-concept of remaining in an occupation that would continue to provide challenging work around those particular skills wherever they were.

Managerial competence: The entire career is organized around climbing an organizational ladder to achieve a position of responsibility in general management in which decisions and their consequences could be clearly related by the individual to his own efforts in analyzing problems, dealing with people, and making difficult decisions in uncertain conditions.

Creativity: The entire career is organized around the same kind of entrepreneurial effort which would permit the individual to create a new service or product, to invent some thing, or to build his or her own business.

Security or stability: The entire career is organized around the location of an organizational niche that would guarantee continued employment, a stable future, and the ability to provide comfortably for the family through achieving a measure of financial independence.

Autonomy: The entire career is organized around finding an occupation such as teaching, consulting, writing, running a store, or something equivalent, which permits the individual to determine his own hours, lifestyle, and working patterns.[9]

In his book, *Career Dynamics*, Schein provides a "self-analysis form," a questionnaire that a person can use to provide information to help determine his or her own career anchor.[10]

Life Goals Exercise

One series of life-and career-planning exercises is shown in the outline that follows. Herbert A. Shepard is generally acknowledged as the author and the originator of these exercises.

1. **First phase**
   a. Draw a straight horizontal line from left to right to represent your life span. The length should represent the totality of your experience and future expectations.
   b. Indicate where you are now.
   c. Prepare a life inventory of important "happenings" for you, including the following:
      1. Any peak experiences you have had.
      2. Things which you do well.
      3. Things which you do poorly.
      4. Things you would like to stop doing.
      5. Things you would like to do well.
      6. Peak experiences you would like to have.
      7. Vales (e.g., power, money, etc.) you want to achieve.
      8. Things you would like to start doing now.
   D. Discussions in subgroups.

2. **Second phase**
   a. Take 20 minutes to write your own obituary.
   b. Form pairs, take 20 minutes to write a eulogy for your partner.
   c. Discussions in subgroups.[11]

The Collage and the Letters

As another example, the outline of activities suggested by Fordyce and Weil had the following steps.[12] First, individuals working in small groups are asked to make a *collage*—a symbolic representation of their lives constructed out of art materials, old magazines and newspapers, and the like; these are posted on the walls for later discussion. Second, individuals write two *letters*, the instructions for which are as follows:

> Now imagine that you have died ten years from now. Write a letter from one of your best friends to another good friend, telling about you and your life. What do you want him to be able to say about you? Next, imagine you have been killed in an auto accident next week. Now write a similar letter. What would he be likely to say about you?[13]

At this point, the group discusses the collages and letters of each individual, giving the individual the chance to get feedback from the rest of the group about their reactions and also allowing the group to learn more about each other.

This third set of public sharing serves to prepare the members for the next step, consisting of building a "life inventory," similar to the "life goals exercise." discussed earlier. After the preparation of the life inventory, each individual prepares a career inventory by writing answers to questions such as the following: What facets of work (my career up to this point) do I like most/least? What do you think are my best skills, abilities, and talents that I bring to the work situation? What kinds of rewards do I seek from my job—money, status, recognition, being a part of a team? What new career areas do I want to pursue? What new skills do I need to develop for the new career areas? These inventories are shared and discussed within the group. As a final step, individuals set down a plan of action steps for achieving the goals they have identified.

Life-and career-planning activities may take one day, an entire week, or, when spread out a few hours at a time, several weeks. These activities involve generating data about oneself, analyzing the data both individually and in-groups, and formulating clear goals and action pans for achieving them. These activities are particularly helpful for those who feel they are on "dead center," who are contemplating a career change, or who have seldom been introspective about their own lifestyle and career pattern.

COACHING AND MENTORING

The OD consultant can be in a position to provide guidance for formal mentoring programs. While coaching by an employee's immediate superior usually focuses on job performance, *mentoring* is usually much broader and focuses on general career and personal development. The mentor role is usually filled by someone other than the immediate superior, and usually by a person of higher rank from outside the employee's department. Mentoring can be accomplished on a person-to-person basis, or the mentor can meet with a small group of four or six protégés, or in both group and one-and-one sessions. With the group approach, the group has the potential to evolve into a learning team whose members can coach each other.[14] The OD consultant can provide valuable training, such as training in active listening or training in small-group process interventions, for example, for those involved in this process.

Mentoring, coaching, counseling, and consulting skills can be enhanced significantly by T-group experiences. In T-group setting, people typically learn to listen more carefully, to pay more attention to emotional content, to feedback what they are hearing in more useful ways, to understand what is going on in a group, and so on. This training is valuable for supervisory coaching at all organizational levels, for team members consulting with each other, and for those wanting to develop OD consultation skills.

A number of Indian organizations have institutionalized the practice of providing mentors to their incoming employees as this also helps to provide a sense of belongingness and anchoring within the organisation. One such example is Tata Consultancy Services where intensive training is provided to the mentors in order to make this practice successful.

INSTRUMENTED TRAINING

Self-diagnostic surveys are widely used in human relations training and in laboratory training settings. When used appropriately, they can also be useful for team building. For a successful intervention, the consultant must have expertise in the use of a particular instrument, it must have reasonably high reliability and validity, its use must be based on a diagnosis of what would be helpful to further the development of the team, and participants must have concurred in its use. Many instruments are available; to illustrate, the second edition of *Instrumentation in Human Relations Training* described 92 instruments with wide application to the behavioral sciences.[15]

One example of a diagnostic instrument, the Myers-Briggs Type Indicator (MBTI), with origins in Carl Jung's concept of personality types, uses combinations of scores from four major scales to identify orientation toward Extraversion or Introversion, Sensing or Intuition, Thinking or Feeling, and Judging or Perceiving. When shared in a group whose members have relatively high trust in each other and relatively high communications skills, this self-disclosed information can further tolerance and understanding between members, can be used by individuals to enhance strengths in deficient areas, and in some instances can be useful in sorting out team assignments.[16] As another example of Grid OD, as discussed in chapter 11, is based on an inventory that assesses one's leadership style and management practices. Using a questionnaire, participants can plot on a two-dimensional grid where their practices appear to be in terms of "concern for production" and "concern for people." Workshops focusing on diagnosed styles can be a springboard for developing more effective leadership and team behaviors.

The advantages of using self-diagnostic instruments are probably in the context of training programs involving strangers or persons from different units than in the context of team building. In the latter case, it would be important to base the use of an instrument on a joint diagnosis of issues and challenges facing a team, an understanding of the theory and research underlying the instrument, and an understanding of any potentially dysfunctional consequences of its use. Some of the dysfunctional consequences might be:

- Using the results to label or stereotype others.
- Distorting responses so that scores produce results assumed to be "socially acceptable" or what management might want.
- Focusing on the analysis of behavior rather than on addressing and solving more fundamental issues facing the team.
- Fostering overdependence on the OD consultant.[17]

One of the dysfunctional aspects of using instrumental training techniques in OD happens when an OD consultant lets his or her "kit bag" of diagnostic surveys drive the selection of interventions. The consultant must make an informed judgment as to what intervention would be particularly useful to the client group at a given time. A self-diagnostic survey might or might not be appropriate.

ROLE EFFICACY LAB (REL)

Prof Udai Pareek has developed an instrument for enhancement of Role Efficacy. This can be used in addition to other instruments in order to generate diagnostic data. One strategy can be to start with the Role Efficacy Labs for the middle management level and then simultaneously for the next higher and lower level.

REL is a short process-oriented programme to diagnose the level of role efficacy in a group of employees (generally managers) in an organisation, and to take steps to raise that level. We have found a three-day REL useful for this purpose, although the lab can be longer, if some other aspects are included in it.

Instruments

An essay on my Role is an important instrument in REL. Role efficacy Scale (REL) or some structured instruments may not be as useful, since the spontaneous feelings and attitudes of the respondents are likely to filter through their conscious thinking (inhabitations and censoring) more easily in a projective device like the essay rather than in structured instruments. However, it may be useful to use a structured, instrument, like RES, to measure the respondents' perception of the role efficacy of the roles they supervise. If possible, the occupants of these roles may be asked to complete RES beforehand. It may then be useful to compare the differences between the perceptions of the role occupants and their bosses, later in the REL.

It may be useful to administer the instruments at the start of the lab, so that further interventions do not affect the responses to the instruments.

Unfreezing

In the beginning some unfreezing activity is useful. A microlab may be a useful activity (for the concept of microlab see Pareek and Rao, 1982, chapter 3). Most of the items in the microlab may be focused on the role.

Scoring of Instruments

The main purpose of "teaching" the participants the scoring system for an essay on My Role and RES or other instruments is to help understand and internalize the various aspects of role efficacy. The more they "search" evidence of the various dimensions of role efficacy in their own essays or those written by their colleagues, the more their thinking will get saturated with these ideas, and will influence their thinking in future, further influencing the way they shape their and their subordinate roles.

Concept Sessions

The concept sessions need to be short and interspersed in the working sessions. It may be useful to give some reading material to the participants, e.g., this book for reading a night, so that the next day they can use the readings to work on their diagnosis and action planning, and in raising conceptual issues.

Small Group Work

A lot of group work is involved in REL. The groups may be changed from time to time. If there are smaller number of participants, they may be divided into three groups (one each to work on role making dimension, role centering dimension, and role linkage dimension). If there are a larger group of participants, 10 groups may be formed, one for each aspects of role efficacy. Similarly, groups may be formed for suggestions for own role, suggestions for subordinate roles, and suggestions (expectations) from the management. However, the groups must work out specific suggestions for their situations, and generate newer ideas.

Force Field Analysis

Before working out suggestions for (or expectations from) the top management, it may be useful to spend some time in understanding the current situation in the organisation, what dimensions promote role efficacy of employees at a particular (e.g., middle management) level. Such an analysis for the different dimensions (or at least three clusters or dimensions) may provide some insight into the action possibilities—strengthening the supporting forces, and reducing or eliminating the retarding forces.

Action Planning

Each individual participant should prepare an action plan to increase his own role efficacy, and the role efficacy of his subordinates. These plans may be duplicated and distributed. This represents the commitment of each participant to himself and to the group. After individual plans are prepared, several common and collaborative action points may be developed, so that a group of people may collaboratively take action to develop their role efficacy. These may also be duplicated and distributed (after all these are shared in the plenary session and generally approved by the entire group).

Dialogue with the Top Management

The last item in the REL is aimed at (a) sharing the thinking and individual and group commitments with the top management, (b) creating an opportunity to get moral support and reinforcement of the top management, (c) generating ideas for action by the top management, (d) creating an opportunity for the top management to comment on and explain why some expectations are unrealistic and cannot be met, and to announce their own action plans to do something on some other suggestions.

It is necessary to ensure that the action suggestions generated for the top management relate to role efficacy aspects. There is a temptation for the group to use an opportunity of the dialogue to settle some other issues. If the latter is done, the purpose of the dialogue is defeated, If may, therefore, be useful to review critically by the total group of what will be communicated to the top management.

The dialogue may be useful if representatives of the management meet with about the same number of participants in the presence of the entire group. An empty chair may be provided for any member who has an urge to speak something, but the dialogue must be confined to the joint group of six to 10 persons.

It is necessary to prepare the top management also for the dialogue. They should be prepared to examine some suggestions, and take action on some of these. It may be useful to communicate such action taken from time to time. The top management should feel as much committed to such action as they expect the participants to honour their own action commitments.

Follow up

After a Role Efficacy Lab follow up and reinforcement may be planned. An annual one-day conference, reviewing expanses of role efficacy attempts may be helpful. In such a conference, top management may also share what they did to increase role efficacy of their employees. Monthly bulletins can be issued to report successful experiences of increasing role efficacy. One aspect may be specially highlighted every month (e.g., centrality, proactivity, etc).

Counselling

As it is important to work on role efficacy by redesigning the role, similarly, it is important to work on role efficacy from the point of view of the role occupant. Role efficacy may be low because the role occupant may either not be able to perceive those aspects in the role, or he may not be able to use his own power to build those aspects in the role. Necessary counselling and help in planning action to build these aspects by the individual himself may be useful. For example, if the person perceives that linkages with other roles are weak, it may be useful to work with him on what he can do to build stronger linkages with the other roles. Or, if he feels that his role does not provide opportunities to learn new things and grow, he can be helped to perceive various parts of the role, which may contribute to learning new things and his growth. The purpose of such counselling is to help the individual realise what prevents him from being effective, and to take necessary steps himself, without waiting for redesigning of the role in order to have higher role efficacy. Such counselling may become a part of performance counselling.

CONCLUDING COMMENTS

T-group training, the educational and social intervention giving rise to the laboratory training movement, typically yields important awareness about the self, interpersonal relationships, group dynamics, and leadership. Behavior modeling is a training technique designed to increase effectiveness in problematic interpersonal situations. Life-and career-planning workshops are less process oriented than T-group experiences, and they emphasize individual examination of personal, career and life plans and then discussion of individuals' analyses and plans in small groups. The use of five career anchors, the life goals exercise, and the collage and letters can be significant experiences for participants in these workshops. Coaching and mentoring can supplement an OD effort, and the OD consultant can play an important role in these processes. Instrumented training sessions using self-diagnostic surveys can be useful adjuncts to team building. One dysfunctional aspect of diagnostic surveys, like any OD or training technique, is that they can drive the OD consultant's interventions when a careful diagnosis of what would be particularly useful to a client group would be more appropriate.

NOTES

1. Sometimes called "L-groups" (learning groups), "D-groups" (development groups), study groups, and sensitivity training. See Edgar H. Schein and Warren G. Bennis, *Personal and Organizational Change Through Group Methods: The Laboratory Approach* (New York: John Wiley & Sons, 1965), p. 14.

2. K. D. Benne, L. P. Bradford, and R. Lippitt, "The Laboratory Method," in L. P. Bradford, J. R. Gibb, and K. D. Benne, eds., *T-Group Theory and Laboratory Method* (New York: John Wiley, 1964), pp. 15–44. This quotation is from pp. 16–17.

3. Marvin R. Weisbord, *Productive Workplaces* (San Francisco: Jossey-Bass Publishers, 1987), pp. 334–335.

4. Peter B. Vaill, "Integrating the Diverse Directions of the Behavioral Sciences," in Robert Tannenbaum, Newton Margulies, Fred Massarik and Associates, *Human Systems Development* (San Francisco: Jossey-Bass Publishers, 1985), p. 558.

5. See Albert Bandura, *Social Learning Theory* (Englewood Cliffs, NJ: Prentice-Hall, 1977); A. P. Goldstein and M. Sorcher, *Changing Supervisor Behavior* (New York: Pergamon, 1974); G. P. Latham and L. M. Saari, "Application of Social-Learning Theory to Training Supervisors Through Behavioral Modeling," *Journal of Applied Psychology*, 64 (1979), pp. 239–246; and J. I. Porras, K. Hargis, K. J. Patterson, D. C. Maxfield, N. Roberts, and R. J. Bies, "Modeling-Based Organizational Development: A Longitudinal Assessment," *The Journal of Applied Behavioral Science*, 18, no. 4 (1982), pp. 433–446.

6. Bandura, ibid.

7. J. I. Porras and J. V. Singh, "Alpha, Beta, and Gamma Change in Modeling-Based Organization Development," *Journal of Occupational Behavior*, 7 (1986), pp. 9–23. This quotation is from page 11.

8. Edgar H. Schein, *Career Dynamics: Matching Individual and Organizational Needs* (Reading, MA: Addison-Wesley Publishing Company, 1978), pp. 126–127.

9. Edgar H. Schein, *Occupational Psychology*, 3d ed. (Englewood Cliffs, NJ: Prentice-Hall, Inc., 1980), pp. 83–84.

10. Schein, *Career Dynamics*, pp. 257–262. See also Edgar H. Schein, "Individuals and Careers," in Jay W. Lorsch, ed., *Handbook of Organizational Behavior* (Englewood Cliffs, NJ: Prentice- Hall, 1987), pp. 155–171.

11. These are representative of the life-planning exercises that have been used in NTL Institute programs for the training of OD practitioners. See also Gordon Lippitt, "Developing Life Plans," *Training and Development Journal* (May 1970), pp. 2–7.

12. Based on discussions in J. K. Fordyce and R. Weil, *Managing WITH People* (Reading, MA: Addison-Wesley, 1971), pp. 109–113.

13. Ibid., p. 131.

14. Gillian Flynn, "Group Mentoring Solves Personality Conflicts," *Personnel Journal*, 74 (August 1995), p. 22. See also Caela Farren, Janet Dreyfus Gray, and Beverly Kay, "Mentoring: A Boon to Career Development," *Personnel* 61 (November–December 1984), pp. 20–24; and the entire issue of *OD Practitioner*, 28, no. 3 (1996). See also the entire issue of *The Leadership and Organization Development Journal*, 17, no. 3 (1996).

15. J. William Pfeiffer, Richard Heslin, and John E. Jones, *Instrumentation in Human Relations Training*, 2d ed. (LaJolla: University Associates, 1976). See also J. W. Pfeiffer and A. Ballew, *Using Instruments in Human Resource Development*, Vol. 2, UA Training Technologies (San Diego: Pfeiffer & Company, 1988).

16. Barbara N. Brown, "It's Not Just Four Letters: Using the Myers Briggs to Improve Organizations," *OD Practitioner*, 29, no. 2 (1997), pp. 17–22. See also Robin N. Amadei and Lyn

Wade, "Government Employees Learn to Work in Sync," *Personnel Journal*, 75 (September 1996), pp. 91–94.

17. See William J. Rothwell, Roland Sullivan, and Gary N. McLean, eds., *Practicing Organization Development: A Guide for Consultants* (San Francisco: Jossey-Bass, 1995), pp. 272–275; and J. W. Pfeiffer and A. C. Ballew, *Using Instruments in Human Resource Development* (San Diego: Pfeiffer & Company, 1988).

CHAPTER 13

Issues in Consultant-Client Relationships

A number of interrelated issues can arise in consultant-client relationships in OD activities, and they need to be managed appropriately if adverse effects are to be avoided. These issues tend to center on the following important areas:

Entry and contracting
Defining the client system
Trust
The nature of the consultant's expertise
Diagnosis and appropriate interventions
The depth of interventions
On being absorbed by the culture
The consultant as a model
The consultant team as a microcosm
Action research and the OD process
Client dependency and terminating the relationship
Ethical standards in OD
Implications of OD for the client

No simple prescriptions will resolve all dilemmas or problems in these aspects of OD, but we have some notions about managing these areas.

ENTRY AND CONTRACTING

An initial discussion that can lead to an OD consulting contract can occur in various ways, but typically events evolve something like this example. The telephone rings: An executive has some concerns about his or her organization and the consultant has been recommended as someone who could help. After a brief description of some of the problems and a discussion of the extent to which the consultant's expertise is a reasonable fit for the situation, an agreement is made to pursue the matter over a meal or through an appointment at the executive's office.

During the face-to-face meeting, the consultant explores with the potential client some of the deeper aspects of the presenting problem. If "communications between managers aren't as thorough and as cordial as they ought to be," the consultant asks for examples to get a better fix on the nature of the problem and its dynamics. Almost inevitably several interrelated problems surface. Or if the potential client says, "I want to move to self-managed teams in Plant B." the rationale and objectives for such a program are explored.

Furthermore, in the first meeting, the consultant and the client probably begin to sort out what group would be the logical starting point for an OD intervention. For example, in a particular manufacturing organization it might be important to focus on the top management team of eight people; or, in a city government it might appear prudent to include 20 key people, which would involve the city manager, assistant city managers, and all the departmental heads. Considerable thought must be given to exactly who is to be included—and thus who is to be excluded—in the first interventions. The exclusion of key people, in particular, can be a serious mistake.

If the problems appear to lend themselves to OD interventions, the consultant describes how he or she usually proceeds in such circumstances. For example, the consultant might say: "If I were to undertake this assignment, here's how I would probably want to proceed. First, I would like to get the cooperation of the top management group to set aside, say, two and one-half days for an off-site workshop and to participate in interviews in preparation for that workshop. I would then like to have individual interviews with the entire group, ask each what's going well with the top management team, what the problems are, and what they like things to be like, I would then extract the themes from the interviews. These themes would be reported to the group at the workshop and the problem areas would become the agenda for our work together."

All kinds of nuances can arise in this discussion. In addition to problems of who can and who should attend a workshop other matters concern when and where it could be held, whether members of the management group can be away from their offices for the desired period, whether the top person is to be briefed about interview themes prior to the workshop, the extent of confidentiality of the interviews, and so on. An overriding dimension in this preliminary discussion is the extent of mutual confidence and trust that begins to develop between consultant and client.

Among the ground rules Marvin Weisbord has for his consulting relationships are the following:

> Any information I collect and present will be anonymous. I will never attach names to anything people tell me. However, in certain situations (e.g., team building) I don't *want* confidential information, meaning anything which you are unwilling for other team members to know, even anonymously....
> All data belongs to the people who supply it. I will never give or show it to anyone without their permission.[1]

If both parties agree, these conditions become part of the overall psychological contract between consultant and client.

The more formal compensation aspects of the initial contract are also important and need to be clarified for the peace of mind of both client and consultant. One course of action is to have an oral arrangement for an hourly or daily fee, with no charge for a brief telephone discussion, and usually no charge for a longer first exploration. Thereafter, a bill might be sent for time spent, or a bill might be submitted for the total agreed-upon price for the particular project.

Contracting, in both a psychological and financial sense, occurs over and over in OD consulting. Again, drawing on Weisbord and focusing on the psychological contract:

> Contracting, like the seasons, is repetitive and continually renewable. If I have a long-term, contract (e.g., four days a month for a year) I also have a separate contract for each meeting, which I present on a flipsheet and discuss at the outset. If I have a contract with a boss to help him build his team, I need to extend it to the team before we go to work....
>
> In short, I'm never finished contracting. Each client meeting requires that reexamine the contract. Does it cover everybody I'm working with? Is it clear what we're doing now? And why?[2]

DEFINING THE CLIENT SYSTEM

The question of who the client is quickly becomes an important issue in consultant-client relationships. (We usually refer to the consultant in the singular, but the points we want to make also tend to apply to consultant teams. Similarly, the initial client may be an individual or a management team.) We think a viable model is one in which, in the initial contact, as single manager is the client, but as trust and confidence develop between the key client and the consultant, both begin to view the manager and his or her subordinate team as the client, and then the manager's total organization as the client.

THE TRUST ISSUE

A good deal of the interaction in early contacts between client and consultant is implicitly related to developing a relationship of mutual trust. For example, the key client may be fearful that things will get out of hand with an outsider intervening in the system—that the organization will be overwhelmed with petty complaints or that people will be encouraged to criticize their superiors. Subordinates may be concerned that they will be manipulated toward their superiors' goals with little attention given to their own. These kinds of concerns mean that the consultant will need to earn trust in these and other areas and that high trust will not be immediate.

Similarly, the consultant's trust of the client may be starting at neutral. The consultant will be trying to understand the client's motives and will want to surface any that are partly hidden. For example, if the client has hopes that a team-building session will punish an inadequately performing subordinate, the consultant and the client will need to reassess the purposes of team building and examine whether that activity is the appropriate context for confronting the matter. On a positive note, the client may see OD as a means of increasing both the client's and the subordinate's effectiveness, plus having hopes that a successful OD effort may bring considerable recognition from superiors. Surfacing such motives and examining their implications for effective behavior will enhance trust between the consultant and the client and will help to assure the eventual success of OD activities.

Trust and resistance problems also center on what we call the "good guy-bad guy syndrome." Internal or external OD consultants, through their enthusiasm for an exciting technology, may signal that they perceive themselves as the carriers of the message, that is, that they are "good guys," and implicitly that others are not, or at least are backward.

This attitude obviously creates all sorts of trust and resistance problems. People usually want to work collaboratively with others in the pursuit of common ends—but people tend to resist being pushed around, or put down, under whatever banner. No one likes being put in the "bad guy" role, and we mistrust and resent those who seem to be doing that to us. This trap can ensnare not only the consultant but also the overly enthusiastic line manager.

Confidentiality must be maintained if trust is to be maintained, as implied in Weisbord's ground rules for contracting. Even unintentional errors can be disastrous to the consultant-client relationship. Gavin gives an illustration in which notes made by consultants on the leadership and communications styles of managers were inadvertently duplicated and circulated to participants along with notes on workshop themes and action steps. The consultants had been asked to do the latter; the notes on the managers' styles had been intended to be used by the facilitators in private counseling session with individual managers. As Gavin reports it, "By the time these notes had been circulated, any semblance of trust in the consultants had been destroyed."[3] We will have more to say about trust later.

THE NATURE OF THE CONSULTANT'S EXPERTISE

Partly because of the unfamiliarity with organization development methods, clients frequently try to put the consultant in the role of expert on substantive content, such as on personnel policy or business strategy. *We believe it is possible, and desirable, for the OD consultant to be an expert in the sense of being competent to present a range of options open to the client*, but any extensive reliance on the traditional mode of consulting, that is, giving substantive advice, will tend to negate the OD consultant needs to resist the temptation of playing the content expert and will need to clarify his or her role with the client when it becomes an issue. However, we think the OD consultant should be prepared to describe in broad outline what the organization might look if it were to go very far with an OD effort. Further, as we will discuss later, central to his or her role, the OD consultant must be an expert on process and naturally wants to be perceived as competent. The consultant, therefore, gets trapped into preparing reports or giving substantive advice, which if more than minimal, will reduce his or her effectiveness. (For alternative metaphors to consider, see C. Ken Wiedner's essay," The Physician-Patient Metaphor Reconsidered."[4])

At least four good reasons should encourage the OD consultant to avoid for the most part the expert role. The first is that a major objective of an OD effort is to help the client system to develop its own resources. The expert role creates a kind of dependency that typically does not lead to internal skill development.

The second reason is that the expert role almost inevitably requires the consultant to defend his or her recommendations. With reference to an initial exploratory meeting, Schein mentions the danger of being "seduced into a selling role" and states that under such conditions "we are no longer exploring the problem.[5] In short, finding oneself in the expert role and defending one's advice tends to negate a collaborative, developmental approach to improving organizational processes.

A third reason for largely avoiding the expert role has to do with trust. As shown in Table 13-1, one criterion for resolving whether to provide confidential reports or advice to top management is how such an intervention would affect various client groups role is a

TABLE 13-1 Is a Given Intervention Compatible With the OD Facilitator Role? Ideas to Consider

Intervention	To or For CEO or Unit Leader	To or For Client Team
Confidential report of advice on qualifications of job incumbents	No.	No.
Confidential report or advice on structure of organization or unit	No.	Usually not; at stake is the trust of the various team members. One question for resolving the issue would be, Who would be hurt?
Technical report or advice in some area of the consultant's expertise, e.g., computer applications, or a wage and salary survey, or training in statistical process control	Usually not. One consideration would be, What would this "purchase of expertise" mode of consulting do to the client's expectations about my role?	Usually not. One consideration would be, What would this "purchase of expertise" mode of consulting do to the client's expectations about my role?
Describing various options open to the client and the implications of those options	Yes and no. Depends on whether the intervention is seen as perspective enlarging or prescriptive for the CEO or other key client, whether the client and consultant are open with others about the request, and whether considerable trust has been earned.	Yes, providing that the intervention is seen as perspective enlarging and not as prescriptive.
Advice on OD strategy	Yes, if it is overall organizational strategy and if shared with top team and more broadly in the organization. Yes, if it is strategy for team, providing that it is shared with team.	Yes, if it is strategy for team. Yes, if it is broad organization strategy providing that advice is shared widely in the organization.
Advice on intervention, e.g., when and how a team-building session should be conducted	Yes, providing that advice is shared with team.	Yes.
Data feedback to CEO or unit leader from interviews or questionnaires	Yes, if it is data about the leader. Yes, if it is a team or organizational data and others have concurred in the strategy of the top person having a preliminary briefing. No, if the understanding was that the data would be fed back to the team first.	Yes, if it is data about the team. No, if it is data about other teams, unless data have been aggregated to present overall organization averages, ranges, etc., and there has been wide concurrence on the strategy.
Guidance or moderating of a team-building session	Yes, if it is with concurrence of team.	Yes, if it is with concurrence of team.
Process consultation or coaching on individual behavior or style	Yes, if it is requested.	Yes, if it is requested.

tenuous one at best. Any impression that the consultant is making recommendations inimical to members of client groups puts the consultant in the role of an adversary. For example, the disclosure that the consultant has made a secret recommendation that the number of divisions and vice presidents be reduced from 16 to 8 is likely to be met with widespread alarm and immediate distrust of the consultant. The question will also immediately arise, What else is the consultant up to that we don't know about? Thus, making recommendations to the top is quite different from confronting the top management group with the data that three-fourths of the members of the top team believe that the organization has serious problems, partly stemming from too many divisions. In the one instance, the consultant is helping the top team to be more expert in surfacing data and diagnosing the state of the style.

A fourth reason has to do with expectations. If the consultant goes very far in the direction of being an expert on substance in contrast to process, the client is likely to expect more and more substantive recommendations, thus negating the OD consultant's central mission which is to help with process.

Some exceptions to these reasons are described in Table 13-1. For example, it is usually desirable and necessary to give advice on the design of a workshop or the design of a questionnaire. Such advice is usually facilitating, providing that the consultant is open to modifications of his or her suggestions by members of the client system. As Schein states it:

> The process consultant should not withhold his expertise on matters of the learning process itself; but he should be very careful; not to confuse being an expert on *how to help an organization to learn* with being an expert on the *actual management problems* which the organization is trying to solve.[6]

In other words, the OD consultant should act in the expert role on the process used but not on the *task*.

Another exception consists of providing a range of options open to the client. For example, if issues include how a unit or organization should be structured in terms of consultant can be helpful by presenting some optional forms and discussing the possible implications of each. However, such an intervention should ordinarily be presented in a team situation so as not to be misinterpreted, must be timely in terms of its relevance and acceptability, and should be essentially perspective-enlarging in contrast to prescriptive. *We believe that the more extensive the OD consultant's knowledge of management and organization, the more effective the OD consultant can be. But beware of the difference between being essentially a facilitator-educator and being essentially an advice-giver.* Even the presenting of options can be overdone. If the consultant's ideas become the focal point for prolonged discussion and debate, the consultant has clearly shifted away from the facilitator role. Obviously, the situation is not an either/or matter; it is a matter of degree and emphasis.

DIAGNOSIS AND APPROPRIATE INTERVENTIONS

Another pitfall for the consultant is the temptation to apply an intervention technique he or she particularly likes and that has produced good results in the past, but may not square with a careful diagnosis of the immediate situation. For example, giving subgroups an assignment to describe "what is going well in our weekly department head meetings" and "what is preventing the meetings from being as effective as we'd like" might be more on target and more timely than launching into the role analysis technique with the boss's role as the focus of discussion. It might be too soon; that is, too much defensiveness on the part of the boss or too much apprehension on the part of subordinates might be the case and prevent any productive discussion from taking place. As Herbert Shepard has said, the consultant has said, the consultant should "start where the system is."[7]

We think a consultant should do what he or she can do, but the intervention should be appropriate to the diagnosis, which requires an intensive look at the data, for example, the themes from interviews. The wider the range of interventions with which the consultant is familiar, of course, the more options the consultant can consider. The more the consultant's expertise and experience, the less agonizing is likely to be required in selecting or designing appropriate interventions.

DEPTH OF INTERVENTION

A major aspect of selecting appropriate interventions is the matter of *depth of intervention*. In Roger Harrison's terms, depth of intervention can be assessed using the concepts of accessibility and individuality. By *accessibility* Harrison means the degree to which the data are more or less public versus being hidden or private and the ease with which the intervention skills can be learned. *Individuality* means the closeness to the person's perceptions of self and the degree to which the effects of an intervention are in the individual in contrast to the organization.[8] We assume that the closer one moves on this continuum to the sense of self, the more the inherent processes have to do with emotions, values, and hidden matters and, consequently, the more potent they are to do wither good or harm. It requires a careful diagnosis to determine whether these interventions are appropriate and relevant. If they are inappropriate, they may be destructive or, at a minimum, unacceptable to the client or the client system.

To minimize these risks, Harrison suggests two criteria for determining the appropriate depth of intervention:

> First to intervene at a level no deeper than that required to produce enduring solutions to the problems at hand; and; second, to intervene at a level no deeper than that at which the energy and resources of the client can be committed to problem solving and to change.[9]

To Harrison, these criteria require that the consultant proceed no faster or deeper than the legitimation obtained from the client system culture and that he or she stay at the level of consciously felt needs.[10] We believe these are sound guidelines.

Harrison does recognize, however, and we agree, that the change agent is continuously confronted by the dilemma of whether to "lead and push, or to collaborate and follow.[11] Harrison's orientation is to the latter, but we are inclined to be slightly less conservative. We think that, to be effective, the consultant needs occasionally but prudently to take minor risks in the direction of leading and pushing, but these risks should not be quantum jumps. As the consultant develops expertise in diagnosis and in making interventions, the risks that run are mainly the risks of a rejected suggestion. We do, however, agree with this essence of what Harrison is suggesting and agree with his criteria.

Another way of viewing depth of intervention might be to think about the performance of units by descending order of systems and subsystems. Data about the behavior and performance of the total organization are perhaps the most accessible and the least personal and perhaps create the least personal anxiety and defensiveness. Performance and behavior data about *me* in an organization are perhaps the least accessible and the most personal. The consultant then, needs to have the skills to intervene effectively down through these progressively smaller systems—frequently simultaneously—according to whether the issue is

How well are we performing as a total organization?
How well are we doing as a large unit?
How well are we doing as a team?
How well are you and I working together?
How well are you doing?
How well am I doing?

The concept of depth of intervention, viewed either in this way or in terms of a continuum of the formal system, informal system, and self-suggests that the consultant needs an extensive repertoire of conceptual models, intervention techniques, and sensitivities to be able to be helpful at various levels. The consultant's awareness of his or her own capabilities and limitations, of course, is extremely important.

ON BEING ABSORBED BY THE CULTURE

One of the many mistakes one can make in the change-agent role is to let oneself be seduced into joining the culture of the client organization. Even though one needs to join the culture enough to participate in and enjoy the functional aspects of the prevailing culture—an example would be good-natured bantering when everyone is clear that such bantering is in fun and means inclusion and liking—participating in the organization's pathology will neutralize the consultant's effectiveness.

One of us recalls an experience in which the most critical issue to surface in preliminary interviews with members of a professional staff group—we'll call it an engineering organization—was who would be the new manager. The current manager's promotion was to take effect in a few weeks, and he was anxious that the group members provide some input on the selection of his successor as well as that they tidy up a number of unresolved communications and administrative matters. One obvious candidate for the promotion was a senior engineer who was highly respected for his professional competency—clearly an engineer's engineer. However, younger members of the staff privately expressed fears to the consultant that the senior engineer would be too authoritarian if he assumed the manager's role, and they did not want to lose his accessibility as professional mentor. On the other hand they had strong concerns that they would seriously hurt the man's feelings by openly confronting the issue of his style and that he might resign if the matter were confronted. As a result, the consultant team acquiesced in feeding back to the group the issue most troubling them. In effect, everyone but the senior engineer conspired to protect him, to pretend that he was a strong candidate for promotion, and to postpone the decision. As a result, the group was partly paralyzed for weeks. The immediate effect of the team-building session was one of frustration for all of the participants. In retrospect, the consultant's view is that the client system could probably have worked through the matter and that the senior engineer would have proved to be the strongest and most adaptable there that day, including the consultants.

The dilemma created when a client subgroup describes an issue to the consultant but says, "We won't deal with it and we won't let you surface it in the total group," is a troublesome one. One way out of the dilemma may be to discuss the likely consequences of not dealing with the issue. One consequence may be that the recipient of unclear communication develops a kind of paranoia from the confusing or distorted signals he or she is receiving. Another consequence is that a norm may be implicitly created that says *all* negative interpersonal feedback is off limits, which has the deeper consequence that the entire group is denied data about problem areas that could be constructively worked on. Another consequence might be that the group may be denied the capability of sharing much positive feedback for fear that such sharing could spill over into qualifying statements that begin to get into negative areas. Confronting the subgroup with the dilemma and outlining the consequences of inaction, then, may be much more constructive than succumbing to the pressures of the culture.

Internal change agents may be even more susceptible to absorption by the prevailing organizational culture than are external change agents. As long as they work with people and units that have considerable "political distance" from their own unit, their objectivity may be any more vulnerable than that of a consultant from the outside. On the other hand, if their own unit (whether they are specialists who are part of a human resources or an OD unit or have a home base in some line department) is somehow engaged in maneuvering for resources or power in competition with their client, they may inadvertently be drawn into the politics of the situation. Rather than helping to surface the dynamics of dysfunctional rivalry under appropriate circumstances, the change agents may become part of the problem, thus helping to submerge an issue or contributing to tactics incompatible with the helping role and thereby alienating the client or potential clients.

THE CONSULTANT AS A MODEL

Another important issue is whether change agents are willing and able to practice what they preach. In the area of feelings, for example, the consultant may be advocating a more open system in which feelings are considered legitimate and their expression important to effective problem solving and at the same time suppressing his or her own feelings about what is happening in the client system. In particular, this problem can be a frequent one for the less-experienced practitioner, and it usually has an impact on this person's feeling of competency: "If only I had said...." The more one learns to be in touch with one's own feelings, the more spontaneous one can be and the greater the options open for interventions. (For this reason, we recommend extensive T-group experience for OD consultants.) However, the client system is not the appropriate ground for working out any problems the consultant may be currently experiencing. On the other hand, being too aloof emotionally will tend to minimize the possibilities of helping the client.

As another example of modeling behavior, the OD consultant needs to give out clear messages—that is, the consultant's words and apparent feelings need to be congruent. The consultant also needs to check on meanings, to suggest optional methods of solving problems, to encourage and support, to give feedback in constructive ways and to accept feedback, to help formulate issues, and to provide a spirit of inquiry. We are not suggesting that the OD consultant must be a paragon of virtue; rather, we are suggesting that to maximize one's effectiveness, one must continuously practice and develop the effective behaviors one wishes to install in the client system.

THE CONSULTANT TEAM AS A MICROCOSM

The consultant-key client viewed as a team or consultants working as a team can profitably be viewed as a microcosm of the organization they are trying to create. In the first place, the consultant team must set an example of an effective unit if the team is to enhance its credibility. Second, practitioners need the effectiveness that comes from continuous growth and renewal processes. And third, the quality of the interrelationships within the consulting team carries over directly into the quality of their interventions. To be more explicit about the last point, unresolved and growing conflict between two consultants can paralyze an intervention. Or simple lack of attention to team maintenance matters can produce morale problems that reduce spontaneity and creativity in planning sessions or in interacting with the client system.

ACTION RESEARCH AND THE OD PROCESS

A related issue is whether the OD process itself will be a subject to the ongoing action research being experienced by the client system. The issue of congruency is, of course, important, but the viability of the OD effort and the effectiveness of the consultants may be at stake. Unless feedback loops relate to various interventions and stages in the OD process, the change agents and the organization will not learn how to make the OD interventions more effective.

Feedback loops do not necessarily have to be complicated. Simple questionnaires or interviews can be very helpful. As an illustration, we recall having lunch with the key people who had been involved in a problem-solving workshop, and upon asking several questions about how things were going "back at the shop," we found that problems had emerged centering on who had been involved to attend the workshop and who had not. This feedback, at a minimum, has caused us to pay even more attention to prework and to helping workshop participants plan how to share effectively what has occurred with those not attending.

THE DEPENDENCY ISSUE AND TERMINATING THE RELATIONSHIP

If the consultant is in the business of enhancing the client system's abilities in problem solving and renewal, then the consultant is in the business of assisting the client to internalize skills and insights rather than to create a prolonged dependency relationship. This issue tends to be minor, however, if the consultant and the client work out the expert versus facilitator issue described earlier and if the consultant subscribes to the dependency and more client growth than the traditional consulting modes, and the notion of a shared technology leads to rapid learning on the part of the client.

The latter notion is congruent with Argyris's admonition that if the consultant intervention is to be helpful in an ongoing sense, it is imperative for the client to have "free, informed choice."[12] And to have this free choice, the client requires a cognitive map of the overall process.[13] Thus the consultant will have to be quite open about such matters as the objectives of the various interventions that are made and about the sequence of planned events. The OD consultant should continuously be part educator as he or she intervenes in the system.

An issue of personal importance to the consultant is the dilemma of working to increase the resourcefulness of the client versus wanting to remain involved, to feel needed, and to feel competent. A satisfactory solution to this dilemma, we believe, is gradual reduction in external consultant use as an OD effort reaches maturity. In a large organization, one or more key consultants may be retained in an ongoing relationship, but with less frequent use. If the consultants are constantly developing their skills, they can continue to make innovative contributions. Furthermore, they can serve as a link with outside resources such as universities and research programs, and more important, they can serve to help keep the OD effort at the highest possible professional and ethical level. Their skills and insights should serve as a standard against which to compare the activities of internal change agents. Some of the most innovative and successful OD efforts on the world scene, in our judgment, have maintained some planned level of external consultant use.

Another dimension of the issues arises, however, when the consultant senses that his or her assistance is no longer needed or could be greatly reduced. For the client's good, to avoid wasting the consultant's own professional resources, and to be congruent, the consultant should confront the issue.

A particularly troublesome dilemma occurs when the use of the consultant, in the judgment, of the consultant, is declining more rapidly than progress on the OD effort seems to warrant. It would be easy to say that here, too, the consultant should raise the matter with the client, even if consultant risks appearing self-serving. In such situations we wish more were known about the dynamics of OD efforts losing their momentum. Such additional knowledge would help consultants and clients to assess more objectively the extent of need for consultant assistance, how to improve the skills of the consultant and the client in managing the OD effort, and how to rejuvenate is warranted.

We also suspect that OD efforts frequently flounder because of internal power struggles that have not been sensed early enough by the consultant or understood well enough for anyone to intervene constructively. For example, some relatively powerful person or group may be fearful of losing status or influence and may be mobilizing support for the status quo through such tactics as distorting information or discrediting whoever is seen as the threat. The threat may be the practitioner or the OD effort or the threat may be wholly unrelated to the OD process. But if people in the organization get caught up in the political power maneuvering, the OD effort may be immobilized. This interference appears to be what happened to the highly successful STS and self-managed team approach that had flourished at the General Foods per food plant in Topeka for several years.[14] While much more needs to be known about these occurrences as they relate to OD efforts, it would seem that these situations, if sensed, need to be surfaced and confronted head on. Such shadowy struggles are usually dysfunctional whether or not an OD effort is under way, and the remedy may need to be a prompt description of reality by the chief executive officer. While a long term OD effort, should replace most such covert maneuvering with an open working through of issues, these situations can and do occur while an OD effort is under way. (For more on power and politics and OD, see chapter 14.)

Sometimes the organization may simply be temporarily overloaded by externally imposed crises occupying the attention of key people. Under such conditions, the best strategy may be one of reducing or suspending the more formalized OD interventions and letting people carry on with their enhanced skills and then returning to the more formalized aspects at a later date. If the dynamics of these and the other circumstances we have described were more defined, the resolution of the problem of what to do when the OD effort seems to be running out of steam might take directions other than reducing or terminating the involvement of the change agent.

CASE STUDY

A medium sized manufacturing company was promoted by the State Government in India in early nineties to manufacture industrial explosives of lower detonating impact.

The state government constituted a top team to lead the formation, project management and putting the plant on stream in record time. The technology was imported from UK and the technical experts came from the Ordinance Department of India. As a matter of principle the organization had an ex-director of explosives as the CMD.

Besides him, the management team comprised senior people from the State Government cadre of Industries Department, Central Government Engineers from Defense and Ordinance Department and some from an MNC in India who also made similar detonators. Some of the staff functions like IR was headed by experienced professionals from private sector textiles company and accountants from auditing firms.

Just when the plant was scheduling to go on stream with test runs, the CMD realized the need for integrating the management team to fall in line with the goals and objectives of the new fledgling company.

An external OD consultant was appointed after a due selection process by the CMD. The terms of contracting went through prolonged dialogues because the financials had to be vetted by the General.

The manager, who held the funds of the State Government allotted for training and development purposes, was negotiating the engagement in terms of a number of sessions of training sessions, while the consultant was talking about number of days to be engaged. Also there was a caste bias and a suspicion that the CMD was choosing a consultant of his own caste and language. The GM was a secular person yet he doubted the choice of the consultant to make an entry.

The second difficulty was in working out the teams of work. Terms like diagnostic survey, open ended meeting across the organization, getting a sense of the operating culture, conflicts and strengths were strange things that made them feel uneasy and doubt the consultant further.

Because the CMD gave unilateral support to the functioning, they obliged the initial meetings with all the seniors.

The first diagnosis revealed that the top team was already concerned of their career path in the new set up. Having been used to the definite jumps in their government jobs where more than merit, seniority decided the promotion, they found their counterparts from the MNC looking at competence in the current job as a measure of performance evaluation.

So the consultant approached the problem strategically. What he did was to take strips of flip chart paper and wrote the variety of titles that senior managers of such manufacturing set up were used to and invited the team to a workshop situation and gave them the task of designing the appropriate organization structure with the help of the strips placing them here and there as they discussed. The dynamics of debates and the discussions threw light on the aspirations of individuals and how they perceived the power relationships between the membership.

This helped them to realise the dynamics of the entire situation and opened them up to further discussions in a more receptive frame of mind.

ETHICAL STANDARDS IN OD

Much of this chapter and, indeed, much of what has preceded in other chapters, can be viewed in terms of ethical issues in OD practice, that is, in terms of enhancement versus violation of basic values and/or in terms of help versus harm to persons. Louis White and Kevin Wooten see five categories of ethical dilemmas in organization development practice stemming from the actions of either the consultant or client or both. The types of ethical dilemmas they see are: (1) misrepresentation and collusion, (2) misuse of data, (3) manipulation and coercion, (4) value and goal conflicts, and (5) technical ineptness.[15] (These five types largely encompass the several ethical dilemmas reported by Susan De Vogel in a survey of practitioners.[16])

We will draw on and modify their categories to suggest what we see as some of the more serious areas for potential ethics violations in OD consulting. Some of these areas apply not only to OD consulting, but to management consulting in general. The illustrations are ours and are only hypothetical.

Misrepresentation of the Consultant's Skills An obvious area for unethical behavior would be to distort or misrepresent one's background, training, competencies, or experience in vita sheets, advertising, or conversation. A subtle form of misrepresentation would be to let the client assume one has certain skills when one does not.

Professional/Technical Ineptness The potential for unethical behavior stemming from lack of expertise is persuasive in OD. To give one example using Harrison's concept of depth of intervention, it would seem to be unethical to ask people in a team-building session to provide mutual feedback about leadership style when neither preliminary interviews nor the client group has indicated a readiness or a willingness to do so. Another example would be as follows: A preliminary diagnosis suggests the appropriateness of a feedback intervention, but the consultant has no experience from which to draw in order to design a constructive feedback exercise. The consultant goes ahead anyway. It would be unethical for the consultant to plough ahead without some coaching by a more experienced colleague. (This situation may call for the "shadow consultant."[17]) Thus, we have hypothesized two violations of ethical standards: (1) using an intervention that has a low probability of being helpful (and may be harmful in this circumstance), and (2) using an intervention that exceeds one's expertise.

Misuse of Data Again, the possibilities for unethical behavior in the form of data misuse on the part of either the client or the consultant are abundant. This is why confidentiality is so important in OD efforts. (See Weisbord's ground rules for contracting earlier in this chapter.) Data can be used to punish or otherwise harm persons or groups. An obvious example would be a consultant's disclosure to the boss the names of those who provided information about the boss's dysfunctional behavior. Another example would be showing climate survey results from Department A to the head of Department B without Department's A's authorization.

Serious distortions of the data would also be unethical. Let's imagine a scenario in which the consultant interviews the top 20 members of management and finds several department heads are angry about the behaviors of fellow department head Z and the practices in Z's department. Further, Z is hostile and uncooperative with the consultant in the data-gathering interview. The consultant is now angry but is not conscious of the extent of the anger. When the consultant feeds back the themes from the interviews to the group, his or her anger takes the form of overstating and overemphasizing the dysfunctional aspects of Z's unit. (In an ironic twist, the group might turn on the consultant and defend Z. As a colleague of ours says, "Never attack the 'worst' member of the group—the group will reject you."[18])

Collusion An example of collusion would be the consultant agreeing with the key client to schedule a team-building workshop when department head Z is scheduled to be on vacation. (This maneuver is hardly the way to deal with the problems created by Z, is likely to create reduced trust in the consultant and the client, Z's boss, and is likely to intensify Z's dysfunctional behavior.) Another example illustrating the power that a consultant with expertise in-group dynamics can wield for good or harm is the consultant colluding with other members of the group to set up a feedback situation in which Z's deficiencies will be all too apparent, particularly to Z's boss. Instead of creating a situation in which everyone, including Z, has a chance of improving performance, this collusion is aimed at Z's undoing. (We've picked on Z enough; if he or she is in this much of a problem, Z' performance should be confronted head on by the boss, outside of the team-building setting, and preferably well in advance. If OD interventions are perceived as methods for "getting" anyone, the OD process is doomed to failure.)

Coercion It is unethical to force organizational members into settings where they are, in effect, required to disclose information about themselves or their units, which they prefer to keep private. The creation of a T-group with unwilling participants would be an example.

A troublesome dilemma occurs in the case of a manager and most of his or her subordinates who want to go off-site for a problem-solving workshop but one or two members are strongly resisting. If friendly persuasion and addressing the concerns of the individual(s)—not painful arm-twisting—do not solve the matter, perhaps a reasonable option is for the manager to indicate that nonparticipation is acceptable and that one will be subject to recriminations, but those individuals should understand that the group will go ahead and try to reach consensus on action plans for improvement without their input.

Promising Unrealistic Outcomes   Obviously, this is unethical and counterproductive. The temptation to make promises in order to gain a client contract can be great, but the consequences can be reduced credibility of the consultant and the OD field, and the reduced credibility of the key client within his or her organization.

Deception and Conflict of Values Deception in any form is unethical and will destroy trust. In chapter 12 we gave the example of a telephone company that embarked on a major reengineering effort giving assurances of job security, and then proceeded to lay off a huge part of the workforce. The layoffs came after the company had promoted team-work and empowerment and secured employee cooperation in streamlining operations. For an OD professional on the scene under such circumstances, the ethical course of action would be to press top management to look at the probable consequences of reengineering, to look at possible options, and to be completely open with employees about the implications of whatever change strategy was selected. And the ethical responsibilities of the OD professional and company management extend, of course, to mitigating the impact of any change effort on the lives of individual employees.

Thus, the values underlying ethical OD practice are honesty, openness, voluntarism, integrity, confidentiality, the development of people, and the development of consultant expertise, high standards, and self-awareness.

IMPLICATIONS OF OD FOR THE CLIENT

An OD effort has some fundamental implications for the chief executive officer and top managers of an organization, and we believe that these implications need to be shared and understood at the outset. Basically, *OD interventions* we have described them, *are a conscious effort on the part of top management*:

1. *To enlarge the database for making management decisions.* In particular, the expertise, perceptions, and sentiments of team members throughout the organization are more extensively considered than heretofore.
2. *To expand the influence processes.* The OD process tends to further a process of mutual influence; managers and subordinates alike tend to be influential in ways they have not experienced previously.
3. *To capitalize on the strengths of the informal system and to make the formal and the informal system more congruent.* A great deal of information that has previously been suppressed within individuals or within the informal system (e.g., appreciations, frustrations, hurts, opinions about how to do things more effectively, fears) begins to be

surfaced and dealt with. Energies spent supporting matters can now be rechaneled into cooperative effort.

4. *To become more responsive.* Management must now respond to data that have been submerged and must begin to move in the direction of personal, team, and organizational effectiveness suggested by the data.

5. *To legitimatize conflict as an area of collaborative management.* Rather than using win-lose, smoothing, or withdrawal modes of conflict resolution, the mode gradually becomes one of confronting the underlying basis for the conflict and working the problem through to a successful resolution.[19]

6. *To examine its own leadership style and ways of managing.* We do not think an OD effort can be viable long if the top management team (the CEO plus subordinate team or the top team of an essentially autonomous unit) does not actively participate in the effort. The top team inevitably is a powerful determinant of organizational culture. OD is not a televised game being played for viewing by top management; members of top management are the key players.

7. *To legitimatize and encourage the collaborative management of team, interteam, and organization cultures.* This broad intervention goal is largely the essence of OD.

We think that these items largely describe the underlying implications for top management and that the OD consultant needs to be clear about them from the beginning and to help the top management group be clear about them as the process unfolds.[20]

THE ROLE OF THE HUMAN RESOURCE SPECIALIST IN ORGANIZATION DEVELOPMENT ACTIVITIES

The role of HR person is more subtle and subjective. The HR person has to bring about a change in the thinking of its employees to bring about a change in the organisation culture. For this the HR person has to constantly strive to create a continuously learning organisation. It must enable the employee to recognise that learning and change are basically the same thing. Thus they have a big role in the development of the organisation.

The change in the mindset has to occur not only at the organisation level but also at the employee level. If a non-managerial person is promoted to a managerial level, then it also involves a change in the mindset and perception. The employee has to develop himself as a manager. For example, he may need more of expertise in dealing with people than his functional expertise. This cannot happen overnight. So such people have to be gradually trained over a period of time to effectively take over at work. This entails succession planning and identification of potential successors. For this the HR person has to plan individual career paths and identify managerial competencies in individuals.

Another important role that the HR person has in organization development is to develop the managers as coaches and mentors. Coaching would deal with the developing of subordinates on the job. Mentoring would deal with the personal development of subordinates.

The Organisation

Jyoti Ltd., began as small unit in 1943, located at Baroda. Presently it is engaged in developing, manufacturing, and marketing a wide range of products in hydraulics, electricals, agriculture, ceramics, renewable energy systems, instrumentation, and laser.

The company employs more than 6000 people working at its R and D, production units in and around Baroda, and a marketing set up all over the country and in Singapore. In January 1983 the company reorganised itself into a product-based divisional structure having more than a dozen divisions. This led to a dual relationship for the branch sales staff where the reporting at the branch level and the other in the functional reporting to the product divisions at head office.

In Bombay where this OD work was in progress, there were two offices, the zonal office and the branch office. The zonal office was headed by a general manager and the branch by a branch manager.

New Human Resources Department

As another organisational innovation a separate and new department of HRD was introduced in Jyoti Ltd., in December 1980. During the incumbency of the first HRD manager, work was done mainly in (a) streamlining training, (b) redesigning the performance appraisal form, (c) redesigning the scheme of prerequisites to managers and other staff, and (d) introducing a management training scheme.

One of the activities under the HR Department was organization development. Most often the literature on OD advocates that OD must begin from the top. An internal HRD OD functionary may find it difficult to initiate such a process at the top. The question was: does he begin OD at all? Th strategy chosen at Jyoti was "to initiate OD in any subsystem of the organisation to improve the effectiveness of that subsystem." The strategy was debatable. The following section gives a rationale for it.

Reasons for Authentic Opportunism during OD with Subsystems

1. The operating culture of a social system of any size or denomination stabilizes over fairly long periods of time. Given the circumstances over the period, members of the system make innumerable choices, some of which get reinforced. These start forming a basis for a culture of the system. Reversing this evolutionary logic for the purpose of changing the culture, it may be equally desirable to encourage and reinforce conscious choices in desirable directions by as many persons as possible. So, a movement towards OD values has to be supported and re-inforced by as many managers as possible and would have to grow in number considerably that in the future, at the appropriate time, the more widespread changes become easier and more stable. This would be especially so if the managers chosen to initiate OD now are likely to become top decision makers in a few years.

2. One way to see OD is to focus exclusively on the human processes underlying any over task or activity (Pareek, 1975; Backhard, 1975). These processes, which are impressed by social theories and intentions upon the minds of people, are not possibly complete. In a subsystem context that these would be (a) interpersonal processes which can encourage empathy, (b) processes that take place when individuals perform their roles in the subsystem and try to cope with the stress which they experience, (c) processes in groups or teams which can help them become more cohesive and effective, (d) decision-making processes in the subsystem which can make each member an integral part rather than alienating him from his work and society, (e) influence processes between the subsystem and its task environment inside the organisation or on its boundary with the wider organizational environment, and (f) the existential pro-

cesses in each person which can either take him in the direction of self-alienation or help him realize this potential in relation to himself to his fellow beings, his organization and his society.

3. Related to the previous reason is the third reason, but there the focus was on the role of the subsystems manager. The difference would lie between thinking of the subsystems manager as a subordinate to his boss and the chief executive of a semi-autonomous organization. If the subsystem manager can be seen as a semi-autonomous chief executive then he has partial rights to allow or disallow an intervention by a person external to the subsystem.

The "selling approach" used by Robin, Irwin, Plovnick, and Fry of Sloan School of Management at the MIT (1977) has similar implications. They applied this approach in the case of a geographically widespread health care system in America. Their rationale was as follows:

"At the beginning of nearly every problem-solving, consulting, or change model there is a felt need. That is, the client system, having experienced a 'hurt' or a problem, is seeking help. In our experience we have found the most effective way of entering an organisation is to be asked in."

"However, we have also found that many health care organisations, though beset with organizational problems, are incapable of summoning a consultant. There are several reasons for this. First, though they are uncomfortable with a situation they may not be aware that there is anything 'wrong ' or unusual about it. In many industrial organizations, for example, a crisis situation often unfreezes the organization and stimulates them to search for help to avoid future crisis. In health care organizations, the crisis mode is the norm, not the exception; it's 'the way things are in the business." Surprised health team members often comment: "Don't all teams work this way." Second, health care organisations may suspect there is a better way to organize themselves but do not know where to find the appropriate resources to help them. Third, though uncomfortable they may choose to ignore "the administrative stuff."

"For these reasons a consultant who is anxious to work at helping create systems may have to initiate the contact and essentially market, or create, the felt need. This might require convincing skeptical administrators and physicians that: (1) there is a better way to manage, (2) a consultant can help them to do so, and (3) it is worth their time, effort, and resources to try to change the way they are doing things."

Based on these reasons, it would be valid to start OD in any part of the organisation. The basic prerequisites for this would be (a) that the part can be seen as a subsystem with specific task and membership, and (b) that the manager-in-charge of the subsystem owns up to the objectives and process of OD. Applying this approach in Jyoti meant that the HRD functionaries would have to continuously remain on the lookout for such subsystems.

CONCLUDING COMMENTS

Numerous issues regarding the client-consultant relationship need to be addressed and managed in a successful OD effort. These issues have to do with establishing the initial contract, identifying who is the client, establishing trust, clarifying the role of the consultant, determining the appropriate depth of intervention, examining the consequences of being absorbed by the organization's culture, viewing the consultant and consulting teams as models, applying action research to OD, terminating the relationship, and ethical standards. These issues have important implications for practitioners top management, and the organization.

NOTES

1. Marvin Weisbord, "The Organization Development Contract," *Organization Development Practitioner*, 5, no. 2 (1973), pp. 1–4.
2. Ibid.
3. James F. Gavin, "Survey Feedback: The Feedback of Science and Practice," *Group & Organization Studies*, 9 (March 1984), p. 46. For more on trust, see Dale E. Zand, *Information, Organization, and Power* (New York: McGraw-Hill, 1981), pp. 37–55.
4. C. Ken Wiedner, "The Physician-Patient Metaphor Reconsidered," *OD Practitioner*, 29, no. 4 (1997), pp. 49–57.
5. Edgar H. Schein, *Process Consultation: Its Role in Organization Development* (Reading, MA: Addison-Wesley, 1969), p. 82.
6. Ibid., p. 120.
7. Herbert A. Shepard, "Rules of Thumb for Change Agents," *OD Practitioner*, 17 (December 1985), p. 2. Shepard calls this the "Empathy Rule."
8. This discussion is based on Roger Harrison's essay, "Choosing the Depth of Organizational Intervention," *Journal of Applied Behavioral Science*, 6 (April–June 1970), pp. 181–202.
9. Ibid., p. 201. [Harrison's emphasis.]
10. Ibid., pp. 198–199.
11. Ibid., p. 202.
12. Chris Argyris, *Intervention Theory and Method* (Reading, MA: Addison-Wesley, 1970), p. 17.
13. See Chris Argyris, *Management and Organizational Development: The Path from XA to YB* (New York: McGraw-Hill, 1971), pp. 58, 108, 137, for a discussion of the importance of "maps."
14. See Art Kleiner, *The Age of Heretics* (New York: Currency/Doubleday, 1996), pp. 73–101.
15. Louis P. White and Kevin C. Wooten, "Ethical Dilemmas in Various Stages of Organizational Development," *Academy of Management Review*, 8 (October 1983), pp. 690–697.
16. See William J. Rothwell, Roland Sullivan, and Gary N. McLean, *Practicing Organization Development: A Guide for Consultants* (San Francisco: Jossey-Bass/Pfeiffer, 1995), pp. 459–464.
17. Mikki Ritvo and Ronald Lippitt, "Shadow Consulting: An Emerging Role," in Walter Sikes, Allan Drexler, and Jack Gant, *The Emerging Practice of Organization Development* (Alexandria, VA: NTL Institute, 1989), pp. 219–224.
18. Conversation with Charles Hosford.
19. Blake and Mouton refer to "confrontation," "forcing," "smoothing," "compromise," and "withdrawal" as the different modes of conflict resolution. See Robert Blake and Jane Mouton, *The Managerial Grid* (Houston: Gulf, 1964), pp. 30, 67, 93, 94, 122, 123, 163.
20. For more on the implications of OD for behavior changes in the client system, see Jerry I. Porras and Susan J. Hoffer, "Common Behavior Changes in Successful Organization Development Efforts," *The Journal of Applied Behavioral Science*, 22, no. 4 (1986), pp. 477–494. For more on consultant-client relationships see Diane McKinney Kellogg, "Contrasting Successful and Unsuccessful OD Consultation Relationships," *Group and Organization Studies*, 9 (June 1984), pp. 151–176.

CHAPTER 14

Power, Politics, and Organization Development

Power and politics, indisputable facts of organizational life, must be understood if one is to be effective in organizations. In this chapter we examine power and politics in relation to organization development. The OD practitioner needs both knowledge and skill in the arenas of organizational power and politics. As Warner Burke observes: "Organization development signifies change, and *for change to occur in an organization, power must be exercised.*[1]

POWER DEFINED AND EXPLORED

Let us examine several representative definitions of power:

"Power is the intentional influence over the beliefs, emotions, and behaviors of people. Potential power is the capacity to do so, but kinetic power is the act of doing so... One person exerts power over another to the degree than he is able to exact compliance as desired." [2]

"A has power over B to the extent that he can get B to do something that B would otherwise not do."[3]

Power is "the ability of those who possess power to bring about the outcomes they desire."[4]

"Power is defined in this book simply as the capacity to effect (or affect) organizational outcomes. The French word "pouvoir: stands for both the noun 'power' and the verb 'to be able.' To have power to be able to get desired things done, to effect outcomes—actions and the decisions that precede them."[5]

Analyzing these definitions shows some common elements: effectance—getting one's way: the necessity interaction between two parties; the act or ability of influencing others; and outcomes favoring one party over the other. We therefore define interpersonal power as *the ability to get one's way in a social situation.*

THEORIES ABOUT THE SOURCES OF SOCIAL POWER

Power exists in virtually all social situations. It is especially salient in coordinated activities such as those found in organizations. In fact, for organizations to function, an authority or power dimension is required.

How do some people come to possess power? How is power generated, bestowed, or acquired? In this section we will examine four different views about who gets power and how: Emerson's "power-dependence theory," French and Raven's "bases of social power," Salancik and Pfeffer's "strategic-contingency model of power," and Mintzberg's observations on the genesis of power in organizations.

Power-dependence theory is related to a broader framework of social interaction called *social exchange theory*, which posits that what goes on between persons is an exchange of social commodities: love, hate, respect, power, influence, information, praise, blame, attraction, rejection, and so forth. We enter into and continue in exchange relationships when what we receive from others is equivalent to or in excess of what we must give to others. When the net balance for us is positive, we will continue the exchange relationships; when the net balance for us is negative, we will terminate or alter the relationship. Social interaction represents an exchange of social goods and services. Viewed in this light, giving someone power over us in the commodity we exchange when we are dependent on that person for something we want.

Closely related to these ideas is the classic statement by John R. P. French and Bertram Raven on the "bases of social power."[6] These authors suggested five sources, or bases, of social power as follows:

1. *Reward power*—power based on the ability of the power holder to reward another, that is, to give something valued by the other.
2. *Coercive power*—power based on the ability of the power holder to punish another, that is, to give something negatively valued by the other.
3. *Legitimate power*—power based on everyone's belief that the power holder has a legitimate right to exert influence and that the power-receiver has a legitimate obligation to accept the influence.
4. *Referent power*—power based on the power-receiver having an identification with (attraction to, or feeling of oneness with) the power holder.
5. *Expert power*—power based on the power holder possessing expert knowledge or expertise needed by the other. Informational power is the form of expert power where the power holder possesses important facts or information needed by the other.

In this theory, power belongs to those persons who control or mediate desired commodities. Exchange theory and power-dependence theory are quite compatible with the ideas proposed by French and Raven.

Henry Mintzberg has developed a theory of organizational power drawn from the organization theory literature and has own creative synthesis abilities.[7] This theory "is built on the premise that organizational behavior is a power game in which various players, called *influencers*, seek to control the organization's decisions and actions."[8] The three basic conditions for the exercise of power are (1) some sources or basis or power, coupled with (2) the expenditure of energy in a (3) politically skillful way. According to Mintzberg, the five possible bases of power are, first, control of a resource; second, control of a technical skill; and, third, control of a body of knowledge. All of these must be critical to the organization. The fourth basis is legal prerogatives—being given exclusive rights to impose choices. A fifth basis of power is access to those who have power based on our first four bases.[9] In addition to a base of power, the influencer must have both the "will" and the "skill" to use it.

An organization has many potential influencers, such as the board of directors, the managers, the top executives, the employees, the unions, suppliers, customers, regulators, and so forth. The important aspects of Mintzberg's theory are that the sources of power derive from possession of a commodity desired by others, that power-in-action requires will and skill, and that the organization is the context for the exercise of power.

ORGANIZATIONAL POLITICS DEFINED AND EXPLORED

Let us now examine the concept of politics on organizations. Following are several representative definitions of politics:

> Harrold Lasswell defined politics simply as the study of who gets what, when, and how.[10]
>
> Organizational politics involve those activities taken within organizations to acquire, develop and use power and other resources to obtain one's preferred outcomes in a situation in which there is uncertainty or dissensus about choices.[11]
>
> Organizational politics involve intentional acts of influence to enhance or protect the self-interest of individuals or groups.[12]
>
> Organizational politics is the management of influence to obtain ends not sanctioned by the organization or to obtain ends through non-sanctioned influence means.[13]
>
> We view politics as a subset of power, treating it... as *informal power*, illegitimate in nature. Likewise we also treat authority as a subset of power, but in this sense, *formal* power, the power vested in office, the capacity to get things done by virtue of the position held.[14]

Analyzing these definitions suggests that the concepts of power and politics are similar. Both relate to getting one's way—effectance. Both relate to pursuit of self-interest and overcoming the resistance of other. For our purposes, organizational politics is power-in-action in organizations; it is engaging in activities to get one's way.

One important feature in these definitions should be examined further. The first three definitions treat politics as a neutral set of activities. We are inclined to consider politics as neither good nor bad per se but believe that *politics, like power, has two faces*.

The negative face of politics is characterized by *extreme* pursuit of self-interest; unsocialized needs to dominate others; a tendency to view situations in win-lose terms—what I win, you must lose—rather than win-win terms; and predominant use of terms—what I win, you must lose—rather than win-win terms; and predominant use of the tactics of fighting—secrecy, surprise, holding hidden agendas, withholding information, information, deceiving. The positive face is characterized by a *balanced* pursuit of self-interest and the interests of others; viewing situations in win-win terms as much as possible; engaging in open problem solving followed by action and influencing; a relative absence of the tactics of fighting; and a socialized need to lead, initiate, and influence others.

Organizations often display consistent patterns of decision making, resource allocation, and conflict resolution. Three patterns identified in the organization literature are the bureaucratic, rational, and political models.[15] In a bureaucratic model, decisions are made on the basis of rules, procedures, traditions, and historical precedents. In a rational model, decisions are made on the basis of rational problem solving; goals are identified and agreed upon; situations are analyzed objectively in relation to goals; alternative action plans are generated and evaluated; and certain alternatives are chosen and implemented. In a political model, decisions are made on the basis of perceived self-interest by coalitions jockeying for dominance, influence, or resource control. Most organizations exhibit all these models, although in some organizations one predominates. A predominantly political orientation is only one of several possibilities.

FRAMEWORKS FOR ANALYZING POWER AND POLITICS

Two conceptual models will provide a picture of the component situations involving organizational power and politics. The first is taken from Pfeffer's book, *Power in Organizations*. The second is derived from the literature on game theory.

Pfeffer's model of the antecedents and conditions for power is shown in Figure 14-1. In this diagram, political activities are seen to be the *outcome* of a number of conditions. When these conditions exist, power and politics result. According to Pfeffer, the environment of the organization imposes demands and constraints that will be accommodated in the form of "means" and "ends"—that is how the organization gets the job done and the goals it pursues. Often heterogeneous or incompatible goals are sought by members of the organization. Likewise, members may seek different or incompatible ways to accomplish the goals. Preferences for different means to the goals is what is meant by the term "heterogeneous beliefs about technology." "Differentiation" refers to the fact that division of labor in organizations creates many subgroups, which, in turn, produces different worldviews, different subgroup goals, and "tunnel vision" of subgroup members.

The primary conditions giving rise to conflict are differentiation, scarcity (in the client resources prevent all parties from having all they want), interdependence (the distribution of resources affects everyone in some way), and incompatible goals and/or means to goals. When these conflicts exist, conflict occurs. And when conflict exists, power and political behavior are likely to result if two additional features are present.

It is possible to *increase* or *decrease* the amount of political activity in organizations by manipulating the conditions of power and politics shown in the model. For example, if resource abundance replaced resource scarcity, conflict would be reduced and politics would be reduced. If organizational actors (became less interdependent) for instance, through the use of profit centers and other structural arrangements), conflict would be reduced. Likewise, increased consensus about goals and means and more centralized power would reduce conflict and hence, reduce political activity.

A second model comes from game theory literature. The conditions giving studied rise to *cooperation and competition* and to the use of power have been studied extensively by

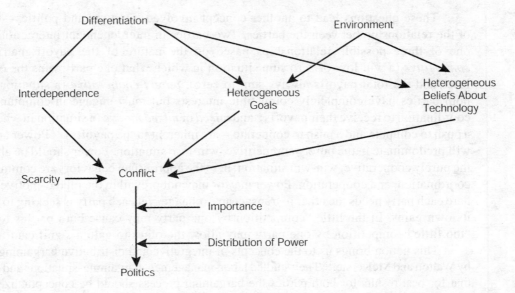

Source: Jeffery Pfeffer, Power in Organizations (Marshfield, MA: Pitman Publishing Inc., 1981), p. 69. Used by permission.

FIGURE 14-1 Model of the Conditions Producing the Use of Power and Politics in Organizational Decision Making

economists and behavioral scientists in an attempt to understand wars, strikes, and arguments as well as cooperation and altruism.[16] Several concepts from game theory provide a framework for understanding power and politics. Some of these concepts are conflict, the payoffs matrix, the nature of interdependent relationships, and integrative and distributive bargaining.

Game theory views conflict as a critical condition leading to power and political behavior. In *conflict of interest*, different parties prefer different goals. In *conflict or competition for scarce resources*, different parties want the same resources but both parties cannot possess them.

Thus conflict arises from the real or perceived nature of the *payoff matrix*, the way in which the goods and services sought by two or more parties are to be distributed. Some payoff matrixes promote cooperation and minimal power use. Understanding the payoff matrix is the key to understanding conflict, which in turn is the key to understanding political behavior. To analyze a particular situation for its potential for organizational politics we want to know answers to the following questions:

What is the commodity or issue that is under decision?
How important is the commodity or issue?
What possible payoffs are available?
What are the likely payoffs?
Can all parties get their desires, or must one party win and one party lose?

These questions lead to another concept involved in power and politics—the nature of the relationship between the parties. Two parties in interdependent interaction can have one of three possible relationships based on the nature of the payoff matrix: *purely competitive* (a win-lose or zero sum situation in which what one party wins the other party loses and the total payoffs always sum to zero), *purely cooperative* (a situation in which both parties have completely compatible interests but must engage in communication or coordination to receive their payoffs), and *mixed* or *mixed motive* (a situation in which both—a push to compete and a push to cooperate—are inherent in the payoffs).[17] Power and politics will predominate in the purely competitive, win-lose situation. Power should be absent from the purely cooperative, win-win situation; here the appropriate behaviors are communication, coordination, and cooperation. Power may or may not prevail in the mixed-motive situation; here each party needs the other to transact an exchange, yet each party is seeking to maximize its own gains. In the little "competition by one party may cause both parties to lose; yet "too little" competition by one party may allow the other to gain a significant advantage.

This notion brings us to the concepts of integrative and distributive bargaining proposed by Walton and McKersie.[18] They studied labor-management bargaining-situations and concluded that for best results for both parties the bargaining process should be conceptualized in two–phases: (1) a problem-solving, collaborative phase in which the total joint payoffs are maximized, and (2) a bargaining phase in which the payoffs are divided between the parties. In the first phase, called integrative bargaining, the parties try to identify areas of mutual concern, search for alternative courses of action, and create the largest joint sum of values possible. It is cooperative, problem-solving phase. In the second phase, called distributive bargaining, the parties are in conflict, as they "divide up the pie" created during integrative bargaining. Here each party tries to establish norms and procedures that will help to maximize its gains while trying to keep the gains of the other party to a minimum. Integrative bargaining calls for problem solving, honesty, open communication, and mutual exploration of all ideas. Distributive bargaining calls for secrecy, suspicion, deception, and not accepting the ideas of the other party. By separating bargaining into these two phases, both parties can achieve better solutions.

THE ROLE OF POWER AND POLITICS IN THE PRACTICE OF OD

We have discussed a number of ideas concerning power and politics. In this section we will attempt to integrate those concepts with organization development and offer advice to the OD practitioner for dealing with the political realities found in organizations.

The Nature of OD in Relation to Power and Politics

Organization development was founded on the belief that using behavioral science methods to increase collaborative problem solving would increase both organizational effectiveness and individual well-being. This belief gave rise to the field and is a guiding premise behind its technology. To increase collaborative problem solving is to increase the positive face of power and decrease the negative face of power. Thus from its perception OD addressed issues of power and politics by proposing that collaboration, co-operation, and joint problem solving are better ways to get things done in organizations than relying solely on bargaining and politics. The nature of OD in relation to power and politics can be examined from several perspectives, its strategy of change, its interventions, its values, and the role of the OD practitioner.

To use the framework of Robert Chin and Kenneth Benne, OD programs implement normative-reeducative and empirical-rational strategies of change, not a power-coercive strategy.[19] The normative-reeducative strategy of change focuses on norms, culture, processes, and prevailing attitudes and belief systems. Change occurs by changing norms and beliefs, usually through education and reeducation. The empirical-rational strategy of change seeks facts and information in an attempt to find "better" ways to do things. Change occurs by discovering these better ways and then adopting them. The power-coercive strategy of change focuses on gaining and using power and on developing enforcement methods. Change occurs when people with more power force their preferences on people with less power. OD practitioners advocate normative-reeducative and empirical-rational strategies of change, and OD interventions are designed to implement these strategies. Organization development thus has a strong bias toward a normative-reeducative strategy of change and against a power strategy.

Virtually, all OD interventions promote problem solving, not politics, as a preferred way to get things accomplished. OD interventions increase problem solving, collaboration, cooperation, fact-finding, and effective pursuit of goals while decreasing reliance on the negative faces of power and politics. We know of no OD interventions designed to increase coercion or unilateral power. For example, OD interventions typically generate valid, public data about the organization's culture, processes, strengths, and weaknesses. Valid, public data are indispensable for problem solving but anathema for organizational politics. OD interventions do not deny or attempt to abolish the reality of power in organizations; rather, they enhance the positive face of power, thereby making the negative face of power less prevalent and/or necessary. Not only is organization development not a power/political intervention strategy, it is instead a rational problem-solving approach that is incompatible with extreme power-oriented situations.

OD *values* are consistent with the positive face of power, but not with the negative face of power. Values such as trust, openness, collaboration, individual dignity, and promoting individual and organizational competence are part of the foundation of organization development. These values are congruent with rational problem solving and incongruent with extremely political modes of operating. "Power equalization" has long been described as one of the values of organization development. Emphasis on power equalization stems from two beliefs; first, problem solving is usually superior to power coercion as a way to find solutions to problematic situations; second power, equalization, being one aspect of the positive face of power, *increases* the amount of power available to organization members, and by so doing adds power to the organization.

The *role* of the OD practitioner is that of a facilitator, catalyst, problem solver, and educator. The practitioner is not a political activist or powerbroker. According to Chris Argyris, the "interventionist" has three primary tasks: (1) to generate valid useful information, (2) to promote free, informed choice, and (3) to promote the client's internal commitment to the choices made.[20] The practitioner works to strengthen skills and knowledge in the organization. But organization members are free to accept or reject the practitioner, his or her program, and his or her values, methods, and expertise. The OD consultant, like all consultants, provides a service that the organization is free to "buy" or "not buy". The facilitator or educator role is incompatible with a political activist role because cooperation requires one set of behaviors and competition requires a different set of behaviors, as we discussed earlier. Cobb and Margilies caution that OD practitioners can get into trouble if they move from a facilitator role to a political role.[21]

In summary, organization development represents an approach and method to enable organization members to *go beyond* the negative face of power and politics. This major strength of OD derives from the strategy of change, the technology, the values, and the roles of OD practitioners.

Operating in a Political Environment

We will present some general observations in operating in a political environment, followed by some rules of thumb for the OD practitioner.

First, organization development practitioners operate from a potentially strong power base they can use to advantage. According to the framework of French and Raven, the OD consultant possesses power from the following bases: legitimate power (the OD program and consultant are authorized by the organization's decision makers); expert power (the consultant possesses expert knowledge); information power (the consultant has a wealth of information about the strengths and weaknesses of the organization); and possibly referent power (others may identify with and be attracted to the consultant). These sources of influence produce a substantial power base that will enhance the likelihood of success. Michael Beer has identified additional means by which an OD group can gain and wield power in organizations.[22]

1. *Competence.* Demonstrated competence is the most important source of power, accept-ability, and ability to gain organizational support.
2. *Political access and sensitivity.* Cultivating and nurturing multiple relationships with key power figures in the organization will ensure timely information and multiple sources of support.
3. *Sponsorship.* "Organization development groups will gain power to the extent that they have sponsorship, preferably multiple sponsorship, in powerful places.[23] This maxim has been recognized for years under the heading of "get top-level support for the program."
4. *Stature and credibility.* Beer notes that power accrues to those who have been successful and effective. Success leads to credibility and stature. Early successes in the OD program and its usefulness to key managers of the organization helps promote this reputation.
5. *Resource management.* Power accrues to those who control resources—in this case, the resources of OD expertise and ability to help organizational subunits solve their pressing problems.
6. *Group support.* If the OD group is strong internally, it will be strong externally. If the OD group is cohesive and free of internal dissention, it will gain power.

Paying attention to these sources of power will enhance the likelihood of success of OD programs.

Second, the models presented in this discussion suggest ways the OD practitioner can help organization members reduce the negative face of power. Creating slack resources, replacing tight coupling of interdependent relationships with more loose coupling, gaining agreement on goals and means for goal accomplishment, centralizing some decision making, and addressing mixed-motive situations in two phases as indicated by integrative and distributive bargaining—all these processes can reduce the negative consequences of intense power and politics. The OD practitioner can help implement these conditions in the organization, thereby modifying the political climate.

Third, the concept of the positive and negative faces of power and political suggests where the practitioner is likely to be more effective. We believe that OD programs are likely to be unsuccessful in organizations with high negative faces of politics and power: the OD program will likely to be used as a pawn in the organization's power struggles, and the OD practitioner can become a scapegoat when conditions require a "sacrifice." On the other hand, OD programs are likely to be highly effective in organizations with positive faces of power and politics: the practitioner helps organization members build multiple power bases in the organization (more power to everyone); he or she promotes collaborative problem solving, which leads to better decisions; and the practitioner teaches organization members how to manage mixed-motive situations to ensure the best outcomes.

Fourth, the OD practitioner should learn as much as possible about bargaining, negotiations, the nature of power and politics, the strategy and tactics of influence, and the characteristics and behaviors of power holders. This knowledge is not for the purpose of becoming a political activist, but rather to understand better those organizational dynamics where power is an important factor. This knowledge will also make the OD practitioner a more competent actor in the organization and a more effective consultant in helping organization members solve their problems and take advantage of opportunities.

Fifth, the OD practitioner realizes that power stems from possessing a commodity valued by others. If the OD program indeed improves individual and organizational functioning, if the OD practitioner has indeed learned his or her craft well, then a valuable commodity has been produced that will be welcomed by the organization power holders.

What advice is available for OD practitioners who want to operate more effectively in a political environment? Several rules of thumb are implied by the fact that power accrues to persons who control valued resources or commodities.

Rule One   Become a desired commodity, both as a person and a professional. Becoming a desired commodity as a person means being interpersonal competence by virtue of their training, experience, and expertise. Skills such as listening, communicating, problem solving, coaching, counseling, and showing appreciation for the strengths of others are components of interpersonal competence. Good OD practitioners will have learned and practiced these skills. Being trustworthy means being reliable, dependable, and honest in dealing with others. These skills and traits are highly valued in social exchanges; persons who possess them become desired commodities and accrue power.

Rule Two   Make the OD program itself a desired commodity. OD programs become desired commodities when they are instruments that allow individuals and organizations to reach their goals. OD programs should be result-oriented. Another way the OD program becomes a desired commodity is by focusing on important issues, those issues vital to the organization's success. Greiner Schein challenge OD practitioners to become more involved in the strategic management process.[24]

Rule Three   Make the OD program a valued commodity for multiple powerful people in the organization. When the OD program serves the needs of top executives, it gains an aura of respect and protection that sets its above most political entanglements. Being of value to multiple power holders rather than a single one both increases support and reduces the likelihood that the program should be of value to persons at all levels, paying special attention to the needs of top executives is a useful rule of thumb. Again the issue is helping people realize their important goals. The power holders can be expected to reciprocate with endorsement, support, and protection of the OD program.

Rule Four Create win-win solutions. The nature of organizations and the nature of organization development suggest this rule. Organizations are social systems in which members have both a history and a future of interacting, and effective conflict management techniques are required to enhance stable, constructive social relationships. Many OD interventions promote win-win solutions for conflict situations. OD professionals who are skilled in conflict management techniques and OD programs that encompass conflict resolution activities become valued commodities.

Rule Five Mind your own business, which is to help someone else solve his or her major problem. Sometimes OD practitioners overlook that they are hired by others, usually managers, to help them achieve their goals and solve their problems. The OD consultant is successful to the extent that the manager is successful; the OD consultant is competent to the extent that the manager's goals are met through collaboration between consultant and key client. OD consultants are not hired to instill OD values in an organization, to cause the widespread use of participative management, or to "do good and expunge evil" (as defined by the consultant). Instead, OD consultants have a formal or informal contractual agreement with managers to help them do what they are trying to do—better. The role of the OD consultant is to help others upon request. Beer and Walton argue that organization development should move from being practitioner-centered to being manager-centered.[25] The *OD program belongs to the manager, not the OD consultant.* A valuable by-product of this fact is that if a program runs into political turbulence, the manager will vigorously defend it.

Rule Six Mind your own business, which is to be an expert on process, not content. Organizational politics revolve around decisions: Should we seek Goal A or Goal B? Should we use Means X or Means Y? Should we promote Mary or John? The proper role of OD consultants is to help decision-makers by providing them with good decision-making *processes*, not by getting involved in the answers. Abiding by this rule keeps the consultant from becoming entangled in politics, while at the same time increasing his or her usefulness to the organization's power brokers. The principle is simple but powerful: know your legitimate business and stick to it.

Rule Seven Mind your own business because to do otherwise is to invite political trouble. A subtle phenomenon is involved here: when people engage in illegitimate behavior, such behavior is often interpreted as politically motivated. Illegitimate behavior encroaches on others' legitimate "turf," which arouses defensive actions. Illegitimate behavior causes others to try to exert greater control over the situation. We believe the legitimate role of the OD practitioner is that of facilitator, catalyst, problem solver, and educator, not power activist or power broker.[26]

We could propose more rules of thumb, but these give the flavor of the issues one must consider when operating in a political environment. Attention to these rules can save OD practitioners' time and energy that can be more profitably invested in the OD program.

PLANNED CHANGE, POWER, AND POLITICS

Now let's look at power and politics through the eyes of a management consultant specializing in planned change. David Nadler and the Delta Consulting Group have twenty years of experience helping leaders implement change in more than 130 organizations. Change always involves power and politics, Nadler states in *Champions of Change*: "Changes ... bring instability, upheaval, and uncertainty.... Change means new patterns of power, influence, and control—and, consequently, high-stakes office politics. That's what change entails—and that's why it's so hard.[27]

Nadler observes that power and politics reach their highest pitch during the transition state—that period after the change program had begun when people know that old structures, procedures, and behaviors are no longer appropriate, but before they know what is appropriate and are confident and competent in new roles and behaviors. In Lewin's three-stage model of unfreezing-moving-refreezing, the transition state is synonymous with "moving." *Managing the transition state is one of the biggest challenges of large-scale change efforts.* Transition states always involve three characteristics: instability, uncertainty, and stress. *Instability* arises because people don't know that jobs, authority, and role they will have in the future; they have given up a stable, known past for a murky, unknown future. *Uncertainty* arises because no one has "the answers" when people ask questions about their place in the "new" organization. The result of instability and uncertainty is stress—for both leaders and followers.

CONCLUDING COMMENTS

In this chapter we have examined power and politics with the goals of understanding the phenomena and deriving implications for OD practitioners. Power and politics are similar in nature, arise from known condition, and are amenable to positive control. Our suggestions for using power to operate effectively in organizations may help practitioners avoid the perils and pitfalls of power that "go with the territory" of organizational change.

NOTES

1. W. Warner Burke, *Organization Development: Principles and Practices* (Boston: Little, Brown and Co., 1982), p. 127.
2. R. G. H. Siu, *The Craft of Power* (New York: John Wiley, 1979), p. 31.
3. R. A. Dahl, "The Concept of Power," *Behavioral Science* (1957), pp. 202–203.
4. Gerald Salancik and Jeffrey Pfeffer, "Who Gets Power—And How They Hold on to It: A Strategic-Contingency Model of Power," *Organizational Dynamics*, 5 (1977), p. 3.

5. Mintzberg, *Power In and Around Organizations*, p. 4. [Mintzberg's emphasis.]
6. John R. P. French, Jr. and Bertram Raven, "The Bases of Social Power," in Dorwin Cartwright, ed., *Studies in Social Power* (Ann Arbor: Institute for Social Research of the University of Michigan, 1959), pp. 150–167.
7. Mintzberg, *Power In and Around Organizations*. This book is an important contribution to the concept of power in general and organizational power in particular.
8. Ibid., p. 22.
9. This discussion is taken from ibid., chapter 3, especially pp. 24–26.
10. Harold Lasswell, *Politics: Who Gets What, When, How* (New York: McGraw-Hill, 1936).
11. Pfeffer, *Power in Organizations*, p. 7.
12. Robert W. Allen, Dan L. Madison, Lyman W. Porter, Patricia A. Renwick, and Bronston T. Mayes, "Organizational Politics: Tactics and Characteristics of Its Actors," *California Management Review*, 22 (1979), p. 77.
13. Bronston T. Mayes and Robert W. Allen, "Toward a Definition of Organizational Politics," *The Academy of Management Review*, 2, no. 4 (October 1977), p. 676.
14. Mintzberg, *Power In and Around Organizations*, p. 5.
15. Pfeffer, *Power in Organizations*, chapter 1. See also Jay M. Shafritz and J. Steven Ott, eds., *Classics of Organization Theory*, 2d ed. (Chicago, IL: The Dorsey Press, 1987).
16. See, for example, J. Von Neumann and O. Morgenstern, *Theory of Games and Economic Behavior* (Princeton: NJ: Princeton University Press, 1947); R. D. Luce and H. Raiffa, *Games and Decisions: Introduction and Critical Survey* (New York: John Wiley, 1957); T. C. Schelling, *The Strategy of Conflict* (Cambridge, MA: Harvard University Press, 1960); and J. W. Thibaut and H. H. Kelley, *The Social Psychology of Groups* (New York: John Wiley, 1959).
17. Schelling, *The Strategy of Conflict*.
18. R. E. Walton and R. B. McKersie, *A Behavioral Theory of Labor Negotiations* (New York: McGraw-Hill, 1965).
19. Robert Chin and Kenneth D. Benne, "General Strategies for Effecting Change in Human Systems," in Warren G. Bennis, Kenneth D. Benne, Robert Chin, and Kenneth E. Corey, eds., *The Planning of Change*, 3d ed. (New York: Holt, Rinehart and Winston, 1976).
20. Chris Argyris, *Intervention Theory and Method: A Behavioral Science View* (Reading, MA: Addison-Wesley, 1970), pp. 17–20.
21. Cobb and Margulies, "Organization Development: A Political Perspective," *Academy of Management Review*, 6 (January 1981), pp. 50–59.
22. Michael Beer, *Organization Change and Development: A Systems View* (Santa Monica, CA: Goodyear, 1980), pp. 258–261.
23. Ibid., p. 259.
24. Larry E. Greiner and Virginia E. Schein, "A Revisionist Look at Power and OD," *The Industrial-Organizational Psychologist*, 25, no. 2 (1988), pp. 59–61.
25. Michael Beer and Anna E. Walton, "Organization Change and Development," *Annual Review of Psychology*, 38 (1987), pp. 339–367.
26. A growing number of authors assert that OD practitioners should be political activists and/or powerbrokers. We disagree. For this other point of view, see: R. G. Harrison and D. C. Pitt, "Organizational Development: A Missing Political Dimension?" (pp. 65–85), and P. Reason, "Is Organization Development Possible in Power Cultures?" (pp. 185–202), both from the book *Power, Politics, and Organizations* edited by A. Kakabadse and C. Parker (Chichester, United Kingdom: John Wiley and Sons, Ltd., 1984). See also W. R. Nord, "The Failure of Current Applied Behavioral Science—A Marxian Perspective," *Journal of Applied Behavioral Science*, 10 (1974), pp. 557–578; Andrew Pettigrew, "Toward a Political Theory of

Organizational Intervention"; Virginia Schein, "Political Strategies for Implementing Organizational Change"; and N. Margulies and A. P. Raia, "The Politics of Organization Development," *Training and Development Journal*, 38 (1984), pp. 20–23.

27. David A. Nadler, *Champions of Change* (San Francisco: Jossey-Bass Publishers, 1998), p. 5.

CHAPTER 15

The Future and Organization Development

N o one is omniscient about the future, but our look at OD history and present practice can help develop a picture of what might lie ahead. And what lies ahead is exciting, rewarding, and full of challenges.

THE CHANGING ENVIRONMENT

The environment in which organizations operate is increasingly turbulent in an era of global, national, and regional commercial competitiveness. But paradoxically that competition is part of a rapidly shifting mélange of competitiveness and interdependencies. Alliances, consortia, mergers, and acquisitions are all common. Production and communications technology are changing at an exponential rate. Furthermore, dislocation of people through downsizing and restructuring is rampant. Simultaneously, a profusion of business startups is taking place. Yesterday's strategies are not likely to work in tomorrow's workplaces.

In large part the old organizational paradigm is dying. It doesn't work well in this emerging environment. Top-down, autocratically directed, rigidly hierarchical, fear-generating organizations is giving way to something new. The new paradigm proclaims that the most innovative and successful organizations will be those that derive their strength and vitality from adaptable, committed team players at all levels and from all specialties, not from the omniscience of the hierarchy.[1] Increasingly, organizations will be flatter, with smaller central staffs and with more delegation to small groups and units. High-performance organizations focusing on the customer and continuous quality improvement and placing high value on human resources, diversity, and high-performance teams will be the norm.[2]

Indian organizations too have realised this and are readying themselves with skill set upgradation and sweeping changes in the mindsets of executives. Companies are increasingly emphasizing on introducing planned interventions which would ultimately lead to achieving strategic goals.

OD will be a major player in assisting organizations to shift to and sustain this new paradigm and to help invent even more effective paradigms in the future. The future of OD is bright, but only if the field continues to evolve. Here are some opinions about that evolution and some of the contingencies that must be faced.

FUNDAMENTAL STRENGTHS OF OD

The central strength of OD is that the processes about which we have written in this book are fundamentally sound. These processes include careful tuning in to the perceptions and feelings of people; creating safe conditions for surfacing perceptions and feelings; involving people in diagnosing the strengths and weaknesses of their organizations and making action plans for improvement; focusing on team and other interdependent configurations; redesigning work so that it is more meaningful and motivating; explicitly training people toward a participative, open, team leadership mode; and using qualified third parties. These and other characteristics of OD have created a powerful and durable process for organization improvement.

A second fundamental strength has to do with the political, governmental milieu. OD is highly compatible with democratic governmental structures and processes that are well established in many parts of the world and emerging elsewhere. Indeed, approaches promote and help sustain democratic processes.

Third, OD practice has been expanding in the last two or three decades to create a blending of attention to people-oriented processes with attention to the design of the human-technical system. More and more examples indicate a melding of what Frank Friedlander and L. Dave Brown in the 1970s were calling "human-processual "and "technostructural" approaches.[3] To illustrate, this blending can be seen in the increasing use of parallel or collateral organizations in large-scale change projects, many of which involve extensive technological changes. It is also evident in the extensive use of employee involvement in sociotechnological systems (STS) programs, and in the use of OD practitioners in the training and development of self-managed teams.

Fourth, almost everywhere organizations are recognizing the need for assistance in getting the right people together to talk constructively about important organizational and transorganizational matters, and for developing processes for making things better. In light of these pressing needs, the OD field clearly has an enormous and vital role to play in the foreseeable future.

OD won't go away; it can't go away. If it did, it would be reinvented under a new label. We believe that OD can only become stronger and more effective through evolving theory, research, and practice.

OD'S FUTURE

How large a role OD will play in the constantly changing organizational, political, and economic milieu of the future will depend upon a number of interrelated conditions. Most of the conditions we are generally favorable to OD, but countertrends and/or uncertainties will have to be addressed. These conditions and contingencies have to do with leadership and values; knowledge about OD; OD training; the interdisciplinary nature of OD; diffusion of technique; integrative practice; mergers, acquisitions, and alliances; rediscovering and recording history; and the search for community.

Leadership and Values

For OD to flourish, top-management—CEOs, boards of directors, top executives, including the human resources executive—and OD consultants must place high value on strong individual, team, and organizational performance coupled with people-oriented values. As O' Toole says, management can *choose* to try to create organizations that have both profitability and humanistic/developmental objectives whether or not the two are necessarily correlated.[4] In an almost schizophrenic situation in the United States, some top managements are highly attentive and committed to this duality of objectives, and others are concerned only with the bottom line/or the price of stock. As George Strauss says, some executives have a "slash and burn" mentality.[5] Most OD consultants, as we have seen in chapter 4, have strong orientations toward organizational effectiveness coupled with democratic and humanistic values.

OD consultants, then, are caught in a major dilemma when top executives in their client organizations begin to demonstrate this "slash and burn" mentality. Does the OD consultant remain silent and assist management in carrying out a large downsizing by helping alleviate some of the pain experienced by organizational members? Or does the OD consultant quickly question the proposed course of action? Warner Burke says the following in a thoughtful article on the future of OD.

> For the good of the organization and its individual members, consultative help may mean confrontation, questioning, and challenging.... When an OD practitioner's client is contemplating downsizing, the intervention of choice is to test the wisdom of such a decision.[6]

He goes on to say that the OD consultant of the future needs to help management look at the social forces that might be operating in downsizing decisions, what the research shows about the consequences, and what alternatives are available.

The OD process will take root and flourish in direct proportion to the prevalence of the dual set of values that O' Toole talks about, or the extent top executives decide to travel Route One, as described by Hackman and Oldham. These value decisions must be coupled with strong leadership skills. By strong leadership skills we are referring to Kotter's notions of "establishing direction," "aligning people," and "motivating and inspiring."[7] The OD practitioner can play a major role in this leadership.

OD Training

The quality of OD training in the United States appears to be high if one looks at the curricula of university programs, NTL's array of training experiences, the training offerings of various consulting and training organizations, and the attention paid to OD matters in conferences of the OD Network, the Academy of Management, the American Society for Training and Development, and other national and international organizations.

We would agrue that the future will hold a need for availability of T-group training—as a training intervention, not as an organizational intervention—particularly for both aspiring OD practitioners and managers. And we should not overlook the utility of T-group training for any or all organizational members, including first-line supervisors.

Accreditation and peer review of OD skill competency has languished. For a few years an implied accreditation of some well-selected professionals was available through NTL

Institute Associate status, and then that approach was shifted to accreditation through Certified Consultants International. But the latter organization did not have the support it needed and closed shop, although some regional professional development groups remained after the national organization closed its doors. Clients, of course, can be encouraged to look at and inquire about credentials and competency. Certainly the attainment of a doctorate with an OD concentration, or a masters such as the Masters of Science in organization Development offered jointly by the American University and NTL Institute for Applied Behavioral Science, are examples of credentials that suggest in-depth training.[8]

Interdisciplinary Nature of OD

OD's future, to a significant extent, is related to other disciplines. Historically, as we noted in chapter 2, OD has been a highly interdisciplinary, eclectic field. It has been built from theory, research, and practice in social psychology, adult education, community development, general systems theory, family group therapy, anthropology, philosophy, counseling, psychiatry, general management, social work, human resources management, large conference management, and other fields.

Are scholars and practitioners looking hard at these early contributing fields to see what else is emerging that might be useful? Should other bodies of knowledge be tracked? Surely much can be learned from such fields as international diplomacy, dispute meditation (including divorce meditation), arbitration, architecture, and religion. Historically, some reciprocal influence has passed between these fields and OD. Undoubtedly more is needed.

Diffusion of Technique

OD techniques and approaches have been widely disseminated in society, at least on the American and Canadian scene, and in many parts of Europe, Asia, Australia, New Zealand, Latin America, and elsewhere. In large measure this positive development demonstrates that OD processes are being widely perceived as having considerable value. It is also a compliment to the professionals of the field, including OD trainers, researchers, and writers.

However, at least two problems may be lurking around the edges of this wide dissemination of technique. One problem is that techniques may be used without sufficient understanding of their theoretical, research, and/or historical foundations. The consequences may be misapplication and, in turn, unnecessary cynicism and resistance on the part of clients.

The other problem is the possibility of a gradual diffusion of the OD field across other specialties, with the resultant loss of some of its integration of values, theory, research, history, and practice. It is not a problem of semantics but a potential problem of loss of focus—OD's central values, what to teach, what to learn, and how to communicate the basics and the subtleties of the field. If OD becomes anything or everything, then what is it?

Perhaps solutions lie in the availability of and support for quality training and research in OD and in the careful selection of consultants. Another partial solution may involve widespread understanding of the OD process, so that participants themselves act as a check on misdirected or ill-considered efforts. The less mystery and the more openness and understanding about OD, the better.

Integrative Practice

It would be a challenge, indeed, for any one person to develop skills in all of the interventions we have described in this book, plus acquiring in the United States at least, to couple OD skills with the growing number of broad structural interventions, and to do further conceptualizing and research about such integrations. We refer to total quality management (TQM), quality of work life (QWL), and reengineering programs, in particular. The emphasis on teams in TQM and QWL makes OD a natural partner in these efforts. The lack of emphasis on participative approaches in reengineering efforts makes OD-practitioner involvement less likely, but not less necessary. Important conceptualization relative to this integration has occurred. For example, Robert Golembiewski and Ben-Chu Sun and Warner Burke have written about OD and QWL.[9] Dan Ciampia, Marshall Sashkin, Kenneth Kiser, Edward Lawler, Susan Mohrman and Gerald Ledford, and others have made contributions toward the theoretical and applied integration of TQM and OD.[10] This work needs to be extended.

OD practitioners need to be as knowledgeable as possible about such structural interventions and these integrations. At the same time, we believe that experts in the technological aspects of these fields also need to be knowledgeable about OD. An ideal arrangement may be for OD professionals to join with such experts on consulting teams. This collaboration is happening, although just how extensively we do not know. Obviously, it requires that such teams pay considerable attention to their own team building and teamwork.

In short, the OD field is closer to the refinement of such a paradigm, but the journey must continue.

Mergers, Acquisitions and Alliances

As the tempo of business transactions worldwide increases, the phenomena of acquisitions, mergers, and alliances will also become more evident. As described in chapter 10, interventions that have grown out of the OD field can be highly relevant in helping two or more organizational cultures meld and in ameliorating the potential dislocation and pain that can occur when organizations are combined. Such interventions will require a high degree of interpersonal, political, and cultural skill of the consultant or consulting team—even more so when than one country and/or language is involved.

Rediscovering and Recording History

The history of OD is indispensable for retaining and improving effective OD interventions and approaches. For example, as we have discussed, numerous practitioners today are rediscovering the utility, in some circumstances, of "getting the whole system in the room," and are drawing on its history, which goes back at least to the 1950s.[11] As another example, some contemporary practitioners are finding that, for a variety of reasons, a successful change effort in one part of an organization can be suffocated by forces in other parts of the system. Knowledge about such resistance was articulated in the 1970s and possibly earlier.[12] Jyotsna Sanzgiri and Jonathan Gottlieb say that "there will be a resurgence in the need to understand more of what the founders of the field of OD were always interested in: participative structures, decision making based on action research, long-term approaches to management, and processes for organizational renewal and change."[13]

Some portions of OD history are in danger of being lost forever, although some are likely to be reinvented from time to time. We are convinced that hundreds of interventions devised by OD consultants have been tremendously successful in particular applications and used perhaps two or three times again, but never recorded and published. Focusing on the broad, fundamental participant action research process is of overriding importance, but nevertheless intervention techniques are extremely important for the OD professional's "tool kit."

The Search for Community

Finally, we believe that the search for community will be increasingly high on the agendas of organizations and OD efforts in the future, either explicitly or implicitly. Before we describe what we mean by "community," however, we want to make some general assertions about the context of the search for community.

Outcomes such as the production of high-quality goods and services, making a profit, and staying viable and competitive are, and must be, superordinate goals for vast numbers of organizations in essentially free-enterprise economies. Consequently, the interests of most organizations of all kinds are clearly served by being productive, efficient, and adaptable, lest they find themselves out of business.

People, almost universally, believe that how work is accomplished and how people relate to each other are highly important matters. People may have different prescriptions for meeting these goals—or narrow versus wide perspectives—but at some level they know that cooperation is better than in-fighting, that friendship is more rewarding than so forth. Thousands of organizations worldwide do pay attention to these matters as evidenced by large amounts of experimentation and research relative to these dimensions. (See, For example, the discussion in chapter 12 on work design and the use of self-managed teams.)

Without a doubt, many people, including top executives in all kinds of organizations, want even more than a profitable, well-managed, reasonably harmonious workplace. Some may have accomplished it, some may be working toward this end, some may be only beginning to articulate what it is. More than a few are talking and writing about it. And that something, which has some spiritual overtones, has been referred to by many thinkers as a *sense of community*.[14]

No one should be surprised to see that OD interventions take people toward a sense of community, because the values underlying OD stem largely from what people have said over and over again in private interviews and safe group settings as to what they want from their organizations and from other people. And desire for a sense of community is evident in organizations as diverse as manufacturing firms, insurance companies, schools, churches, government units, the military, private clubs, and charitable institutions.

What words would describe a "sense of community?" From what we have experienced in our own lives, including managerial and OD consulting roles, from interacting with OD and group dynamics professionals, from membership in various organizations, from family interactions, and from reading and conceptualizing, we believe that people tend to experience some or a lot of each item on the following list when a sense of community is present.

- We interact frequently within at least one cohesive group, perhaps several.
- We feel included, and we work hard at making others feel included.

- We like what we are doing, and we like each other.
- We participate in setting goals, solving problems, and in organizational direction.
- We value individuality, creativity, and differences of opinion.
- We're all pursuing the same general objectives.
- We believe in strong service to our customers and other stakeholders.
- We maintain high standards of achievement.
- We hold each other mutually accountable for effective contribution.
- We feel fairly rewarded and recognized.
- We trust one another to be cognizant and supportive of our individual interests.
- We act ethically and with integrity in our relationships.
- We see ourselves in others and others on ourselves;[15] we are empathic listeners and observers; we are attentive to each other's emotional needs.
- We each assume responsibility for effective leadership and effective group processes.
- We work hard at intergroup cooperation and teamwork.
- We reinforce our culture with much listening, recognition, expressions of appreciation, humor, ceremony, and tradition.
- We all have a sense of purpose that includes and transcends the job and the organization.[16]

The last item on the preceding list—the sense of transcendent purpose—takes us into the realm of spirituality, which perhaps can be defined as a continuous searching for the true, for the good, for meaning, and for wholeness. Based on traditional OD values, and with skill, organization development efforts would seem to be on the same search. We see this search continuing, and perhaps intensifying, into the future.

High Performance and Community

High organizational performance can be congruent with and supportive of a sense of community, and vice versa. Obviously it requires vision, time, empathy, skill, commitment, and hard work to achieve either or both. An assessment of where a group or various units of an organization are on each of the dimensions in the preceding list and then moving on to ask "Where do you want to be?" are steps toward a shared sense of community as well as toward higher organizational performance.

We believe future OD efforts increasingly will be aimed at *both* high organizational performance and a sense of community. In many ways, the pioneers and major thinkers in the field have been saying this same thing all along.

CONCLUDING COMMENTS

Enormous opportunity and potential exist for the OD movement in the future. Organizations throughout the world need the unique help that can be provided by highly trained interventionists using people-oriented, action research approaches. The future of OD is bright, as long as the high-quality, hard work of the past continues, and providing it does not become fashionable for top leaders to revert to autocratic or capricious practices in times of high turbulence or crises. Much challenging, difficult work remains to be done, but also great fun and many rewards in working with people in making their organizations more successful and satisfying.

What is OD all about? OD is really about people helping each other to unleash the human spirit and human capability in the workplace.

NOTES

1. See also Tom Peters, *Liberation Management* (New York: Alfred A. Knopf, 1992), pp. 208–209, 238–239; and A. J. Vogl and David A. Nadler, "It Could Happen to Us," *Across the Board*, 30 (October 1993), pp. 27–32. For more on paradigms, see Joel Arthur Barker, *Future Edge* (New York: William Morrow and Company, 1992).
2. See Walter Kiechel III, "How We Will Work in the Year 2000," *Future* (May 17, 1993), pp. 38–52; Richard A. Melcher, "How Goliaths Can Act Like Davids," *Business Week* special issue, *Enterprise: How Entrepreneurs Are Reshaping the Economy and What Big Companies Can Learn* (1993); and Thomas A. Stewart, "The Search for the Organization of Tomorrow," Fortune (May 18, 1992), pp. 92–98.
3. Frank Friedlander and L. Dave Brown, "Organization Development," *Annual Review of Psychology*, 25 (1974), pp. 313–316, 320–321, and 336–341. See also Marshall Sashkin and W. Warner Burke, "Organization Development in the 1980s," *Journal of Management*, 13 (Summer 1987), pp. 395–417; and Michael Beer and Elise Walton, "Developing the Competitive Organization: Interventions and Strategies," *American Psychologist*, 45 (February 1990), p. 160.
4. James O'Toole, "Do Good, Do Well: The Business Enterprise Awards," *California Management Review*, 33 (Spring 1991), p. 21.
5. George Strauss, "President's Column," *Industrial Relations Research Association Series Newsletter*, 35 (September 1993), p. 2.
6. W. Warner Burke, "The New Agenda for Organization Development," *Organizational Dynamics*, 26 (Summer 1997), p. 11.
7. John P. Kotter, *A Force for Change: How Leadership Differs from Management* (New York: The Free Press, 1990), p. 7.
9. Robert T. Golembiewski and Ben-Chu Sun, "Positive-Findings Bias in QWL Studies," *Journal of Management*, 16 (September 1990), p. 667; and W. Warner Burke, *Organization Development* (Boston: Little, Brown and Company, 1982), p. 323.
10. Dan Ciampa, Total Quality (Reading, MA: Addison-Wesley Publishing Company, 1992); Marshall Sashkin and Kenneth J. Kiser, *Total Quality Management* (Seabrook, MD: Ducochon Press, 1991); Marshall Sashkin and Kenneth J. Kiser, "What Is Total Quality Management and How Does It Relate to OD?" *Academy of Management ODC Newsletter* (Winter 1992), pp. 16–19; and Edward E. Lawler III, Susan Albers Mohrman, and Gerald E. Ledford, Jr., *Employee Involvement and Total Quality Management* (San Francisco: Jossey-Bass Publishers, 1992).
11. See Marvin R. Weisbord, *Productive Workplaces* (San Francisco: Jossey-Bass Publishers, 1987), p. 283.
12. See Paul S. Goodman, *Assessing Organizational Change* (New York: John Wiley, 1979).
13. Jyotsna Sanzgiri and Jonathan Gottlieb, "Philosophic and Pragmatic Influences on the Practice of Organization Development, 1950–2000," *Organizational Dynamics*, 21 (Autumn 1992), p. 64.

14. Philip H. Mirvis, "'Soul Work' in Organizations," *Organizational Science*, 8 (March–April 1997): pp. 193–206. See also Francis J. Gouillart and James N. Kelly, *Transforming Organizations* (New York: McGraw-Hill, 1995); and Gilbert W. Fairholm, "Spiritual Leadership: Fulfilling Whole-Self Needs at Work," *Leadership and Organization Development Journal*, 17, no. 5, (1996), pp. 11–17.

15. Ibid., p. 194.

16. This list is consistent with what can be found in John Nirenberg, *The Living Organization: Transforming Teams into Workplace Communities* (Homewood, IL: Business One Irwin; and San Diego, CA: Pfeiffer & Company, 1993); and John Nirenberg, "From Team Building to Community Building," *National Productivity Review*, 14 (Winter 1994–95), pp. 51–62.